ANTISEMITISM

Deborah Lipstadt is Dorot Professor of Modern Jewish History and Holocaust Studies at Emory University. Her books include *The Eichmann Trial*, *Denial: holocaust history on trial* (a National Jewish Book Award-winner), *Denying the Holocaust: the growing assault on truth and memory*, and *Beyond Belief: the American press and the coming of the Holocaust*, 1933–1945. She lives in Atlanta.

BOOKS BY DEBORAH LIPSTADT

Beyond Belief: The American Press and the Coming of the Holocaust, 1933–1945

Denying the Holocaust: The Growing Assault on Truth and Memory

Denial: Holocaust History on Trial

The Eichmann Trial

Holocaust: An American Understanding

DEBORAH LIPSTADT

ANTISEMITISM

HERE AND NOW

SCRIBE

Melbourne • London

Scribe Publications
2 John St, Clerkenwell, London, WC1N 2ES, United Kingdom
18–20 Edward St, Brunswick, Victoria 3056, Australia

First published by Scribe 2019

Book design by Iris Weinstein
Printed and bound in the UK by CPI Group (UK) Ltd, Croydon CR0 4YY

Scribe Publications is committed to the sustainable use of natural resources
and the use of paper products made responsibly from those resources.

9781925228670 (UK edition)
9781925322675 (Australian edition)
9781925307580 (e-book)

CiP records for this title are available from the National Library of Australia and British Library.

scribepublications.co.uk
scribepublications.com.au

To the memory of my mother, Miriam bat Natanel and Rebecca.

God was her "refuge and her fortress" (Psalm 91).

She was my greatest fan.

CONTENTS

A NOTE TO THE READER

This has been a challenging project. I was surprised by the difficulties I encountered in writing this book, for it was hardly my first foray into addressing painful topics. I have been writing, teaching, and speaking about the *Shoah,* one of the most all-encompassing examples of state-sponsored genocide, for decades. Given that I have already spent so much of my scholarly and personal time skulking in the sewers of antisemitism and genocide, why should this project have been any different from the many others that preceded it? The answer became clear as I wrote. As horrific as the Holocaust was, it is firmly in the past. When I write about it, I am writing about what was. Though I remain horrified by what happened, it is history. Contemporary antisemitism is not. It is about the present. It is what many people are doing, saying, and facing *now.* That gave this subject an immediacy that no historical act possesses.

But it is not just about the present. It is also about the future. Where are the troubling phenomena addressed here leading? And that question points to yet another difficulty. Most historians avoid speculating about the future. We eschew predictions because we know how quickly things can change. Often, those historians who have relied on their knowledge of the past to prognosticate have erred. And yet, when one writes about a contemporary problem, it is hard not to predict. Aware of this, I try very hard in this book to avoid doing so. After addressing some basics of the issue— defining antisemitism, categorizing the antisemite, and figuring out how best to spell the word—I try to unpack what it is we are witnessing. Is today's antisemitism the same or different from what we have seen before? Where is it coming from: the right or the left?

Is it, as some would contend, all about Israel? Are we seeing anti-semitism where it is not? Are others refusing to see antisemitism where it clearly is?

While there seems to have been a decided increase in both physical acts and rhetorical expressions of antisemitism in recent years, our conversation should not be rooted in or motivated by numbers or by antisemitic acts. This would suggest that, if the numbers decrease, our worries should abate. I remember that during the 2000 American presidential campaign many Jews predicted that Al Gore's selection of Joseph Lieberman as his running mate would precipitate a rise in antisemitism. It didn't happen. Some pundits then opined that perhaps antisemitism was dead. They looked at the American social landscape and saw Jewish presidents presiding over universities that once had strict quotas. They saw Jews sitting on the boards of major corporations and being elected to public office from regions without a significant Jewish population. Even the skyrocketing rate of intermarriage, a source of angst within the Jewish community, could be spun into something positive. If so many non-Jews are so willing to have Jews in their families, how prevalent could antisemitism be? But today, antisemitism is "back." (I am not sure it ever really went away.) An accurate accounting of the uptick in antisemitic incidents is important because it does provide necessary empirical evidence. Nonetheless, *numbers should not be what drive us.* What should alarm us is that human beings continue to believe in a conspiracy that demonizes Jews and sees them as responsible for evil. Antisemites continue to give life to this particular brand of age-old hatred. They justify it and the acts committed in its name. The historical consequences of this nefarious passion have been so disastrous that to ignore its contemporary manifestations would be irresponsible.

Another reason numbers should not drive us is that antisemitism is a worldview, a conspiracy theory. It therefore cannot simply be measured by the number of recorded antisemitic acts or by the number of people being categorized as antisemites. A recent study in Great Britain called the approach I have taken the "elastic" view of antisemitism. If Jew-hatred is an attitude, it exists, like all attitudes, "in society at different levels of intensity, and with different shades to it. . . . Some people may be strongly antisemitic, others less so; and while still others may not fit into either of these categories, they may still hold certain [antisemitic] attitudes—even if these are small in number and weak in intensity."[1]

Since antisemitism affects Jews, some readers may be inclined to think that only Jews should be concerned. That would be a mistake. Jews, as the intended target of the antisemite, may indeed be more sensitive to it. Such is the case with any expression of particular hatred and prejudice. But the existence of prejudice in any of its forms is a threat to all those who value an inclusive, democratic, and multicultural society. It is axiomatic that if Jews are being targeted with hateful rhetoric and prejudice, other minorities should not feel immune; this is not likely to end with Jews. And, conversely, if other minority groups are being targeted with hatred and prejudice, Jews should not feel immune; this is not likely to end with these groups, either. Antisemitism flourishes in a society that is intolerant of others, be they immigrants or racial and religious minorities. When expressions of contempt for one group become normative, it is virtually inevitable that similar hatred will be directed at other groups. Like a fire set by an arsonist, passionate hatred and conspiratorial worldviews reach well beyond their intended target. They are not rationally contained. But even if the antisemites were to confine their venom to Jews, the existence of Jew-hatred within a society is an indication that something about the entire society is amiss. No healthy society harbors extensive antisemitism—or any other form of hatred.

·   ·   ·

I have organized this book as a series of letters to two fictional people with whom I have become "acquainted" at the university at which I teach. One is "Abigail," a whip-smart Jewish student who has taken many of my courses and who is trying to understand the phenomenon of antisemitism. The other is "Joe," a colleague who teaches at the university's law school. A non-Jew, he has a deep appreciation for both the successes and travails of the Jewish people, and he counts some of his Jewish colleagues as his most important conversation partners on campus. Abigail and Joe are composites of many people who have turned to me during the past few years to express their confusion, worries, and distress about antisemitism in general and about what they are personally witnessing. They may be fictional figures, but the questions they ask and the concerns they express belong to very real people. I have structured the letters to reflect the situation as of summer 2018.

While the contemporary nature of the events discussed made this a challenging book to write, the pace of recent events made it an almost impossible book to finish. It seemed that every day a new development—the murder of a Holocaust survivor in Paris, elections in Hungary in which the winning side relied on overtly antisemitic tropes, a Polish law rewriting the history of the Holocaust, white power demonstrations in the United States, campus anti-Israel campaigns that easily morphed into expressions of antisemitism, Labour Party antisemitism in the United Kingdom, the growing resiliency of white supremacist groups, and so much more—demanded analysis and inclusion in this work. Sadly, given the unending saga that is antisemitism, I feel comfortable predicting that by the time this book appears there will have been new examples of antisemitism that should have been part of the narrative.

Some readers may find themselves agreeing with me at one point and being outraged by what I say at another. Irrespective of my readers' positions on various issues, I ask that they read with nuance, the same nuance with which I have tried to write. Some may think that I have either exaggerated or understated the severity of the situation. Some may accuse me of finding antisemitism at the "wrong" end of the political spectrum. Should some consider me too willing to see the glass as half empty and others consider me too willing to see it as half full, I (ever the contrarian) will then assume my analysis is just right.

I know from personal experience how easy it is to make pronouncements and to declare others wrong, particularly when the subject is so disturbing. I have tried hard to avoid doing that here. I have attempted, as much as possible, to set my passions aside and see matters with a scholar's analytical perspective. But we are who we are. I cannot, therefore, claim to have been totally dispassionate about what I have encountered. I have tried to avoid writing a call to arms or a cri de coeur, but I recognize that on some level this book is precisely that. It is written with the conviction that action starts with understanding, which will be applied differently by different people in different circumstances. My attempt to explore a perplexing and disturbing set of circumstances is written with the hope that it will provoke action. What precisely that action is remains in the hands of the reader.

ATLANTA, GEORGIA
AUGUST 2018

· I ·

Antisemitism: A Conversation

THE PERPLEXED

Dear Professor Lipstadt:

I write to you because I am worried and confused. I hope you don't mind this intrusion, but after studying with you these past few years, I feel that you are the person to whom I should turn.

Over the last few months I've had a number of extended conversations about anti-Semitism with classmates, most of whom are not Jews. I have asked them to speak freely. And they have. One, somewhat hesitatingly, posited that given that anti-semitism has lasted so long, the Jews must, at least on some level, be responsible for it. Another picked up on this theme and, with great hesitancy, wondered if a people who has been so hated for so long might have done something to cause it. They both kept repeating that they consider me a good friend and meant nothing personal. And I don't think they did. But I felt uncomfortable. The most distressing part of this entire encounter was that I didn't know what to say to them without sounding defensive. I guess I am asking for your help in both understanding what is happening and figuring out how to respond.

They did listen soberly as I told them that Jews must take precautions in Brussels, Paris, and a myriad of other cities. I explained how on a trip to Europe some years ago, I visited Jewish sites without a second thought. In contrast, this summer I shall join a small group of Jewish students for a tour of major European sites. One member of our group wears a *kip-pah* and, without our even asking, he assured us that he would wear a baseball cap during the trip. The other guys, in a show of solidarity, agreed to wear caps as well. I promised not to take along my backpack that has the name of my Jewish youth group emblazoned on it. The fact that outward manifestations of Jewishness have become something one has to keep under wraps in many places in the Western world is both troubling and puzzling to me.

I have no reason to fear for my physical safety here on campus. I feel comfortable as a Jew, except maybe when Israel is the topic of discussion. But this encounter with my friends has left me feeling confused and, I admit, a bit insecure. I'm not sure exactly what I'm asking you to tell me, but I thought that after three years of classes and conversations with you, I would ask for your help in making sense of all this.

Yours,
Abigail

Dear Deborah:

It was good to see you, however briefly, on campus. You were correct in your observation that I didn't seem to be quite my usual self. Though my semester has been productive, I've been in a funk as I've continued to ponder the ever-increasing divisiveness in the United States and throughout so much of the world. While I've long been aware of inequities in our country, I believe that the level of contempt that various groups have for one another has become far more open and mainstream over the past few years. I trace much of it to the 2016 presidential campaign. The campaign and subsequent events didn't create this animosity, but they certainly encouraged it. Expressions of racism, homophobia, Islamophobia, and, of course, Antisemitism seems to be escalating on a daily basis.

I have a strange request. Antisemitism is something I've long abhorred, but also something that I fear I do not fully understand. I know there is much on your plate, but if you would be willing to help me try to comprehend it, I would be very grateful.

Yours,
Joe

Dear Joe and Abigail:

Joe, meet Abigail Ross, a rising senior who has been one of my students for the past few years. She has taken a number of courses relating to different aspects of the Holocaust. Abigail, meet Joe Wilson, a professor at the law school who teaches about law and religion. Joe and I have been in frequent conversation about prejudice and hatred.

Both of you have written to me with questions about the seeming rise in antisemitism in the United States and beyond and have asked if we might engage in an exchange on the topic. I'm happy to do so, not just because two people about whom I care deeply are perplexed about it but also because I believe such an exchange will help all of us get a handle on this vexing situation. Since our schedules are so varied, let's do it in writing. And, if you are both willing, let's share all of our letters with one another. That way, we can all be part of this ongoing conversation.

And because I believe things should have a beginning, a middle, and an end, let's set a time frame of a year for this exchange.

Yours,
DEL

A DELUSION

Dear Abigail and Joe:

Both of you are looking for a way to explain "why anti-semitism?" and to figure out what we can do about it. At the risk of disappointing you, let me start by saying caveat emptor, by which I mean that I don't think I can satisfactorily answer either of these questions. It is hard, if not impossible, to explain something that is essentially irrational, delusional, and absurd. That is the nature of all conspiracy theories, of which antisemitism is just one. Think about it. Why do some people insist that the moon landings took place on a stage set someplace in the American West? Despite the existence of reams of scientific and personal evidence to the contrary, they believe this because they subscribe to the notion that the government and other powerful entities are engaged in vast conspiracies to fool the public.[1] Governmental chicanery is the prism through which their view of the world is refracted. However irrational their ideas may seem to us, they make sense to them. Conspiracy theories give events that may seem inexplicable to some people an intentional explanation. If we were to provide these conspiracy theorists with evidence that proves the landing was indeed on the moon, they will a priori dismiss what we say and assume we are part of the conspiracy. To try to defeat an irrational supposition—especially when it is firmly held by its proponents—with a rational explanation is virtually impossible. Any information that does not correspond with the conspiracy theorists' preferred social, political, or ethnic narrative is ipso facto false. Social scientists have described such theories as having a "self-sealing quality" that makes them "particularly immune to challenge."[2] Conspiracy theories reduce complex issues to the simplest denominator and infuse them with heated exaggerations, suspicions, and fantasies that have no connection to facts. Some people are inclined to dismiss conspiracy theories as relatively benign. They consider people who promulgate them to be mentally unbalanced, right up there with folks who wear tinfoil hats to protect themselves from pernicious radio signals emitted by the government. While one can indeed question how rational these people are, they can still cause real damage.

The delusional aspect of antisemitism became strikingly clear to me in 1972, during my first trip to the Soviet Union. "Refuseniks," those Soviet Jews who were openly fighting the government for the freedom to emigrate, marveled at how the Communist regime managed to blame so many of its problems on Jews. At the same time that the government was persecuting Jews and spreading antisemitism, many Soviet citizens who hated the Communist regime believed it was a conspiracy of Jews. In a not atypical Jewish reaction to persecution, Refuseniks created a genre of jokes to ease their pain and illustrate the delusions of their oppressors. One has stayed with me. I share it with you in the hope of getting what will inevitably be a sobering exchange off to a humorous—or, more properly put, ironic—start.

> The USSR suffered chronic shortages of consumer goods. Early one morning a rumor circulated in Moscow that a store was to receive a shipment of shoes. A

queue formed immediately outside the store and continued to grow exponentially. After people had been
waiting for an hour or so, the manager emerged and
announced, "We will not receive enough shoes to
accommodate everyone. Jews, leave the queue and go
home." And they did. A few hours later he emerged
again and said, "We will not receive enough shoes to
accommodate everyone. All non-veterans, go home."
And they did. A few hours later he emerged yet again
and said, "We will not receive enough shoes to accommodate everyone. All those who are not members of
the Communist Party, go home." And they did. As dusk
was falling, he emerged for a final time and said, "We
will not receive any shoes today. Everyone go home."
Deeply disappointed, two exhausted and shivering loyal
Communist Party members, both of whom were World
War II veterans, walked away from the store. As they
did, one turned to the other and bitterly proclaimed,
"Those Jews, they have all the luck!"

Delusional? Irrational? Antisemitic? All of the above? Let's
try to figure it out.

Yours,
DEL

P.S. Abigail, I smiled when I read about the suggestion that
the guys on your European jaunt wear baseball caps instead of
kippot. During a recent trip to Berlin, a friend gave me directions
to an out-of-the-way synagogue. After some intricate explanations, he added, "When you get to the street that it's on, look out
for the police with submachine guns; they're standing in front

of the synagogue. But if you have trouble finding the street, just watch for men in baseball caps and follow them. They will lead you to the synagogue." I smiled. Sometime later, my friend and I passed a group of tourists. The men were all in baseball caps. He leaned over to me and whispered, "Jews." I smiled at his certitude. The next day I saw the same group in a synagogue. The caps had been replaced with *kippot.* As you may well know, in recent years many local Jews have encouraged their coreligionists not to wear *kippot* in Berlin and other major German cities. Lest you think this is only a German phenomenon, let me disabuse you of that notion. During a recent trip to Italy I was looking for a highly recommended kosher restaurant. I got tangled up in a maze of old circuitous streets and alleyways. Then I saw some guys in baseball caps. On a whim, I followed them and, sure enough, they led me right to the restaurant.

So, baseball caps might not do the trick. But maybe a fruitful exchange of ideas will.

Yours,
DEL

A DEFINITION

Dear Professor Lipstadt:

Thanks for the response. Your focus on the delusional, irrational, and conspiratorial aspects of antisemitism was very helpful. What you seem to be saying is that antisemitism is illogical and, therefore, cannot be explained. I accept that. But if we can't explain it, can we at least define it? Is every negative thing that is written or uttered about Jews an expression of antisemitism? I know that not everything negative written or said about Israel is necessarily antisemitic, but where does one draw the line? Is antisemitism always intentional? Can someone be an unintentional antisemite? I am a bit embarrassed to ask this. My roommate, who is reading this over my shoulder, insists that, given that I have taken your courses and am Jewish, I should know the answers to these questions. She's right. I feel as though I should know. But I don't.

I do remember your recounting in class that old joke that an antisemite is someone who hates Jews more than is absolutely necessary. But now I'm looking for a more substantive answer.

Yours,
Abigail

Dear Deborah:

As you had predicted, I'm already learning from Abigail, who may be surprised to know that, despite all of my writings about prejudice, I've never systematically thought about how to best define antisemitism. It would seem that I should be able to define something about which I am so perturbed. Is it simply hatred of Jews? I believe it's more complex than that. "Someone who hates Jews more than is absolutely necessary" is certainly an intriguing place to start the conversation.

Yours,
Joe

Dear Abigail and Joe:

Let me reassure both of you that you need not be the least bit uncomfortable or frustrated by the fact that you can't quite define antisemitism. You are hardly alone. Much of the general public can't define it. Even scholars in the field can't agree on a precise definition. In fact, there are people, particularly Jews, who eschew definitions and argue that Jews can feel antisemitism in their bones, the same way that African Americans recognize racism and gays recognize homophobia. Their position is best articulated by United States Supreme Court Justice Potter Stewart's famous comment about hard-core pornography as set forth in the Court's 1964 decision on whether Louis Malle's film *The Lovers* fit that category and, according to the law at the time, could therefore be banned because it was not considered "protected speech." In his opinion that the film should be considered protected speech, Stewart set down one of the most quoted phrases in Supreme Court history:

> I shall not today attempt further to define the kinds of material I understand to be embraced within that short-hand description [hard-core pornography], and perhaps I could never succeed in intelligibly doing so. *But I know it when I see it,* and the motion picture involved in this case is not that.[1] [Emphasis added.]

We should be grateful to Justice Stewart not only for expanding the boundaries of artistic expression but also for giving us this highly utilitarian concept. We may at times find it hard to precisely define antisemitism, but we certainly know it when we see or hear it.

Equally useful, though slightly less elegant than Justice Stewart's formulation, is the term "Click!" which was introduced by Jane O'Reilly in an article in the inaugural issue of *Ms.* magazine, in December 1971. In her groundbreaking essay, O'Reilly described those moments in the workplace when a woman realizes that her opinion is being ignored, a man is being credited for her ideas, or she is expected to do something—serve refreshments or watch the boss's child—that no man is ever asked to do. If she complained to her male colleagues, they would be completely befuddled. Oblivious to the obvious gender discrimination, they might declare her oversensitive, if not a bit paranoid. O'Reilly dubbed that moment of her recognition "Click!"[2]

Abigail, I am glad you remember my aside that "an antisemite is someone who hates Jews more than is absolutely necessary." It makes us laugh, but it should also make us think. This pithy observation, which is often attributed to the late philosopher and intellectual giant Isaiah Berlin, provides a simple and useful tool for identifying prejudice.[3] Imagine that someone has done something you find objectionable. You may legitimately resent the person because of his or her actions or attitudes. But if you resent him even an iota more because this person is Jewish, *that* is antisemitism. Let's concretize this by considering a hypothetical example. Imagine a driver who has been deliberately forced off the road by an erratic driver who happens to be black. The person who has almost been hit can legitimately complain to the other people in the car about the dangerous driver. But if he decries "that black guy" who has done this, he has crossed the line into racism. The driver's race is unrelated to his driving skills. Mentioning it can be considered a racist "dog whistle" that subliminally telegraphs the speaker's contempt for black people in general. (However, including the driver's race in your description of him to a police officer is of course not racist; it is simply one of the ways the driver can be physically identified by the cops who are trying to apprehend him.)

Now imagine someone telling his friend about a person whom he feels has cheated him in a business transaction. Complaining about that "crooked real-estate developer" is one thing. Complaining about that "crooked Jewish real-estate developer" is—Click!—antisemitism. But this example of the need to distinguish between a justifiable private grievance and a group-defaming prejudice may not take us far enough. I think it's important to recognize it as a Jewish joke complete with its implicit derogation of Jews in the midst of its defense of them. "Absolutely necessary" in Jewish hands means "Of course we are annoying but don't get carried away and try to kill us."

But "knowing it when you see it" and "Click" work only if we can identify antisemitism's essential elements, its building blocks. We need to unpack the contents of this hatred. Once it's identifiable, we can allow our instincts to check in. If you cannot define something, you cannot address it or fight it. So let's move on to more formal definitions. The International Holocaust Remembrance Alliance's descriptor, which has now been adopted by the European Parliament, identifies it as:

> A certain *perception* of Jews, which may be expressed as hatred toward Jews. *Rhetorical* and *physical* manifestations of antisemitism are directed toward *Jewish* or *non-Jewish* individuals and/or their property, toward Jewish community institutions and religious facilities.[4] [Emphasis added.]

Non-Jews, too? Yes, indeed. In Arthur Miller's 1945 novel *Focus,* a man, who himself is passively antisemitic, develops blurred vision and must start wearing glasses. His boss and his neighbors decide that, based on his new look, he must be Jewish, and they subject him to prejudice and, eventually, physical violence.[5] Though not a Jew, he is, ironically, the object of antisemitism.

The historical sociologist Helen Fein includes in her definition some additional important elements:

> A persisting latent structure of hostile beliefs towards *Jews as a collectivity* manifested in *individuals* as attitudes, and in *culture* as myth, ideology, folklore, and imagery, and in *actions*—social or legal discrimination, political mobilization against Jews, and collective or

state violence—which results in and/or is designed to distance, displace, or destroy Jews as Jews.[6] [Emphasis in original.]

Note the operative word here: *persisting*. It doesn't go away; it's not a onetime event. Though its outer form may evolve over time, its essence remains the same. It is not unlike a stubborn infection. Medication may alleviate the symptoms, but the infection itself lies dormant and may reemerge at an opportune moment in a new incarnation, a different "outer shell." While the shape of the hatred may be adapted and massaged, the basic ideas or illusions that are at its core remain constant. In ancient and medieval times antisemitism was religious in nature. Jews were hated because they refused to accept Christianity and, later, Islam. In the eighteenth century, racial and political rationales were added to the religious one. Voltaire was contemptuous of the Church's hierarchical structure, but he was equally contemptuous of Jews. ("You have surpassed all nations in impertinent fables, in bad conduct and in barbarism. You deserve to be punished, for this is your destiny."[7])

By the nineteenth century, those on the political right were accusing all Jews of being Socialists, Communists, and revolutionaries. Those on the political left were accusing all Jews of being wealth-obsessed capitalists who were opposed to the social and economic betterment of the poor and working classes. Further complicating the matter, the pseudoscience of the eugenics movement posited that Jews were inferior in their genetic makeup. Some of those who subscribed to this pseudoscientific claim simultaneously argued that Jews possessed not just these inferior traits but superior ones as well. Jews were maliciously intelligent, and because they were able to easily mix with non-Jews, they used those traits to wreak havoc with non-Jews' lives. That this was a contradiction in terms—simultaneously superior and inferior—presented no problem for the antisemite. This toxic brew of race, religion, politics, and pseudoscience became the cornerstone of Nazi antisemitism and is today a cornerstone of the white power movement and white supremacist antisemitism.*[8]

The *structure* of antisemitism means that it's not just a bunch of haphazard ideas, but it can result in, as Fein notes, "actions—social or legal discrimination, political mobilization . . . and collective or state violence." It also has an internal coherence. This coherence might be delusional and absurd—just like the Communist who was sure Jews had all the luck because they were kicked off the line first and did not have to wait hours in the freezing cold—but it makes perfect sense to the antisemite. Irrespective of whether the antisemitic manifestations were religious, political, social, racial, or some amalgam of them all, the same themes or tropes remain embedded in them. We know them well: Jews may be small in number, but they have the ability to compel far more powerful entities to do their bidding. That bidding invariably involves aiding Jews at the expense of non-Jews. Jews, over the course of millennia, irrespective of whether they lived in close proximity to one another or were separated by continents, have honed a cosmopolitan alliance that facilitates their evil deeds. The historical template for these charges

---

* I have chosen to use the terms "white power" and "white supremacist" interchangeably. While the two terms may have shades of difference between them, they both speak to the racism, separatism, violence, hatred of Muslims, opposition to immigrants, and antisemitism that is fundamental to these movements.

is to be found in the New Testament's depictions of the death of Jesus. Irrespective of the fact that everyone involved in the story was Jewish—except for the Romans who did the actual crucifixion—the way the story has been told by generations of Church leaders is that "the Jews" killed Jesus, thereby depriving humanity of his wisdom, goodness, and glory. They did so because he demanded that the money changers be evicted from the Temple area, which would have threatened the income of the Temple hierarchy. According to Christian doctrine as it was taught for millennia, Jesus was crucified because, among other things, he threatened Jews' power and financial well-being.

The Church had an institutional motivation in blaming and castigating the Jew. Judaism and Christianity were competing faiths. Christianity was Judaism's "offspring," and its success was threatened by the fact that there were Jews who refused to accept the new "truth." A related historical building block in the evolution of this animus was the declaration by the apostle Paul that a "man is justified by faith without the deeds of the law" and that for Jesus "neither circumcision nor uncircumcision accomplishes anything." In other words, belief in Jesus and his teachings replaced Jewish law and tradition. Supersessionism, or replacement theology—the declaration by Paul that Christianity is the one true faith and therefore supersedes or replaces Judaism, both in belief and in deed—became an essential tenet of the new faith. Pauline doctrine marginalized Jews, particularly those who continued to practice Jewish traditions, and depicted them as blind to the truth. Jews, Paulists argued, repudiated this new faith because of their inherent maliciousness. This formulation rendered Judaism more than just a competing religion. It became a source of evil. It is this that makes antisemitism different from other prejudices. Antisemitism is not simply the hatred of something "foreign," but the hatred of a perpetual evil in the world. Jews are not *an* enemy but *the* ultimate enemy.[9] This hatred is ubiquitous. It has persisted through the millennia, through different cultures. It has been present in many geographic areas—including those with no Jews in residence. It has permeated an array of ideologies, even the resolutely atheistic Marxism.

It's important for you to understand that antisemitism, as is the case with any prejudice, exists independently of any action by Jews. Sometimes, an accusation against a particular Jew, or even a group of Jews, may be correct. There are some Jews who are obsessed with money or who mistreat their employees. But the same can be said about certain non-Jews. Saying that "of course X is obsessed with money; he's a Jew, isn't he?" is antisemitic. Antisemitism is not the hatred of people who *happen to be* Jews. It is hatred of them *because* they are Jews.[10]

Given the absurdity of antisemitic accusations, why do they gain any traction? One explanation may be that, having been embedded in society for millennia, they have gained a staying power that is hard to eradicate. Antisemitism also became a means of explaining otherwise inexplicable situations. For example, when the bubonic plague raged across Europe in the fourteenth century, Jews were accused of poisoning the wells and spreading the disease. For people schooled in millennia of Church-based antisemitism, it provided an easy, straightforward, and logical explanation for a seemingly inexplicable disease. Economic downturns, political tensions, unsuccessful military actions, and a myriad of other crises were explained away by attributing them to the interference of Jews. This blaming of the Jews for the suffering of others served only to further reinforce the power of antisemitism.

Some, however, argue that there is no internal coherence to antisemitism. Jean-Paul Sartre, for example, insisted that antisemitism is a "passion" and rejected the notion that it was an empirical idea. Antisemitism, according to Sartre, made no intellectual sense and thus should not be dignified by being called an "idea."[11] Sartre's notion of the irrational seems to discount the historical and religious origins of Jew-hatred. Echoing and expanding on Sartre is Anthony Julius who, while fully cognizant of the historical lineage of this hatred, argues that antisemitism must ultimately be seen as a "discontinuous, contingent aspect of a number of distinct *mentalities* and milieus.... It is a heterogeneous phenomenon, the site of collective hatreds, and of cultural anxieties and resentments."[12] By rejecting the notion that antisemitism possesses an intellectually credible framework or unified field theory, Sartre and Julius call attention to both the irrational nature of this animus and the reason it's so hard to fight.[13] Julius adds something else to our discussion. He refuses to elevate the antisemite in stature and importance. Consider the exchange I had with Julius, who was my lawyer when I was sued for libel by David Irving for calling him a Holocaust denier, an antisemite, and a racist. Shortly before the trial was to begin, upset at the personal burden of this legal battle, I told Julius that I was intent on decimating Irving. "He's not that important," Julius replied. I was flabbergasted. He and his firm had worked on my case pro bono for close to two years. He despised the way Irving fabricated history and spread antisemitism. How could he say he was unimportant? Sensing my confusion, he explained what he meant. It's not antisemitism that is inconsequential, it's the antisemite himself. "Think of fighting Irving as the equivalent of what you must do when you step in dirt left by a dog on the street," he said—except he used a far more graphic term than "dirt." "The dirt has no intrinsic value. There is nothing interesting about it. Nonetheless, one must carefully clean it off one's feet prior to entering one's home. If you fail to do so and track it into the house, then you face a serious and long-term problem. So, too, with the antisemite." Julius was right. He knew the lies and prejudice Irving spewed had to be relentlessly fought. Our challenge was and continues to be to fight the antisemite without elevating him or her in stature.[14] Antisemites must be fought, especially if there is a chance that their passion or ideology stands a chance of becoming part of a national policy, but they are people of no consequence.

Can something have a coherent structure while at the same time be a heterogeneous passion? I would argue that it can. This is part of its "elastic" quality. Sometimes it may present itself as a passion. In other instances, it may present itself as normative. But whatever form it takes, we must always insist that antisemitism has never made sense and never will. Fight it. But don't elevate it or its purveyors in importance.

Yours,
DEL

A SPELLING

Dear Professor Lipstadt:

Thank you so much for that explanation. Things are beginning to fall into place. I do have a question that I think I need answered before we proceed further. It might seem a bit strange. What is the correct way to spell anti-Semitism? I've seen and used it in so many different ways: as one word, either upper- or lower-case (Antisemitism, antisemitism), and also hyphenated, but in different ways (anti-Semitism, Anti-Semitism, anti-semitism, Anti-semitism). I notice that Professor Wilson goes with "Antisemitism" and that you use "antisemitism." Is this just a question of style or, as is often the case, is there something embedded here that I am missing?

Thanks,
Abigail

Dear Abigail and Joe:

This is an excellent question, and not simply an arcane academic argument. Rarely has so much meaning been vested in a hyphen and an uppercase letter. It's far more significant than the well-known medieval debate over how many angels can dance on the head of a pin. The etymology of this word is part of its ugly history and its contemporary reality.

Let's first address the hyphen. In most cases the right side of a hyphenated word can stand alone as a word in its own right: for example, anti-immigration, anti-trade, or anti-taxes. A hyphen in anti-Semitism suggests that one opposes "Semitism." In recent decades, as the Arab–Israeli crisis has intensified, some Arabs, upon being accused of engaging in antisemitic rhetoric, have posited that it's impossible for them to be anti-semites because they themselves are "Semites." This argument is based on three faulty notions.

First, it assumes there is such a thing as a Semitic people, when in fact there is not. The word "Semitic" was coined in 1781 by a German historian to describe a group of languages that originated in the Middle East and that have some linguistic similarities; they include Arabic, Hebrew, Aramaic, Amharic, ancient Akkadian, and Ugaritic. There's nothing that binds the speakers of these different languages together as a people. (In the nineteenth century, Ernest Renan, a French linguist and cultural historian, compared and contrasted the cultural achievements of people who spoke Semitic languages with speakers of Indo-European languages—which is to say, Europeans.[1] His comparisons were riddled with prejudice, but that's another conversation.) Second, even if one were to posit that there *is* such a cultural or ethnic entity as Semites, this argument assumes that members of a group cannot be prejudiced against their own. In fact, one of prejudice's most debilitating legacies is how the people targeted come to believe that the negative stereotypes thrown at them are true. There are racist African Americans, sexist women, and antisemitic Jews.

Finally, arguing that antisemitism means exhibiting hostility toward all "Semitic" peoples obscures the meaning that has been ascribed to it for virtually all its history. Wilhelm Marr, a German journalist who was a Jew-hater, popularized the term in the late nineteenth century. He contended that Jews, including those who had converted to Christianity, were incapable of assimilating. Once a Jew, always a Jew. According to Marr, Jews were dangerous because their goal was "to harm Germanic identity" and to destroy "the Germanic." Nothing could alter their foreign-ness, including changing their religion. Consequently, Marr rejected the term *Judenhass*, Jew-hatred, because even Jews who now considered themselves Christians were still objects of his hatred. Seeking a word that had a racial and "scientific" connotation rather than a religious one, he chose *Antisemitismus* (capitalized because all nouns are capitalized in German). For him and the legions of people who adopted this word, it meant one thing and one thing only: hating members of the Jewish "race." (In one of those bitter ironies, at the end of his life Marr recanted his antisemitic accusations and, in a final essay entitled "Testament of an Antisemite," acknowledged that the faults he attributed to the Jews were, in fact, the result of the Industrial Revolution and the political debates of the times.[2] His remorse notwithstanding, the damage had already been done.)

Now, about that hyphen: For some reason, when the word first appeared in English in 1893 it was given a hyphen— "anti-Semitism." But in French and Spanish it has always appeared without a hyphen and all lowercased—*antisémitisme, antisemitismo*.[3] In my own English-language usage I choose not to go with the hyphen because the word, both as its creator had intended and as it has been generally used for the past one hundred and fifty years, means, quite simply, the hatred of Jews. It does not mean hostility toward a nonexistent thing called "Semitism." When Marr coined the word, he was most definitely *not* referring to people who spoke Arabic, Aramaic, Amharic, Akkadian, or Ugaritic. That is why I find it particularly offensive when people who speak any of those languages claim that they cannot possibly hate Jews because the language that they speak is linguistically linked to Hebrew.

Finally, am I making any sort of statement by going with the lowercase "antisemite" as opposed to the uppercase "Antisemite"? Yes, I am. It's my small way—and I am certainly not alone in this—of validating Sartre's and Julius's contention that antisemitism is an illogical, delusional passion full of self-contradictions and absurd contentions. It doesn't deserve the dignity of capitalization, which in English is reserved for proper names. I am reminded of the joke purportedly told by Jews living in Germany in the 1930s.

> Two Jews were sitting on one of the few park benches permitted to Jews. One was reading the *Berliner Gemeindeblatt,* a Jewish communal newspaper; the other, the virulently antisemitic Nazi publication *Der Stürmer.* "Why on earth are you reading that thing?" the *Gemeindeblatt* reader asked his friend. "When I read a Jewish publication," his friend replied, "I hear of our woes and terrible fate. When I read *Der Stürmer,* I read how we control the banks, world media, international governments, and how powerful we are. I much prefer the latter."

> Something this absurd does not deserve a capital letter.

Yours,
DEL

·II·

A Taxonomy of the Antisemite

THE EXTREMIST:
FROM THE STREETS TO THE INTERNET

Dear Deborah:

We began our exchange because I was in such a funk about the divisions in our society in general and the rise of antisemitism in particular. One of the catalysts for this funk was the events in Charlottesville, Virginia, in August 2017. I remember watching the television coverage of the neo-Nazi march there and being unable to fathom what I was seeing. Watching a mélange of white supremacist and white power groups march with their tiki torches chanting "Jews will not replace us" left me, a committed Christian who takes his faith very seriously, shaken to the core. Nazi-like flags, placards declaring "Jews are Satan's children," and the murder of a counterdemonstrator by a marcher who used his car as a weapon left me stunned beyond measure.[1]

I broke down in tears when I read about the local synagogue that was holding Shabbat services that morning. Three of the heavily armed neo-Nazis positioned themselves with their arms crossed in front of the entrance to the building. The rabbi and the synagogue president decided to send everyone in the building out the back door in small groups, taking the Torah scrolls with them for safekeeping. I know you are one of those who eschews using Hitler/Third Reich/Nazi Germany analogies when discussing contemporary events. As you have told me, easy ahistorical analogies to the Holocaust and Nazism cheapen the genocidal actions of the Germans and often create an unwarranted angst among people today. But I couldn't stop myself from thinking about Nazi Germany when I read about these Jews who had to sneak out of their synagogue for their own safety. I don't ever remember reading about such an event, except in literature about the Third Reich. I have certainly never heard about it happening in America.

I feel that I need to have a better understanding of the situation. What is it that we are witnessing? Are these young men who paraded through the streets of Charlottesville simply terribly misguided thrill seekers, or is something really serious going on here? I never dreamed we would see people marching in a bucolic college town, freely chanting such vile and hateful slogans.

On the other hand, I have friends—Jews among them—who have told me in the past that all the concerns about antisemitism today are overblown. Not surprisingly, I haven't heard from them since Charlottesville. Can you, who have spent so much time in what you describe as the "sewers" of antisemitism, help me understand what happened there?

Joe

Dear Professor Lipstadt:

Professor Wilson's letter reminds me of how I sat glued to the television for that entire weekend, watching the analyses of the events in Charlottesville. It was frightening to hear things like "Jews will not replace us." Thanks to your class, I recognized the Nazi origins of "blood and soil." What's this all about? Were these just extremist crazies? Are they worth worrying about? Do they have a following? Have they suddenly appeared on the horizon, or have they been lurking beneath the surface, unnoticed by the rest of us? Is this Nazi Germany redux?

Abigail

Dear Joe and Abigail:

Charlottesville left me dumbfounded, too. It was hardly the first of such events. There have been a series of such white nationalist violent demonstrations in the past two years. Though these marchers ostensibly came to "protect" the statue of Confederate general Robert E. Lee from being removed, there is little doubt that this was not their real motive. They were there to stoke their fellow extremists and make a display of their power. They were also there to spread antisemitism and racism. The overt antisemitism of the marchers was evident as they took their first steps across the campus. "Jews will not replace us" is self-explanatory. "Blood and soil" may sound benign, but, as Abigail knows from our class, it's a German slogan *(Blut und Boden)* that was central to Nazi ideology. It idealizes a racially defined nation, and its subtext is that only those people with "pure" or "white" bloodlines can be true citizens of the nation. Only they are rooted to the soil. Jews, on the other hand, are "cosmopolitans," not nationalists, and as such are interlopers and threats to the well-being of the nation. The demonstrators paraded with the Confederate flag, which symbolized far more than a link to a statue of Robert E. Lee. It represents a cultural and political position that melds white power with opposition to liberalism and multiculturalism.[2] While these chants were chilling, something else scared me even more. It wasn't what *was* there that frightened me, but what *wasn't* there. No KKK robes, Nazi-inspired uniforms, or white supremacist paraphernalia were evident. No T-shirts with neo-Nazi slogans were to be seen. Most of the marchers wore neatly pressed khaki pants and smart-looking shirts. Had they not carried flags with swastika-like and white supremacist symbols or the Confederate "stars and bars" and raised their arms in a Nazi-like salute, they might have looked as though they had just walked out of a J.Crew or Brooks Brothers catalog.[3] This was even more evident a few months later when they held another flash protest march. White polo shirts and khaki pants were the uniform du jour. This was not by chance. It was to make them appear to be "ordinary Americans." As Richard Spencer, one of the organizers of the march, noted, "We have to look good." People are not attracted to those who appear "crazed or ugly or victims or just stupid."[4]

Let's step back for a moment from Charlottesville and try to figure out who these marchers are and what they represent. The ideologies motivating them are white power and white supremacy, ideologies that include a foundational belief in the evil nature of the Jews, Muslims, and people of color. According to the supremacists, these minorities are intent on harming "regular Americans." They find one another at white power gatherings. They visit websites that promote neo-Nazism, white nationalism, and antisemitism.[5] Many of them adhere to Christian Identity, a racist interpretation of Christianity that posits that there were two creations—one that failed, which explains the existence of people of color, and one that produced Adam and Eve. Eve was first impregnated by Adam and produced Abel, whose descendants are white folks. She was then impregnated by the snake (i.e., Satan) and produced Cain, whose descendants are Jews, who are therefore, quite literally, "satanic." Some of these people are members of anti-big-government "resistance" groups that engage in violent hate crimes, particularly against government institutions and officials.

Among the groups at the Charlottesville rally was the National Socialist Movement (NSM), which is probably the largest American neo-Nazi group. It reveres Adolf Hitler and the Third Reich. At rallies and protests its members often appear in Nazi-like uniforms and sport swastika armbands. Not, however, at Charlottesville. There were lots of NSM flags visible. But those who carried them looked like clean-cut college students. Also present in Charlottesville was Vanguard America, a group with increasingly strong ties to neo-Nazis. Its members believe that the United States is exclusively for white Americans and not for non-Christians, Jews, Muslims, or people of color. The car used to murder the counterdemonstrator sported a Vanguard America decal.[6] Other participants were people with no apparent ideology who, for a range of personal reasons, just hate those who are different than they are. Brian Levin, a specialist on American extremism, has described them as "thrill offenders with more shallow prejudices." They are part of "informal associations of young people that commit hate crimes for excitement and social engagement." But we increasingly see them acting on these latent or shallow prejudices. They may well eventually join the ranks of what has been called the mission offender, or hard-core hatemonger, who engages in outright acts of violence.[7] As then FBI director James Comey observed in an address to the Anti-Defamation League in May 2017, "in a heartbeat, words can turn to violence. Because hate doesn't remain static too often."[8]

In fact, the hate has not remained static and the words have already turned to violence. In May 2017 Richard Collins, a young African American who was about to graduate from the University of Maryland and be commissioned as second lieutenant in the U.S. Army, was murdered while waiting for an Uber near the campus. His attacker was a member of a white supremacist group, alt-Reich. Using a four-inch blade, he stabbed Collins in the chest. A few days later a white supremacist riding on a streetcar in Portland, Oregon, began verbally assaulting two female passengers, one who was black and one who was wearing a hijab. When two men came to the young women's defense, the assailant slashed their throats. At his arraignment, he declared: "You call it terrorism. I call it patriotism."[9]

These right-wing extremist groups and individuals serve as rallying points for a wide range of people, some more violent than others.[10] In the United States, these groups regularly contend that their country is ruled by what they call the ZOG (Zionist Occupied Government), an international group of wealthy Jews intent on ending American sovereignty and bringing about a one-world government that they alone will rule. ZOG, they proclaim, already controls the media, the banks, and America's foreign policy, and is now working on world domination.[11]

While the views expressed by these people are not new, they tend to proliferate during times when there is populist resentment against what is regarded as an "elite" class of people—usually highly educated men and women with liberal political and social views. This is what we are now seeing in many parts of the world. In the United States, for the first time in many decades—perhaps for the first time ever—these haters believe that they have sympathetic allies in the White House.

Until a few years ago, it could be said that these groups had fallen on hard times in the United States, in part because of lawsuits brought against them by those they have harassed and threatened. Ironically, the government had previously not seen them as a significant threat, in great measure because they were white. After the bombing of the Federal Building in Oklahoma City in 1995 (at the time, the deadliest attack on American government property since Pearl Harbor), the government became more vigilant about monitoring the activities of white power groups. Nonetheless, it still took the House of Representatives Subcommittee on Crime close to six months after the Oklahoma City bombing to hold a hearing on militias. No other committee took up the issue. Timothy McVeigh, the Oklahoma City bomber, was seen more as a lone wolf terrorist than as someone who had been influenced by a white power movement. Although some white supremacist groups were stripped of their resources, their members simply scattered to other small groups, formed new organizations, and became increasingly active on newly emerging social media.[12] They did not go away. This kind of extremism is now experiencing a resurgence, especially as its adherents add hatred of Muslims to their long-standing antisemitism and racism. There are differences among the panoply of groups that constitute the Far Right, but hatred of Muslims, utter contempt for African Americans and Latinos, support of racial segregation, and deep-seated antisemitism are essential to all of them.[13]

It's social media that has really given these extremists a new lease on life. Publications attacking anyone they considered an enemy used to be mailed in plain envelopes from anonymous post office boxes to recipients who would furtively collect them. Today, they are easily accessed with a basic computer search engine. Proponents of these noxious ideas can also use social media to anonymously spew their hatred. With unprecedented ease, they find like-minded people and use Internet platforms to robustly amplify and spread their views. In fact, our perception that the number of antisemites and antisemitic events have markedly escalated may at least in part be governed by the ubiquity of social media. Incidents that we might not previously have heard about are now celebrated on racist websites. Social media allows the extremists not only to communicate more easily with one another but also to make their voices and views heard beyond their adherents. Through the various social media platforms, these hate-mongers can reach a wider audience of people, including those who might previously have not been exposed to these messages of hate. In so doing, they are normalizing open expressions of hatred.[14] Many people are uncomfortable with the white nationalists' and supremacists' open adulation of Nazis, love of violence, and overt antisemitism and racism. They will not join up with them. But influenced by the extremists' spread of hatred on social media, people who might not join a supremacist organization will nonetheless begin to repeat some of their arguments.

Charlottesville did not come out of the blue. We saw these extremists at work during the 2016 presidential campaign. They took particular aim at those Jewish journalists who they believed were either opposed to Trump or insufficiently supportive of him. During the primaries, Bethany Mandel, a self-described political conservative who has written for, among other publications, the *Federalist* and *Commentary,* tweeted what she described as "an offhand remark" about Donald Trump's "legions of antisemitic fans." She described the responses she received as "unlike anything [she had] seen before on Twitter." She received messages branding her a "Jewess" who "deserves the oven." Another message ominously asserted, "Missed one, you slimy Jewess." Not satisfied with these postings, her attackers also began to "dox" her, which means to find and post online private identifying information about her. She subsequently received explicit death threats, including some that were posted on her private Facebook page. She bought a gun.

Were Mandel the only journalist or commentator to be subjected to this barrage of online threats, accusations, and antisemitism, this would be a disturbing anecdote but nothing more. But she was not alone.[15] The cyber-antisemites began to place an echo symbol—((( )))—around the surnames of prominent Jewish journalists and commentators who adopted positions with which they disagreed. The echo symbol originated in 2014, on a podcast called *The Daily Shoah* that is hosted by *The Right Stuff,* a white nationalist blog. The echo began to be used in earnest to identify Jewish reporters who were critical of Donald Trump. Those who relied on it described the symbol as "closed captioning for the Jew-blind." It ensured that the journalist's Jewish identity was immediately evident.[16] In May 2016, Jonathan Weisman, deputy Washington editor for the *New York Times,* mentioned an article by the historian Robert Kagan that linked Donald Trump to fascism. He quickly received a response—"Hello (((Weisman)))"—from someone who utilized the screen name @CyberTrump. Sensing that the parentheses had some connection to his Jewish identity, Weisman asked for an explanation and received the following response: "What, ho, the vaunted Ashkenazi intelligence, hahaha! It's a dog whistle, fool. Belling the cat for my fellow goyim." (The term "belling the cat" comes from a medieval fable in which a group of mice conspires to hang a bell around a cat so that they would have fair warning when she came close to them.) Weisman observed that the belling had its intended impact. "The horde was unleashed," he wrote. Just like Mandel, he received an avalanche of antisemitic comments and accusations. Some messages focused on Holocaust denial, while others depicted the Jew as a fifth columnist conniving to lead America into a war for Israel. One message came from an individual who tagged himself "a proud future member of the Trump Deportation Squad." Weisman was also sent various antisemitic images, including one of the iconic gates of Auschwitz with the words "Arbeit Macht Frei" replaced with "Machen Amerika Great." Other images showed a path of dollar bills leading to a gas chamber, or a smiling Donald Trump in a Nazi uniform about to "flick the switch on a gas chamber." Inside the gas chamber was the body of a man with Weisman's face Photoshopped onto it. In an effort to expose, publicize, and possibly shame these cyber-haters, Weisman posted every message he received. The only image he chose not to post was one of his disembodied head, adorned with a skull cap and side curls, being held aloft.[17]

Julia Ioffe, a Jewish reporter, who in an April 2016 article in *GQ* about Melania Trump mentioned that she had a half brother with whom her family had no contact, was bombarded with antisemitic threats and images, including one with her face superimposed onto that of an Auschwitz prisoner.[18] Other reporters and commentators—including those who these extremists among Trump's supporters mistakenly assumed were Jewish—were also subjected to these kinds of attacks. After writing an article about Trump's racist expressions, *New*

York Times columnist Nicholas Kristof (who is a Christian of Armenian extraction) was besieged with antisemitic messages, including one suggesting that he be sent to the ovens for writing "a typical Jewish hit piece."[19] *Atlantic* editor Jeffrey Goldberg, who was inundated with such attacks, described the message-senders as "neo-Nazis on Twitter." The recurring theme in the approximately one hundred messages he received every day was "[I] should be gassed and my family should be put in the ovens." Goldberg has long had a prominent public profile, but he began to receive these messages only during the 2016 presidential campaign. They came from people who explicitly "advertise[d] themselves as Trump supporters."[20] I'm not suggesting, of course, that they represent all of Trump's supporters. We must be careful about making those sweeping generalizations. The fact that so many of them hide behind online names and false identities suggests that they are cowards who are emboldened by the anonymity of cyber-warfare. But it's worth noting that the vehemence, intensity, and overt antisemitism of these cyber-antisemites caught even these experienced journalists, as well as those who monitor antisemitism, by surprise.

Social media is not the only new tool in the extremists' kit bag. The Charlottesville protests were coordinated by a group that included Richard Spencer, a leader of the alt-right movement. A loose conglomeration of organizations that espouse white nationalism and white supremacy, the alt-right aims to have these views become part of the broader public discourse and to mainstream their ideas in a way that long-established neo-Nazi and other racist groups have been unable to do. An amalgam of far-right positions, the alt-right is just as extreme as any of the long-established racist groups that preceded it. In fact, many of its political objectives are direct legacies of the ideas promulgated by twentieth-century white power movements. They echo the political platforms of former KKK leader David Duke during his various campaigns for public office.[21]

What is different about the alt-right and similar groups is the way they package their ideas, as they try to project a decidedly "normal" image—not as neo-Nazis or Jew-haters, but as "white nationalists" who simply (and, by their way of explaining, rather benignly) believe that white people are being marginalized in society by other racial and ethnic groups. That's why I don't think that, going forward, we'll be seeing swastikas or Nazi-like uniforms at these rallies. We may even see Confederate flags replaced by American flags. (After all, who can object to the American flag?) Though one may not find an overtly racist or Nazi symbol among the clean-cut and well-dressed adherents of these new groups, their views are just as extremist as those of the most committed member of the KKK. They advocate a race-based white supremacism. For them, an American citizen is someone who is white and Christian. In the days after the 2016 presidential election, at an alt-right conference in Washington, D.C., Spencer, referring to liberals and critics of the alt-right, declared that "one wonders if these people are people at all or instead soulless Golems." He saluted "white America," which must "conquer or die," and then declared that "America was, until this past generation, a white country, designed for ourselves and our posterity. It is our creation, it is our inheritance, and it belongs to us." Spencer concluded his remarks with an outstretched arm (containing a strategically placed glass of water) and the cry "Hail Trump! Hail Our People! Hail Victory!" As the audience enthusiastically jumped to its feet and began to cheer, many among them saluted him with outstretched arms and cheers of "Sieg heil" and "Hail Trump."[22] These Nazi-inspired expressions of support were also visible in a video of an event held at a karaoke bar in Dallas, Texas, in April 2016, in which these activists raised their arms in the Nazi salute as another of the movement's ideologues, Milo Yian-nopoulos, sang "America the Beautiful."[23]

Although these and similar groups abroad present themselves as Americanists, Europeanists, white nationalists, and patriots, a closer look at their writings and public statements reveals plain old racism and antisemitism.[24] The *National Review,* a magazine that is considered the voice of the conservative movement in America, described these groups as a "motley crew of white nationalists and wannabe fascists."[25] While the *National Review* may consider them a "motley crew," not having a formal organization has served them well. Alt-right and similar groups may splinter and regroup. Many of their leaders have been disgraced and new ones have replaced them. But their adherents will not disappear. More importantly, they have managed in recent years to establish direct links to people with influence, including those in high-level government positions. President Trump and some of his associates have retweeted and reposted videos, cartoons, memes, and comments on various social media platforms that come from the alt-right and those affiliated with them. The retweeters give license to people who share these sentiments to engage in racist, antisemitic, and extremist rhetoric. And the more this kind of invective is repeated, the more it has a way of bleeding beyond its original borders and becoming part of the national discourse. As that happens, ideas that were once considered to be outside the pale of civil conversation become mainstreamed.

Regards,
DEL

BEYOND THE EXTREMIST

Dear Deborah:

Thanks so much for that explanation and description. I used to think of extremists as those who wore KKK robes or skinhead paraphernalia. Obviously, the problem is far broader and subtler than that. Do you think that the reason some of my friends think contemporary concerns about antisemitism, especially among Jews, are really not credible is that the individuals and groups who are active today don't present as extremists? I think they would agree that what we saw at Charlottesville was antisemitic, because, despite the anodyne way the protesters were dressed, their other manifestations of antisemitism were so blatant. I'm not sure that they would recognize the less openly threatening manifestations of antisemitism that you warn about.

Joe

Dear Joe and Abigail:

Joe, you are so right. We recognize and abhor the extremists. There is no ambiguity about who they are and what they believe. Most people (with an emphasis on the word "most") respond to them with visceral disgust. But our focus on them can some-times distort the landscape because they're not the only ones poised to do harm. In the wake of the Holocaust, Adolf Hitler has become the template for the archetypal antisemite. When someone does not present as an out-and-out Nazi, observers often fail to recognize him or her as an antisemite. But to be an antisemite one need not be a Hitler or Nazi equivalent. You need not even be prone to violence. There are many antisem-ites who would never dream of even using offensive rhetoric. Audiences saw prime examples of this type of person in *Gentleman's Agreement,* a novel by Laura Z. Hobson that, in 1947, became an Academy Award–winning film starring Gregory Peck (playing a non-Jewish journalist named David Green who is passing as a Jew to research an article on antisemitism) and Dorothy McGuire (playing his very proper and wealthy WASP girlfriend). When Green's young son comes home from school one day crying because some kids called him a "dirty Jew and a stinking kike," McGuire's character impulsively gathers him up in her arms and says, "Darling, it's not true! You're no more Jew-ish than I am. It's just a horrible mistake."

She's not a Nazi, of course. And she bears no resemblance to a Hitler or a David Duke. But by telling the boy that he need not worry because he is in fact *not* a Jew, she reinforces both degrading and hateful conceptions of Jews and the notion that there is something inherently wrong with being a Jew. And so—as she herself acknowledges at the end of the film—she is antisemitic. As we'll explore further, there is more than one pro-totypical antisemite. There are many subgroups in this category.

Yours,
DEL

ANTISEMITIC ENABLERS

Dear Abigail and Joe:

I want to share with you an exchange I just had with a group of students studying at Oxford University. Their query introduces us to two additional categories of antisemitism. In one, expressions of antisemitism do not stem from deep ideological commitment but serve a utilitarian purpose, as a means to a political end. In the other, antisemitism is rooted in an ideology that itself has nothing to do with Jews but that sweeps Jews up into it. Both enable this hatred to enter the mainstream.

Yours,
DEL

Dear Professor Lipstadt:

We write to you from Oxford. We are a diverse group of students: British and American, black and white, Jew and non-Jew, wealthy and of limited means. We've been sitting here in a pub discussing the nature of antisemitism, a topic that has become quite newsworthy in the U.K. in recent months, and debating whether it is more likely to come from the Right or the Left. Divisions quickly emerged, but not between the Jews and non-Jews. It was far more political. Those on the left insist that the Left has a proud tradition of fighting against prejudice and has always been at the forefront of movements for inclusion, whether it pertains to feminism, ethnic and religious minorities, or the LGBT community. They contend that, while antisemitism has always found a fertile field on the right, their liberal ideology is by definition averse to it. They believe that a genuinely progressive person could not be an antisemite. Those on the right guffawed at that and insisted that antisemitism has a long history on the left—they reminded us that the USSR persecuted its Jews—and is today securely and structurally embedded there.

The conversation became more heated when the debate turned to President Donald Trump and Jeremy Corbyn, the leader of the Labour Party here in the U.K. Some of the progressives contended that Trump is a prime example of an antisemite. The conservatives insisted that we did not have to look across the pond for an example of an antisemitic political leader. Corbyn fits that bill. During the conversation, your work was repeatedly cited by people on both sides of the political divide. Those on the right and those on the left claimed that you were on their side. And so we decided that you should settle our argument. We thank you in advance and look forward to hearing from you.

Yours,
Students in an Oxford pub

Dear Oxford Students:

Thanks for writing. The questions you raise about Trump and Corbyn are important and it is on them that I will focus.

But first let me note that I was amused and rather pleased that people at both ends of the political spectrum cited me as a compatriot. Rather than claim allegiance to one group or the other, I hope that I will, in my answers to you, challenge everyone in your group to think more critically about their political allegiances. Most important, I hope that those on both the right and left are a bit discomforted by what I say. More about that later.

I don't know if either of these men is an antisemite, which is to say that he harbors personal contempt for Jews. While neither of them may be, both have facilitated the spread of antisemitism. They claim to be deeply perplexed when they are accused of doing so. But their denials notwithstanding, they are directly responsible for the legitimization of explicit hostility toward Jews. One of these men acts out of purely political motives. The other seems to be motivated by a combination of political and ideological motives.

Let's start with Donald Trump. During the presidential campaign Trump used classic antisemitic stereotyping in a speech he delivered to the Republican Jewish Coalition. He left his audience reeling when he asked, "Is there anyone in this room who doesn't renegotiate deals? Probably ninety-nine percent of you [do renegotiate]. Probably more than any room I've ever spoken in. . . . I'm a negotiator, like you folks." And then: "But you're not going to support me because I don't want your money. . . . You want to control your own politicians." In those few sentences, Trump hit almost every millennial-old antisemitic stereotype: Jews have an unnatural desire for money, power, control, and haggling, and an innate deviousness (renegotiating a deal after it is made).[1] I am not suggesting that Trump has contempt for Jews. If asked, he would probably say that he admires what he considers the Jewish quality of being cunning in business dealings.[2] But the fact that he could be so tone-deaf to antisemitic stereotypes left many people baffled. It reminded me of Franklin Foer's observation that philosemites are antisemites who like Jews.[3]

Far more significant than this kind of stereotyping was Trump's refusal to seriously address the antisemitic behavior of his supporters. For example, after Julia Ioffe's article on Melania Trump appeared in *GQ,* Trump supporters went after her with a vengeance. Almost immediately, the leaders of the violently antisemitic website *InfoStormer* called on its followers to let Ioffe "know what you think of her dirty kike trickery." The *Daily Stormer,* a white supremacist and antisemitic website, instructed its followers to "make sure to identify her as a Jew working against White interests." Followers of these sites were encouraged to conduct "a trolling effort against the evil Jewish bitch." And that is precisely what happened. Ioffe was subjected to an outpouring of antisemitic venom and threats, some so vile that they left her concerned for her physical well-being. She was threatened with rape. Her picture was Photoshopped onto that of an emaciated concentration camp victim whose body was on top of a pile of other victims. Another troller Photoshopped her face onto the body of a kneeling Jew with a Nazi guard holding a gun to her head.

When the attacks on Ioffe became public, reporters asked candidate Trump if he had a message for those who were threatening her. Trump shook his head, indicating that he had none. When pressed, he said, "I don't have a message to the fans. A woman wrote an article that's inaccurate."[4] He wouldn't say that what was being done to Ioffe was unacceptable.

Trump adopted a similar stance in response to former Ku Klux Klan leader and Holocaust denier David Duke's endorsement of his candidacy. Trump insisted he could not condemn

Duke because he knew nothing about either Duke or the Klan. He said this despite the fact that ten years earlier he had labeled Duke "a bigot, a racist, a problem. I mean, this is not exactly the people you want in your party."[5] It may have been coincidental, but in the weeks following his refusal to condemn the KKK, there was a significant rise in antisemitic incidents.[6]

Trump and those around him did more than signal to these white supremacists that their comments were acceptable. They amplified their sites. In January 2016, then candidate Trump retweeted a message from an anonymous Nazi sympathizer and white supremacist who uses the twitter handle @White GenocideTM. His profile contained a link to a pro–Adolf Hitler documentary and his site featured a photograph with red lettering proclaiming "Get the F— Out of My Country" with the location of "Jewmerica."* Many of @WhiteGenocideTM's tweets concerned violence allegedly committed by African Americans as well as anti-Arab posts. In February 2016 Trump again retweeted something from @WhiteGenocideTM. Two days later he retweeted a message from a user whose Twitter header image included the term "white genocide." None of these retweets were antisemitic. They generally were contemptuous of his Republican opponents. But the fact that Trump was drawing from these sites and relying on their contents generated great enthusiasm among white supremacists. Consider the response of @TheNordicNation. "You can say #WhiteGenocide now, Trump has brought it into the mainstream."[7]

In the summer of 2016, candidate Trump retweeted an image of Hillary Clinton in front of piles of money and along-

---

*   White supremacists claim that "whites" face a looming genocide. They, not the minority groups they attack, are the true victims.

side a six-pointed star on which were emblazoned the words "Most Corrupt Candidate Ever." The message seemed relatively unambiguous: Clinton had close connections with crooked Jews. When they were criticized for posting this image, the Trump campaign quickly changed the star to a circle, even as they contended that the star was actually a sheriff's star (which can variously appear with either five or six points).[8] More telling than the image itself was the fact that it originated with a group that has a long history of posting racist, antisemitic messages. Left unexplained by the campaign was what it was doing uncritically republishing such accounts.

As president, Trump continued to publicize these dubious sources. In July 2017, he retweeted a doctored video that showed him body slamming and overpowering a man with a large CNN logo superimposed on his face. (The original video had been of Trump body slamming the head of the World Wrestling Entertainment company.) While there was nothing antisemitic about the video, it emerged that the person who had altered it had also posted a photo board of all the CNN executives and journalists who he assumed were Jewish. In the corner of each photo was a Star of David. Lest his message not be clear, he wrote: "Something strange about CNN . . . can't quite put my finger on it."[9]

Equally disturbing were Trump's remarks at a rally shortly before the election. He proclaimed that his campaign was a message for "those who control the levers of power in Washington and for the global special interests." This was a "global power structure that is responsible for the economic decisions that have robbed our working class, stripped our country of its wealth, and put that money into the pockets of a handful of large corporations and political entities." According to Trump, those behind this cabal were "international banks [that] plot the destruction of U.S. sovereignty in order to enrich these global financial powers." The thematic elements upon which Trump relied played on traditional antisemitic stereotypes of the "international Jew" who dominates global financial institutions.[10] He reinforced this notion a few days later in his campaign's final television ad. The ad featured Democratic candidate Hillary Clinton and three Jews: financier George Soros, Federal Reserve chair Janet Yellen, and Goldman Sachs CEO Lloyd Blankfein. As their images flashed onto the screen, Trump's voice could be heard thundering: "The establishment has trillions of dollars at stake in this election for those who control the levers of power in Washington and for the global special interests. They partner with these people who don't have your good in mind." The word "Jew" did not have to appear in the ad for the insinuation that Clinton was an ally of a cabal of greedy global Jewish capitalists to register with white supremacists and nationalists. These tropes and stereotypes about Jews' control of the levers of power remind us of the unique nature of antisemitic prejudice: It is focused equally on the personal attributes of members of the group and on their ability to wreak havoc with the well-being of multitudes of people.[11]

Irrespective of how Trump intended it, his white supremacist and antisemitic supporters heard all this as a ringing endorsement. The editor of the *Daily Stormer* informed his readers that

Our Glorious Leader and ULTIMATE SAVIOR has gone full wink-wink-wink to his most aggressive supporters. After having been attacked for retweeting a White Genocide account a few days ago, Trump went on to retweet two more White Genocide accounts, back to back.

> Where as [*sic*] the odd White genocide tweet could be a random occurrence, it isn't statistically possible that two of them back to back could be a random occurrence. It could only be deliberate.
>
> There is no way that this could be anything other than both a wink-wink-wink and a call for more publicity on his campaign. . . . If it gets brought up in an interview he'll just say . . . "we retweet a lot of people, a lot of people feel strongly about my campaign and want to make America great again, everybody likes me." Today in America the air is cold, and it tastes like victory.[12]

In a September 2016 interview with the BBC, Richard Spencer praised Trump for having "brought nationalism into the campaign." At a time when white Americans were in danger of becoming "a hated minority," Trump had, according to Spencer, moved the arrow, so it was now "pointed in our [white supremacists'] direction."[13] William Regnery, the wealthy founder of Spencer's National Policy Institute, a white nationalist/supremacist think tank, believes that candidate Trump and now President Trump has helped his cause. "I think Trump was a legitimizer," he has said. "White nationalism went from being a conversation you could hold in a bathroom to a front parlor."[14]

Even though there is no evidence of a direct relationship between Trump and these extremist groups, *Fortune* magazine assessed the impact of the interactions between them. Using social media analytics software, it tracked the campaign's connections to white supremacists. Locating the white supremacists who were considered social media "influencers," *Fortune* discovered that a significant number of Trump campaign workers followed the leading #WhiteGenocide influencers. The study concluded that "the data shows . . . that Donald Trump and his campaign have used social media to court support within the white supremacist community, whether intentionally or unintentionally."[15] Not only did Trump's campaign workers regularly follow influential white supremacists on social media, they were also spreading their hate-filled messages to the millions of people who followed Donald Trump on social media. This is the normalization or mainstreaming of white supremacy and its panoply of attendant prejudices.

Trump's ambiguous relationship to antisemitism extended beyond his social media activities. At a press conference following his meeting with Israeli prime minister Netanyahu, President Trump was asked about the rise in antisemitic threats against Jewish institutions. It was a relatively straightforward and benign question:

> Mr. President, since your election campaign and even after your victory, we've seen a sharp rise in antisemitic incidents across the United States. And I wonder what you say to those among the Jewish community in the States, and in Israel, and maybe around the world who believe and feel that your administration is playing with xenophobia and maybe racist tones.

Had Trump issued a ringing condemnation of antisemites and the reprehensible things they do, he could have hit this softball question out of the park. Instead, and most peculiarly, he began by referencing the size of his electoral victory, and then promised to end crime and "long-simmering racism and every other thing that's going on." He went on to mention that he has a Jewish daughter, son-in-law, and grandchildren. And he concluded by declaring that "a lot of good things are happening, and you're going to see a lot of love." The rambling, slightly incoherent nature of the answer aside, he never expressed any contempt for these antisemites and racists.

His response in the summer of 2017 to the terrible events in Charlottesville, Virginia, was more troubling. A few hours after the demonstrations Trump condemned the "egregious display of hatred, bigotry, and violence on many sides." Many sides? His equation of the neo-Nazi, KKK, and white supremacist marchers with those who had come to protest against them left even Trump's political allies distressed. Only one side carried Confederate flags and flags with Nazi-like and swastika-inspired symbols. Only one side shouted racist and antisemitic insults. The only fatality was caused by a self-proclaimed white supremacist. Why was Trump suggesting that there was a moral equivalency between racists and the counterdemonstrators? Two days later, in an apparent effort to walk back his absurd statement, Trump, uncharacteristically relying on a teleprompter, read a statement declaring that "racism is evil" and condemning those who came to Charlottesville to cause violence, "including the KKK, neo-Nazis, white supremacists, and other hate groups." He declared them "repugnant to everything we hold dear as Americans."[16] But he was apparently unable to leave it at that. The next day, at a news conference, he brought up Charlottesville again and reverted to an evenhanded approach. "You had a group on one side that was bad. You had a group on the other side that was also very violent. Nobody wants to say that. I'll say it right now." He then added that there were "very fine people" marching with the white supremacist protesters.[17] A few days later, while events at Charlottesville were still in the headlines, Trump retweeted a message from Jack Posobiec, a Trump supporter known for spreading malicious conspiracy theories about Democratic political figures, including the utterly false and reprehensible claims that high-ranking officials in the Democratic Party were trafficking in children and that Seth Rich, a twenty-seven-year-old employee of the Democratic National Committee and the victim of an unsolved murder on July 10, 2016, was in some way responsible for the leaked DNC emails that were published by WikiLeaks a few weeks later. The tweet asked why there was so much attention being paid to Charlottesville when that same weekend there had been shootings in Chicago and "there was no national media outrage." Once again, the question must be asked: Why was Trump following and giving a much-desired retweet to a man who in the aftermath of Charlottesville had already described it as "massive propaganda" and argued that the mainstream media was "fanning the flames of this violence"?[18]

To add fuel to the fire, Trump ridiculed Kenneth C. Frazier, CEO of the pharmaceutical company Merck & Co. and an African American, for resigning from the American Manufacturing Council, a White House–sponsored group, to protest Trump's comments. A few weeks later, Trump again insisted that there were good people on both sides of the Charlottesville protest.[19]

The simple fact is that Donald Trump was, and still seems to be, unwilling to castigate, much less mildly criticize, actions by the white supremacists, racists, and antisemites who voted for him and who continue to support him. Rather than be outraged by what they say and do, he enables and emboldens them because it serves his political purposes. While Trump is probably not an antisemite, enabling antisemites is itself an antisemitic act that causes as much damage as something that comes from an ideological antisemite. When challenged, antisemitic enablers will often cite their personal relations with Jews. But the rationalization that "some of my best friends/relatives are Jewish/black/gay so therefore the antisemitic/racist/homophobic things that I say cannot possibly be antisemitic/racist/homophobic" is both ridiculous and deplorable.

On some level, I find the utilitarian antisemite—the pot-stirrer who enables haters—to be more reprehensible than the ideologue who openly acknowledges his antisemitism. Because he is not affiliated with any extremist group, the utilitarian stands a better chance of both plausibly denying his antisemitism and influencing an audience that would never listen to an extremist. The unapologetic hater is, at least, honest about his feelings. With him, we know what we are up against.

Trump has not created these white supremacist extremist groups or the sentiments to which they adhere. But he has let these reprehensible genies out of the bottle. They are convinced that they have his imprimatur. And he has not disabused them of that notion. Once they are out, it will be very difficult to get them back in. In my next letter I will deal with Jeremy Corbyn, the British Member of Parliament and head of the Labour Party in the United Kingdom.

Yours,
DEL

Dear Oxford Students:

Jeremy Corbyn's record in politics is not only far more extensive than Trump's, it's also more deeply rooted in firmly held ideological beliefs. As the Brits among you well know, Corbyn has been part of Britain's labor and trade-union movement since the beginning of his political career. In the 1970s he worked as a trade-union organizer and was active in the antiapartheid movement in South Africa. During the years of the "troubles" in Northern Ireland, he showed great sympathy for the Irish

Republican Army, which was waging active opposition—many called it terrorism—against the British presence in Northern Ireland. Consistently on the far-left end of the Labour Party, Corbyn became the unexpected head of the party, due in some measure to an internal political and electoral surprise, in 2015.

Fundamental to Corbyn's political weltanschauung is an automatic—critics might call it knee-jerk—sympathy for anyone who is or appears to be oppressed or an underdog. Those who fight with rocks are always preferred to those who use tanks. Coupled with that is a class- and race-based view of the world. Anyone white, wealthy, or associated with a group that seems to be privileged cannot be a victim. Anyone who is or claims to be victimized by those who are white, wealthy, and/or privileged deserves unequivocal support. It is doubtful that Corbyn deliberately seeks out antisemites to associate with and to support. But it seems that when he encounters them, their Jew-hatred is irrelevant as long as their other positions—on class, race, capitalism, the role of the state, and Israel/Palestine—are to his liking.

Longtime Labour MP and a member of the more moderate wing of the party Alan Johnson aptly described Corbyn as someone who does not "indulge in antisemitism himself. It is that he indulges the antisemitism of others." The only type of antisemite Corbyn seems to have no trouble noticing and condemning is the neo-Nazi or right-wing extremist.[20] James Bloodworth, writing in the *Independent,* observes that although Corbyn might not be an antisemite, "he does have a proclivity for sharing platforms with individuals who do." His problem is compounded by the fact that, as Bloodworth put it, "his excuses for doing so do not stand up."[21]

In August 2015, Corbyn defended Stephen Sizer, a former

Church of England vicar who has publicized an avowedly anti-semitic website, *The Ugly Truth,* which contends that Jews were responsible for 9/11, the Iraq and Afghanistan wars, the daily murder of Palestinian children for sport, harvesting organs from Gentiles at gunpoint, domination of the media, and the complete corruption of a myriad of political offices. *The Ugly Truth* declared that in this world there were "God's people," who are "all those who do His will, who are righteous, who are compassionate and who do not submit themselves to the false gods of voracity, vengeance, vulgarity, and viciousness, which pretty much leaves the Jews out."[22] In a post on his church's website, Sizer asserted that "Zionism seeks exclusive Jewish sovereignty over much of the Middle East."[23] Despite all this, Corbyn remained a Sizer supporter, even after Sizer attended a conference in Iran in 2014 that, according to Iranian Press TV reports, included sessions on the "Mossad's role in the 9/11 coup d'états" and "9/11 and the Holocaust as pro-Zionist 'Public myths.'"[24] Corbyn did more than defend Sizer. He attacked Sizer's critics by claiming that the vicar was under attack only because he "dare[d] to speak out against Zionism." When the Church of England banned Sizer for six months because, it concluded, he used his Internet accounts for "clearly antisemitic" purposes, Corbyn seemed to suggest that Church authorities were part of a pro-Israel smear campaign.[25]

Corbyn has come to the defense of other questionable personalities. One month after 9/11, Raed Salah, a Palestinian Islamist preacher, contended that American Jews working in cahoots with Israel planned and carried out the attacks as a means of "divert[ing] the attention of the media" away from Israeli wrongs and directing sympathy "towards the American continent." Salah asserted that four thousand Jews had been warned not to come to work and were saved as a result.[26] In 2007, Salah revived the pernicious accusation that Jews used the blood of gentile children in making matzah.[27] When the British Home Office announced that it was denying Salah permission to enter the United Kingdom, Corbyn protested, declaring him an "honored citizen." Corbyn publicly invited Salah to Parliament, where he promised not only to introduce him to his colleagues but also to serve him tea on the terrace, because he "deserves it."[28] While some people were not surprised that Corbyn was willing to keep company with a person who had such radical views about Jews, they were a bit perplexed that he would welcome a man who had declared homosexuality to be "not only a crime, but a great crime . . . [that] brings [Allah's] wrath and is liable to cause the worst things to happen."[29]

Even though the European Union and the United States have classified Hamas and Hezbollah as terrorist organizations, Corbyn has described them as "friends," attacked the notion that they were "terrorists," and invited them to meet with him at the Parliament. (Corbyn eventually backed down from his "friends" description, but only after repeatedly refusing to do so.)[30] Corbyn also worked with Dyab Abou Jahjah, an Arab political activist who, two months after 9/11, described his sense of "sweet revenge" as he watched the attack on the buildings.[31] In 2006 Jahjah described the "cult of the Holocaust and Jew-worshiping" as Europe's "alternative religion."[32] Corbyn subsequently invited him to speak at a London antiwar rally. During the political campaign leading up to the 2015 general election in the United Kingdom, Jahjah praised Corbyn's "common belief in dialogue, justice and equality of all," which made their "collaboration" possible. When questioned about this by reporters, Corbyn again claimed ignorance and said he could not remember ever having worked with Jahjah. Reporters quickly produced pictures of the two of them together, prompting Corbyn to withdraw his claim.[33]

In 2010, he hosted a call-in show on Iranian Press TV—the Islamic Republic's only legal television station. Corbyn responded to a caller who described Israel as a "disease" that Arabs must "throw out" and "get rid" of from the Middle East with, "Okay. Thank you for your call." Another caller described the BBC as "Zionist liars." Corbyn responded by noting that the caller had "a good point" and should complain to the BBC. That same year on Holocaust Remembrance Day he hosted an "Auschwitz to Gaza" event in Parliament at which repeated comparisons were made among Jews, Israelis, and Nazis. (In 2018, as party leader, he apparently thought better of having done so and apologized for his participation in this event.) In 2011, he proposed that Holocaust Remembrance Day be renamed Genocide Remembrance Day because "every life is of value." Of course every life is of value. Of course every genocide is deplorable and must be unequivocally condemned. But his determination to erase the specific Jewish connection to this day was striking. (Again in 2018, he issued a public statement on the day, one that bemoaned the loss of "victims of evil," but did not mention Jews or antisemitism. After an avalanche of criticism, he amended the statement.)[34]

In 2012, an American artist named Kalen Ockerman (who goes by the name Mear One) painted, on the side of a privately owned building in the Brick Lane neighborhood in London's East End, a mural that he titled *Freedom for Humanity*. It depicted elderly, formally dressed men (described by the artist himself as an "elite banker cartel") playing Monopoly on a table that rested on the backs of naked, darker-skinned men. The hook-nosed, repulsive-looking characters at the table could have come straight out of the notoriously antisemitic Nazi publication *Der Stürmer*—a point that was made by local media. The city's mayor stated that the "images of the bankers perpetuate antisemitic propaganda about conspiratorial Jewish domination of financial institutions," and the local council ordered the mural removed. Ockerman himself acknowledged these were Jews with his comment "Some of the older white Jewish folk in the local community had an issue with me portraying their beloved #Rothschild or #Warburg etc., as the demons they are." When Corbyn learned that the mural was about to be removed, he praised the artist and defended his artwork in a Facebook post: "Why [remove it]? You are in such good company. Rockerfeller [*sic*] destroyed Diego Viera's [*sic*] mural because it included a picture of Lenin." (In 1934, the Rockefeller family ordered a mural that it had commissioned for Rockefeller Center by the artist Diego Rivera chiseled off because it included a portrait of Vladimir Lenin.)

Corbyn's comments resurfaced in March 2018, when screenshots of his Facebook post appeared in the media. When Labour MP Luciana Berger asked Corbyn's staff about the post, they replied, "In 2012 Jeremy was responding to concerns about the removal of public art on the grounds of freedom of speech. However, the mural was offensive and used antisemitic imagery, which has no place in our society, and it is right that it was removed." Shortly thereafter, possibly recognizing the insufficiency of the initial statement, Corbyn's office released a second statement, contending that his post was "a general comment about the removal of public art on grounds of freedom of speech," and that the Diego Rivera mural was "in no way comparable" with Ockerman's. "I sincerely regret that I did not look more closely at the image I was commenting on," the statement continued, "the contents of which are deeply disturbing and antisemitic. The defence of free speech cannot be used as justification for the promotion of antisemitism in any form. That is a view I've always had."[35]

But this isn't only about Jeremy Corbyn. Were he to retreat into the political wilderness, this problem would not disappear. It's far too entrenched within the current Labour Party leadership and the not-insubstantial Corbyn wing of the party. Shortly before Corbyn became head of the party in 2015, Scottish columnist Stephen Daisley, who does not think Corbyn is an antisemite, observed, "How much easier it would make things" if he were. One could then simply attribute political developments in the Labour Party to the prejudices of one man. But, he continued, "this isn't about Jeremy Corbyn; he's just a symptom and a symbol. The Left, and not just the fringes, has an antisemitism problem."[36] Events at the 2017 Labour Party conference confirmed that this was indeed the case. Some party members called for the expulsion of Jewish groups. Others refused to condemn Holocaust denial and questioned whether someone who harbored antisemitic attitudes should necessarily be barred from the party. At a Labour Party antisemitism training session in September 2016, Jackie Walker, a far-left Labour Party activist, was recorded saying, "I still haven't heard a definition of antisemitism that I can work with."[37]

Film director Ken Loach, a longtime party member and leading Corbyn supporter, dismissed the charges of antisemitism as "mood music" designed to create hostility toward Corbyn and told the BBC that he could not condemn Holocaust denial because "history is for us all to discuss." He then segued into a condemnation of Israel and the original sin of its founding.

Loach and other party leaders (those closest to Corbyn) refuse to acknowledge the existence of antisemitism within the party, despite the fact that the official who had been charged with investigating the matter insisted that the comments he received from Labour Party members on this topic made his "hair stand up" and were "redolent of the 1930s."[38]

This attitude has spread to the campus. In February 2016, Alex Chalmers, the co-chair of the Oxford Union Labour Club (OULC), resigned when the club decided to endorse Israel Apartheid Week on campus. "The attitudes of certain members of the club towards certain disadvantaged groups was becoming poisonous," he said in a Facebook post. "Whether it be members of the Executive throwing around the term 'Zio' (a term for Jews usually confined to websites run by the Ku Klux Klan) with casual abandon, senior members of the club expressing their 'solidarity' with Hamas and explicitly defending their tactics of indiscriminately murdering civilians, or a former co-chair claiming that 'most accusations of anti-Semitism are just the Zionists crying wolf,' a large proportion of both OULC and the student left in Oxford more generally have some kind of problem with Jews."[39]

Labour faced new criticism in April 2018 when it was revealed that Sameh Habeeb, founder and editor of the *Palestine Telegraph,* a journal that had published 9/11 conspiracy theories, antisemitic cartoons, and Holocaust-denial stories, was put forward as a Labour council candidate in Northwood, a community in northwest London. An article in the *Palestine Telegraph* contended that World War I and World War II "were planned in advance for the sake of a group following the dictates of Zionism." The journal's website posted a video of David Duke asserting that Israel was a terrorist threat to America.[40]

The spread of this tolerance for antisemitic sentiment was further revealed when reporters discovered that more than a dozen senior staffers who worked for Corbyn and the Labour Party's shadow chancellor were members of social media sites that contained antisemitic and violent messages, including posts that called Hitler a great man and threatened to kill Prime Minister Theresa May. More than twenty Facebook pages associated with Corbyn and Labour contain Holocaust denial, antisemitic, misogynist, and violent messages. These sites have more than four hundred thousand members. One of them, a Facebook group called Jeremy Corbyn Leads Us to Victory, contains an Israeli flag on which the Star of David had been replaced with a swastika. The flag had been posted by a former Labour candidate for office. A former Labour Party candidate posted a picture of *New York Times* journalists with their faces obscured by Jewish symbols. Another site carried a post stating that "six million is a fallacy." Yet another contended that "the holocaust was a big lie." Some of the posts were so laced with expressions of violent extremism that a former Independent Reviewer of Terrorism Legislation suggested that they be investigated by the police.[41]

When confronted with evidence that proves their assertions wrong, Corbyn and his associates routinely fall back on a number of familiar explanations, which include claims that the comments and articles in question are not antisemitic but merely anti-Israel, or that they had simply not seen the offensive posts. Another one of his close allies dismissed the allegations of antisemitism as coming from Jewish "Trump" supporters who were "making [it] up." When it was first reported that he said this, he denied having done so and argued that he had been misquoted. Then the tape surfaced. The fact that he made these comments in response to a letter signed by sixty-eight U.K. rabbis from across the religious spectrum only made matters worse. Recently, Labour was faced with the need to do another about-face. Though Corbyn's office has insisted that he does not support blanket boycotts and sanctions on Israel, but only on items produced in West Bank settlements, footage emerged from 2015 of his participation in a panel in Ireland in which he called for a blanket boycott of Israel "to be part and parcel of the legal process and for sanctions against Israel." This array of self-contradictory stances, convoluted corrections, and reversals leave many people, including some of Corbyn's closest allies, unsettled.[42]

In March 2018, the Board of Deputies of British Jews and Jewish Leadership Council decided that they'd had enough and sent an open letter to the Labour Party in which they stated, "Again and again, Jeremy Corbyn has sided with anti-Semites rather than Jews. At best, this derives from the far left's obsessive hatred of Zionism, Zionists and Israel. At worst, it suggests a conspiratorial worldview in which mainstream Jewish communities are believed to be a hostile entity, a class enemy."

Corbyn's response to the rabbis' letter was conciliatory. "I recognize that anti-Semitism has surfaced within the Labour Party," he said in an open letter of his own, "and has too often been dismissed as simply a matter of a few bad apples." But others in the party were not as conciliatory. That same month, Diane Abbott, the Labor Party's shadow home secretary, retweeted a Twitter message that claimed that "more and more people are joining the Labour Party because they are so disgusted by the constant smearing of Jeremy Corbyn." In an appearance in May 2016 on a BBC television program, Abbott had said that it was a "smear against ordinary party members" to suggest "that the Labour Party has a problem with antisemitism."[43] Rank-and-file Labour Party members weighed in as well, in an open letter posted on the "We Support Jeremy Corbyn" Facebook group that referred to the Board of Deputies of British Jews and Jewish Leadership Council as "a very powerful special interest group mobilizing its apparent, immense strength against you [Corbyn]. It is clear this group can employ the full might of the BBC to make sure its voice is heard very loudly and clearly. It is a shame not every special interest group can get the same coverage."[44]

The summer of 2018 saw the Labour Party enmeshed in new controversies. One was over Corbyn's attendance as an observer at a conference in Tunis in September 2014 called the International Conference on Monitoring the Palestinian Political and Legal Situation in the Light of Israeli Aggression. During the conference, Corbyn joined a delegation paying respects at a memorial to PLO members who died in 1985 when Israeli jets bombed the organization's headquarters in Tunis. He was photographed standing in the background as wreaths were being laid. But in August 2018, the *Daily Mail* published photographs of Corbyn participating in another wreath-laying ceremony at the same event, this one held a few miles away, to honor members of the Black September faction of the PLO who were the architects of the massacre of Israeli athletes at the 1972 Olympics in Munich. Initially commenting, "I was present at that wreath-laying [of the 1985 victims], I don't think I was actually involved in it," Corbyn had to acknowledge his participation in the second ceremony when he was shown the photographs and reminded of a column he wrote in the *Morning Star* in 2014 on his return to the United Kingdom from the conference, in which he referred to "wreaths laid at the graves of those who died on that day [in 1985] and on the graves of others killed by Mossad agents in Paris in 1991." Never mind that he got the facts wrong (three of the four men buried at the second site were killed by a rival Palestinian faction in Tunis; the fourth was reportedly killed by Mossad agents in Paris in 1992), what infuriated people was Corbyn's refusal, in retrospect, to apologize for honoring the memory of men universally regarded as terrorists. This firestorm did not appear to threaten his followers' faith in his innocence and his attackers' guilt. They dismissed it as an attempt to "smear" him.[45]

Then, at the end of August, the *Daily Mail* reported that in 2013 Corbyn gave a speech at a conference by an organization called the Palestinian Return Centre in which he declared that British Zionists "clearly have two problems. One is that they don't want to study history, and secondly, having lived in this country for a very long time, probably all their lives, they don't understand English irony."[46] Corbyn may have said "Zionists" and not "Jews," but listening to the speech, the two seemed interchangeable. This was a cut to the quick. For what is it but a sense of history and irony that has gotten Jews through the vicissitudes of their collective experience? It was this statement by Corbyn, more than anything else, that left many Jews utterly convinced that this was a man whose contempt for them runs deep.

The difficulty Corbyn and his associates have in recognizing and acknowledging antisemitism on the left seems to be rooted in their foundational claim that because being a progressive means being opposed to any form of racism, oppression, or group hate—including antisemitism—therefore, by definition, a true progressive cannot be an antisemite. Their claim runs into trouble when they are confronted by progressive compatriots who include blanket statements about Jews in their excoriation of wealthy capitalists who oppress and exploit the poor, who imply that Jews exert undue influence on the media, who deny that Jews can be the victims of race-based hatred in the same way that people of color are, and who include offensive, hate-filled Jewish stereotyping in their criticism of Israeli government policies regarding the Palestinians.

So, to return to your original question: Is Jeremy Corbyn an antisemite? My response would be that that's the wrong question. The right questions to ask are: Has he facilitated and amplified expressions of antisemitism? Has he been consistently reluctant to acknowledge expressions of antisemitism unless they come from white supremacists and neo-Nazis? Will his actions facilitate the institutionalization of antisemitism among other progressives? Sadly, my answer to all of this is an unequivocal yes. Like Trump, Corbyn has emboldened and enabled antisemites, but from the other end of the political spectrum. Trump's antisemitic followers believe that his dog whistles give them free rein to openly acknowledge their contempt for racial minorities, Muslims, homosexuals, and Jews. They are convinced, not without reason, that they have had a direct impact on government policy and on various politicians' stance on a range of issues. Their access and potential influence has never been greater. Corbyn's followers believe that his support of them legitimizes their trafficking in the worst antisemitic stereotypes while at the same time vigorously denying that they are antisemitic.

I'll close by referring to a comment I made at the outset of this exchange, when I expressed the hope that my answers would leave both those on the right and the left discomforted. That discomfort should be caused by an acknowledgment on everyone's part that extremism and antisemitism are found not only among people on the other side of the political spectrum. As long as we are blind to it in our midst, our fight against it will be futile.

Yours,
DEL

THE DINNER PARTY ANTISEMITE

Dear Deborah:

Thanks for sharing your exchange with the students in the pub. Now that I have a better understanding of antisemitic enablers, there is another type of antisemite that doesn't seem to fall into that category.

I'm not sure I ever told you that I grew up in a small American town that was populated by many "good ol' boys" who were open about their white supremacism, racism, and antisemitism. I knew them but didn't interact with them all that much because I lived on the "other" side of town. They hated anyone—Jew, black, Latino, gay—who did not fit their image of what America should be. Some of them were angry about their difficult personal circumstances and were looking for someone to blame. Others were just ordinary bigots. There were only a few Jews in our town. Most owned small retail establishments, many of which had been in their families' hands for generations. They were successful but not particularly wealthy. These Jews were good neighbors—even to the bigots. Some of the store owners among them extended credit to the same folks who engaged in overt expressions of antisemitism. A man who did some electrical work for my parents once told my mother how much he hated Jews. But in the same conversation he also told her how decent the Jewish owner of one of the local dry goods stores had been to his family when they got into a financial bind. He never acknowledged the contradiction in his statements. I'll bet that if my mother had pointed it out, he would have said something like "Well, the owner of the store was a 'good Jew,' not like the rest of them." I have no doubt that some of the townsfolk whom I am describing would find resonance in the antisemitism of the right-wing extremists whose bigotry you have depicted.

I also encountered another form of bigotry. My parents were members of the local country club, and while none of the "nice folks" there ever said or did anything overtly antisemitic—and would loudly condemn blatant expressions of antisemitism—there was an unmistakable undercurrent of it throughout the place. I suppose it's possible that the reason the club had no Jewish members was that none had ever applied, but I doubt that was the case. If a member ever invited a Jewish guest to play golf or dine, while no one ever said, "You can't bring some-one like him in," through body language and mumbled asides ("looks like we're letting everyone in nowadays") it was com-municated that Jews were not welcome on the premises. Even members who boasted of their connections to Jews did it with a tinge of antisemitism. I remember someone telling my par-ents that he had invested money with a particular stockbroker, who was a Jew. "He'll certainly make some money for me," he said. "Not sure precisely how, but I am sure he will. They do have that knack, you know." What do you make of people like these?

Yours,
Joe

Dear Joe and Abigail:

Joe, you are describing what I would call the dinner party, or polite, antisemite. He's got Jewish business associates, perhaps even a Jewish friend or two, was horrified by Charlottesville, and has donated to the local Holocaust museum. But when the town council is considering a zoning variance to allow for the construction of another synagogue in his neighborhood, this fellow is at the head of the opposition. "Let's just think for a minute about what this will do to the character of the neighborhood," he'll say. "I mean, things are fine just the way they are, aren't they? Let's consider the long-term ramifications, in terms of population balance." He will mention that he has hired a new associate, casually mention that she is a Jew, but assure those listening to him that she's not a "typical Jew." When told that what he has just said is antisemitic, he will reply with considerable indignation. "That's ridiculous. You know that some of my best friends are Jews." That may well be, but he is still an antisemite. Someone who feels the need to boast that he has Jewish (or African American) friends is more often than not someone who has problems with Jews (or blacks) who aren't his friends.

A corollary to the "some of my best friends" assertion is the increasingly familiar, "How can I be antisemitic? My son [daughter, brother, grandchild, etc.] is married to a Jew [or is Jewish]." Others will cite the Jewish employee whom they always treated fairly and even let leave early on Fridays for Shabbat. This "defense by relative (or employee)" rings hollow. If you make bigoted statements about Jews, you are antisemitic, regardless of how many Jews you are related to or provide with kosher food in your company's commissary.

We may think dinner party antisemites are a dying breed—who would be so stupid as to say such things in public nowadays?—but they are still very much out there. They generally know better than to make their sentiments public, but sometimes they slip up. Consider what happened in 1996, during the divorce negotiations between the lawyers representing Prince Charles and the Princess of Wales. Charles had chosen Fiona Shackleton, a partner at the royal family's law firm, to represent him. Diana chose Anthony Julius, a Jewish intellectual from a decidedly middle-class background. (He also represented me when I was sued for libel by David Irving.) Many British publications, obsessed with this royal divorce case, wrote profile pieces on the two lawyers. According to Julius, they "tended to be uncertain how to assess the significance of my Jewish identity, save that they all took it to be of *immense* significance."[1] But on the day after the divorce settlement was announced by Buckingham Palace, the *Telegraph,* a decidedly conservative newspaper, made perfectly clear why they thought Julius's religious background was significant.

> It became clear almost immediately that the incompatibility of the Prince and the Princess of Wales stretched even to the solicitors they had employed. The Prince, as expected, had chosen the bridge-playing Fiona Shackleton, 39, of Farrer and Co., who had also represented the Duke of York in his separation agreement. One of the country's most respected family law specialists, much of Shackleton's career has been geared to arranging favorable divorce settlements for her clients. She adopts a conciliatory approach.
>
> Unfortunately, her softly-softly approach is at odds with the more bullish attitude of the Princess's solicitor. Anthony "Genius" Julius, 39, is not a divorce lawyer but a specialist in media law, acting for Robert Maxwell and

*once employed by the Daily Mail. His background could
not be further from the upper-class world inhabited by his
opposite number. He is a Jewish intellectual and Labour
supporter, and less likely to feel constrained by consider-
ations of fair play. "I'd be very worried if I were the Royal
Family," says a Cambridge don who taught him. "He'll get
lots of money out of them."[2]* [Emphasis added.]

Pretty impressive. In a few sentences, the *Telegraph* managed to slur Jews, members of the middle class, and people with
liberal political views—all of whom seemed to have no scru-
ples at all. Beset by criticism, the paper tried to explain away
what it had done. The *Telegraph*'s legal director called Julius to
explain that the reporter had originally written "*outmoded* con-
siderations of fair play" and a copy editor had mistakenly eliminated the "outmoded." It remains unclear precisely why the
legal director thought the inclusion of "outmoded" would have
made the article less offensive. Maybe he meant that, nowadays,
when the rules of fair play no longer apply, Jews—who have a
long history of not playing fair—have a decided advantage over
non-Jews, who are still getting used to not having to play fair.
The legal director then hastened to add that the editor of the
Telegraph was herself Jewish, possibly implying that, therefore,
nothing that appeared in the newspaper could be considered
antisemitic or, if somehow this was indeed antisemitic, it was
her fault. The Cambridge don's comment, that Julius's Jewishness makes him particularly qualified to wring a lot of money
out of the royal family, did not seem to trouble the legal director. When he asked Julius what he wanted the paper to do, Julius
told him they could do whatever they wished and ended the
conversation.[3]

Calling a prejudice "polite" does not in any way lessen its significance. In fact, in some respects the polite form of prejudice—irrespective of whom it is directed at—is more insidious than the overt, unapologetic, easily identifiable kind. Polite antisemitism is easily camouflaged; it's subtle and allusive. And when it's exposed for what it is, people who are not clued in to these types of slurs may be appeased by the polite antisemite's very polite—and, more often than not, highly unsatisfactory—"apology." A case in point is the apology that the *Telegraph* ran a few days later. Though ostensibly an apology, it revealed that the newspaper didn't really think there was anything wrong with how Julius had been described.

> Our royal divorce coverage last Saturday included profiles of the legal principals involved. Anthony Julius, of Mishcon de Reya, for the Princess of Wales, and Fiona Shackleton, of Farrer and Co., for Prince Charles.
>
> Intended to compare and contrast their styles but without in any way seeking to question his professional integrity, we referred to Mr. Julius's background as a Jewish intellectual in a context, which we now recognize, to our profound regret, to have *appeared* pejorative. [Emphasis added.]
>
> Many of our readers have taken the strongest exception to this paragraph, making clear that they regard it as a racial slur. In acknowledging the force of this criticism, we offer our sincere apologies to Mr. Julius and to all those who took offense.[4]

Not good enough. Linking Julius's Jewish background to his lack of concern for the principles of fair play and his inborn ability to get a big financial settlement from the royal family did not *appear* to be pejorative. It *was* pejorative. The *Telegraph* was simply unwilling to flat-out admit it. And if many readers had not taken the strongest exception to the paragraph, would the newspaper have in fact recognized that what they said was pejorative?

I recently heard a story that further illustrates this kind of "polite" antisemitism. I was in Aspen leading a seminar for a group of Jewish communal leaders about my research on antisemitism. At the end of the session a participant whom I'll call Marie shyly approached me and asked if she could share with me the story of her personal encounter with antisemitism. Marie told me that she came from a Catholic, French Canadian family in Quebec and had never heard expressions of antisemitism in her parents' home. After a divorce and a bout with cancer, she came home to tell her mother that she had met a wonderful Jewish man who made her happy and whom she was planning to marry. Marie assumed her mom would be thrilled, and so she was completely flummoxed when her mom responded by saying, "But my father said never to shop at Steinberg's." (Steinberg's, Marie explained, was a large, family-owned supermarket chain in Canada.)

In the years since her conversion to Judaism and marriage, Marie and her mom have reached a cautious truce. "But," she said, "I will never forget her first response." When I thanked her for sharing with me what was obviously a painful memory, she again mentioned that she had never noticed any antisemitism in her parents' home. "But," she concluded wistfully, speaking more to herself than to me, "it probably was there."

Joe, it's doubtful that your parents' friends at the club, Marie's mom, or the *Telegraph* editors would ever personally threaten anyone. But these kinds of "polite" antisemites sow the seeds of contempt among those who can do real harm. And they do it in a way that makes their antisemitism especially hard to call out and combat.

Yours,
DEL

THE CLUELESS ANTISEMITE

Dear Deborah:

Thanks for these explanations. I think the following story will introduce yet another category of antisemite.

I was having lunch with a colleague who is Jewish. After hearing about our exchange of letters, she told me a story about her sister Sandra. Sandra had just completed an intense graduate program in New York and had gone out for a celebratory lunch with a small group of fellow students with whom she had become close during the program. Most of them came from cities in which there was a very small Jewish population. She was the only Jew at the table. The four other women had been to her parents' home for more than a few Shabbat dinners and Passover Seders. Most had never really interacted with Jews before and had a great time learning about Jewish customs with Sandra's welcoming family. During lunch, one of the women described an unadvertised sale at a store nearby. When she finished, she turned to Sandra and said, with great excitement, "I'm really looking forward to seeing what they have. You're going, of course, aren't you, Sandra? Can I come along with you? I just know *you'll* know a bargain when you see one." When Sandra stared at her, flabbergasted, the woman became flustered. Sandra took a deep breath and said with a small smile, "I don't think Jews are the only people predisposed to find great ways to save money. Personally, I do most of my shopping online." The woman stammered out an apology, which Sandra graciously accepted.

What would you have said in that situation?

Regards,
Joe

Dear Professor Lipstadt:

I just read Professor Wilson's last letter. I could share with you far too many similar examples. So many of my dorm mates or sorority sisters have said to me, "Abigail, you are going to want to hear about this sale (or bargain or other money-saving opportunity)." I always want to ask them, "Why me, specifically?" But I don't. I feel that there is some clever thing I should say in reply that would convey how insulted I am, but I can never think of what it should be. Are these people aware that what they are saying is antisemitic, however subtle it may be?

Yours,
Abigail

Dear Joe and Abigail:

These are perhaps the saddest and most personally hurtful manifestations of antisemitism. The clueless antisemite is an otherwise nice and well-meaning person who is completely unaware that she has internalized antisemitic stereotypes and is perpetuating them. The only proper response, however hard it may be for you, is to politely tell this person that what she said comes under the category of an insidious and insulting ethnic stereotype.

It's so easy to internalize these prejudices. A number of years ago, I was co-teaching a course on film and the Holocaust. We were discussing the Nazi claim that Jews used their nefarious skills to control world economies. A student raised her hand and said, "But all the German bankers *were* Jews, weren't they?" I immediately began to flood her with details and statistics demonstrating that this was simply not true. My co-instructor, a film specialist, interrupted my flow of facts and figures, turned to the student and quietly said, "So what?" Then, after a pause, she continued: "They actually weren't, but what if they had been? Would that have been a legitimate reason to hate all Jews and attempt to annihilate an entire people from the face of the earth?" Her "So what?" and not my fact-laden jumble, was the correct response. The student had asked a question that was rooted in a false premise: that all the major German banks were owned by Jews, and that one can learn from this that Jews, as a people, aimed to control the world's economies. By citing facts and figures, I had responded to an irrational question in a rational fashion, thereby giving the claim in her question the gravitas it did not deserve. The answer from my colleague (who happened to be a non-Jew, and a former nun, at that) exposed its fundamental irrationality.

There are of course also Jews who—intentionally or unintentionally—traffic in antisemitic stereotypes. When this seeps into the larger culture, it signals that it's okay for non-Jews to do likewise. The Jewish American Princess, or JAP, entered popular culture in the decades after World War II in the works of Jewish novelists (Herman Wouk, Philip Roth), comedians (Joan Rivers, David Steinberg), and filmmakers (Mel Brooks, Woody Allen).[1] The anthropologist Riv-Ellen Prell describes her as a materialistic, conniving, self-centered, and sexually withholding Jewish woman, the product of wealthy, indulgent, and smothering Jewish parents.[2]

Are there Jewish women who fit this stereotype? Certainly, but there are Catholic, Protestant, Muslim, and Asian women who do so as well. Not to mention the fact that there are more than a few men—both Jewish and non-Jewish—who could also be characterized as "spoiled, whiny, selfish, money-grubbing, conniving, and malicious."[3] But there's something about the JAP that just won't let her vanish into pop culture history, regardless of how many notable Jewish women nowadays proudly defy this stereotype (Ruth Bader Ginsberg, Elena Kagan, and Gal Gadot are three who immediately spring to mind). Jews like to laugh at themselves, and JAP jokes are, unfortunately, a part of that. But as Abe Foxman—the former national director of the Anti-Defamation League and a vigorous critic of antisemitism—points out, JAP jokes started as something Jews told one another but then they got "away from us" and ultimately "took on a life of their own."[4] When groups that have been subjected to discrimination and prejudice denigrate themselves, they do more than internalize a negative self-perception. They give license to others to do likewise. This is not harmless humor. It belittles Jews and women. The fact that it has its roots among Jews makes it no less debilitating.[5] Whether coming from Jews or non-Jews, this manifestation of latent antisemitism spreads hateful and hurtful tropes and ideas.

Well, that's quite a taxonomy we've assembled: the extremist, the enabler, the dinner party, and the clueless antisemite. Sometimes the categories blend into one another. We've also seen that sometimes the most harm can be done, not by the violent, in-your-face, self-professed Jew-hater, but by ordinary people who have acquired these views almost through cultural osmosis.

A recent careful and well conducted study in Great Britain found that only 2.4 percent of the British public "open[ly] dislike[d] Jews." These people had a set of "developed negative ideas" about Jews and their characteristics. They "readily and confidently" express antisemitic views. Another 3 percent hold multiple antisemitic attitudes, though they are less pronounced about them. While this total of 5.4 percent is quite small, approximately 30 percent subscribed to or agreed with a few stereotypical antisemitic ideas. Though the members of this larger group are not "committed political antisemites," they do disseminate antisemitic ideas into the broader public sphere.[6] More than the extremists, they keep antisemitism alive and flourishing, and pass it on to future generations.

Though I started with a description of the most virulent type of antisemite and concluded with the person who may not even know she is expressing antisemitism, they all invoke, in one form or another and to one degree or another, the standard antisemitic themes: money, power, and conspiratorial control.

Be well,
DEL

·III·

Contextualizing Antisemitism

A COGNITIVE FAILURE?

Dear Professor Lipstadt:

These categories have been very helpful, but they lead me to another question. Is fighting antisemitism simply a matter of showing people how ridiculous their antisemitic theories are? If, as you so convincingly say, antisemitism is irrational and delusional, is there any way of educating the haters?

Abigail

Dear Abigail and Joe:

If only I had an easy answer to give you. Joe, you and I are both educators. Abigail, you are headed to a prestigious PhD program and hope to become an academic. We all reflexively fall back on education as an antidote. Education will certainly work in many instances. But, I must sadly acknowledge, education will be of limited value for committed antisemites. Their contempt for the Jew is not the result of a "cognitive error."[1] It's not that we simply need to rationally show them that Jews do not in fact control the banks or the media, or shape the foreign policy of whichever country they live in. Their view of Jews is, unfortunately, refracted through a preestablished prism of hatred. That's why these irrational and absurd charges make sense to them.

Consider, for example, the ridiculous claim that the night before the 9/11 attacks four thousand Israelis and/or Jews were called and told not to come to work at the World Trade Center the next morning. The notion that four thousand people could have received a phone call and that none of them ever, to this day, mentioned it to anyone else—family, friends, or coworkers—defies logic. Who are these four thousand people? Not one among them has ever been identified. Moreover, who would have had a telephone list of every Jew working in those huge buildings? Only the most delusional conspiracy theorists would believe there exists a central registry of all Jews working in a given location and that four thousand people were so well disciplined that they never spoke of this.

A French bestseller, *L'Effroyable Imposture (The Horrifying Fraud)*, contended that the 9/11 attacks were directed by American Jewish neoconservatives to get public support for military invasions of Iraq and Afghanistan. Two hundred thousand copies of the book were sold in France in the space of a few months. The book was subsequently translated into more than two dozen languages. Even though virtually every French newspaper observed that reams of forensic and eyewitness evidence contradicted the book's conclusions, French readers enthusiastically embraced it. But this kind of delusion was not limited to France. At one point, 20 percent of the American public believed that the attacks were an "inside" job.[2]

As I noted in a previous letter, at the heart of all conspiracy theories is the notion of a secret cabal of powerful people, a demonic elite who control crucial elements of a particular society. Conspiracy theorists rely on circuitous reasoning, contending that the fact that the conspirators cannot be precisely identified "proves" the conspiracy. Only an exceptionally powerful cabal could conceal its manipulative powers.[3] In an effort to disprove the 9/11 Jewish/Israeli conspiracy theory, some media outlets combed the 9/11-related death notices and announcements of memorial services, and reviewed the names of the victims and their biographies to come up with an estimated Jewish death toll. They found that Jews constituted approximately 12 percent of the victims, a number that corresponds to the Jewish population in the New York City area.[4] But such well-intentioned efforts rarely lay conspiracy theories to rest because they offer a rational answer to an irrational accusation. As it happens, we know the precise starting point for this particular accusation. Four days after the 9/11 attack, the Syrian government–controlled newspaper, *Al-Thawra,* reported, without any proof, that "four thousand Jews were absent from their work on the day of the explosions."[5] In an attempt to discredit this "report," the United States State Department identified *Al-Thawra* as its unsourced creator. But, as is often the case regarding conspiracy theories, the debunkers' attempt to disprove the conspiracy was simply seen as "proof" of their own involvement in it.[6] Ironically, the claim that the Mossad was behind the 9/11 attacks was challenged by an unexpected source: Al Qaeda itself. Osama bin Laden's chief deputy, Ayman al-Zawahiri, claimed that this false rumor started with Al-Manar, the Hezbollah-affiliated television station in Lebanon, and was quickly picked up and repeated by the Iranians. Zawahiri, noting that Hezbollah and Iran are Shiite while Al-Qaeda is Sunni, indignantly claimed that the purpose of this "lie" was to suggest "that there are no heroes among the Sunnis who can hurt America as no one else did in history."[7]

Despite both Al-Qaeda's protestations and extensive evidence to the contrary, the notion that the Mossad and/or the American government was responsible for 9/11 continues to hold sway.[8] In 2016, Joy Karega, at the time an assistant professor at Oberlin College, endorsed this assertion. On her blog, she quoted a speech by the avowed antisemitic minister Louis Farrakhan, in which he declared that this was all a Jewish and Zionist plot.

> They say that the World Trade Center building [sic] were brought down by carefully placed explosives, not by planes. They say that all three buildings had to have been wired with explosive charges long before September the 11th and this is something that took tremendous sophistication to do, and that sophistication was not with Osama bin Laden or his followers. Listen. But if it was not Muslims then who? . . . It is now becoming apparent that there were many Israeli and Zionist Jews in key roles in the 9/11 attack.

Karega did not limit her accusations to 9/11. She insisted, without providing evidence to substantiate her claim, that "the same people behind the massacre in Gaza" were also complicit in the 2014 downing of a Malaysian airliner over Ukraine and the murders in Paris of the *Charlie Hebdo* cartoonists. In fact, she contended that Israeli prime minister Netanyahu went to Paris right after the massacre in order to "bend Hollande and French governmental officials over one more time in public just in case the message wasn't received via Massod [sic] and the 'attacks' they orchestrated in Paris." In November 2015, Karega claimed that "ISIS is not a jihadist, Islamic terrorist organization. It's a

CIA and Mossad operation, and there's too much information out here for the public not to know that."[9] According to Karega, Israelis and, by extension, Jews could seamlessly compel the CIA to bend to their will, create ISIS, and lure thousands of Muslims to its ranks. When Israel brought down the Malaysian plane, it was acting, she charged, in cahoots with Jewish bankers. According to Karega, "the Rothschild-led banksters [*sic*] exposed and hated and out of economic options to stave off the coming global deflationary depression, are implementing the World War III option." Karega "quoted" these Rothschild-led banksters: "We own nearly every central bank in the world. We financed both sides of every war since Napoleon. We own your news, the media, your oil and your government." Reacting to a report that the Obama administration was about to assist Holocaust survivors living below the poverty line, Karega wrote: "One of these days some of My Peoples gonna [*sic*] learn who ALL American presidents work for and why they are chosen and placed in office." She planned to try to look at some of these "[Jewish] Federations that handle the money and resources. We can probably look deep and try to trace it."[10]

These are not the claims of someone who is simply "misinformed." Karega was on the faculty of a prominent American academic institution. Although some of her colleagues at Oberlin condemned her remarks, there were others who fiercely defended her and condemned the "irresponsible hostility drummed up against her."[11] Claiming that she had been made a "scapegoat" who was "specifically targeted" because of her gender and race, her defenders argued that the attacks on her "reinforce[d] oppressive anti-Black" narratives and "antiBlack racism" on Oberlin's campus.[12]

Even more troubling than Karega's remarks was the fact

that Oberlin had assigned her to teach Writing for Social Justice, a course in which students were to "develop, negotiate, and revise their own . . . ethics . . . on social justice issues." As someone who has participated in numerous faculty searches, I find it baffling that Karega's racist and antisemitic beliefs did not surface during Oberlin's vetting and interview process. While she may have been fully qualified to teach many topics, social justice does not appear to be one of them.[13]

I return to the point that I made at the outset of this letter. Karega's views are not the product of a cognitive error—in other words, that she is simply unaware that the world economic system is not controlled by "Rothschild-led banksters." Karega and others who subscribe to these conspiratorial notions weaponize them and use them as a means of attacking their critics. I fear, Abigail, that there is little we can do to enlighten those who hold such repugnant beliefs. For the most part, they are not interested in hearing rational explanations. We can, however, try to reach those whom they might influence. The National Institute of Standards and Technology (NIST) acknowledged this when, in 2006, it issued a fact sheet to disprove the conspiracy theorists' claims that the World Trade Center had been blown up by controlled demolition from within the buildings and not by the explosions caused by the airplanes that crashed into the Twin Towers. Four years earlier, a NIST 10,000-word report had reached a similar conclusion. Not surprisingly, it did not convince the conspiracy theorists. In light of the persistence of these unfounded and disproved claims, the NIST acknowledged that "this fact sheet won't convince those who hold to the alternative theories that our findings are sound. In fact, the fact sheet was never intended for them. It is for the masses who have seen or heard the alternative theory claims."[14]

I hate ending on such a pessimistic note. I'm reminded of the definition of a Jewish optimist as someone who thinks things cannot get any worse. I'm a historian and, as such, I am loath to predict what will happen in the future, though I am increasingly pessimistic. And so, I conclude this letter by contending that, even though we cannot convince the conspiracists, we must work to create firewalls between them and those whom they might influence. Those firewalls are the facts that conclusively demonstrate how delusional their perceptions of Jews are.

Be well,
DEL

DELEGITIMIZING ANTISEMITISM:
JEWS CAN'T BE VICTIMS

Dear Professor Lipstadt:

I've just come from a seminar on American Ethnicity, Religion, and Race, where I think I encountered antisemitism head-on. As part of a discussion, one of the students referred to "prejudice, including racism, sexism, and homophobia," at which point another student calmly but deliberately interjected, "and antisemitism." The first student accepted the point and was trying to proceed when, from somewhere around the seminar table, came a mutter: "Yeah. Right. Jews are really suffering. Talk about privilege." When the students sitting on either side of the Mutterer glanced at him, he added a bit defensively, "Jews aren't suffering. They have good jobs, get into good schools, and have no problem succeeding in life. Antisemitism is not in the same category as racism. Certainly not in this country. Yet Jews are always referencing the Holocaust and what they call 'antisemitism.' They're always playing the Holocaust card. Suffering? They're just trying to hitch a free ride on the backs of people of color who face real racism. They are white and they are privileged." I was stupefied by what he said and by the confidence with which he expressed it. The professor asked for responses. Feeling compelled to say something, I was about to jump into the fray when the class ended.

I must admit that I'm not sorry the class ended before I

could speak. I have no idea, even after our exchange of letters, precisely what I would have said. I'm a bit ashamed that, even though I'm Jewish, I didn't have a cogent answer at the ready. Some of what he said rings true. For the most part, Jews do live better lives than people of color. I know we don't experience prejudice in the same way at all. But I also know that there was something very wrong with both what he said and how he said it. The whole thing left me deeply unsettled.

Yours,
Abigail

Dear Abigail and Joe:

Abigail, please don't feel discouraged that you didn't know how to respond to the Mutterer. It's an ongoing challenge even for those of us who are considered "experts" in the field. The fact that you have a Jewish heritage does not automatically equip you—or anyone else, for that matter—to know what to say when challenged by someone who minimizes the significance of antisemitism today.

Your Mutterer contends that while antisemitism may exist in some parts of the world, it's not a problem of the same magnitude as other prejudices—racism in particular. It's something separate, apart, and of little—if any—consequence. My response may surprise you: In certain respects, he's right. Antisemitism *is* different in structure, history, and contemporary impact than other forms of racism. Then again, he's also wrong. Antisemitism is an ongoing phenomenon that must be taken very seriously. In the case of the Mutterer, what's unclear to me is whether his mistake is perceptional or ideological in nature.

Before we turn to the Mutterer's argument, let's think about the etymology of the word "prejudice," which comes from the Latin *praejudicium,* or prejudging. Prejudice is the act of negatively prejudging or assessing someone's personal characteristics and behaviors based on stereotypical beliefs about the racial, ethnic, religious, cultural, political, or geographic group to which she belongs.[1] And regardless of how many people a prejudiced person may encounter who do not conform to their group stereotype, this person continues to hold his racist beliefs. Are there Jews who are obsessed with money? Are there feminists who are perpetually angry and shrill? Yes, just as there are Jews on fixed incomes who spend time doing volunteer work and feminists who are mellow and laid-back. But that doesn't interest the racist, who is often an insecure and/or angry person who needs to deprecate groupings of people who are different from his group in order to feel good about himself. In the best of all worlds, antisemites would be pitied for their ludicrous ideas. But they are capable of doing real harm, as can be seen by what happened in Germany in the 1930s and throughout Europe in the 1940s—those events that the Mutterer is so tired of hearing about.

The Mutterer is not wrong in his opinion that racial minorities are affected by prejudice today in a fashion that is different from the way Jews are affected by it. Racial minorities can cite very real ways in which their day-to-day lives are shaped by prejudice and hatred. Such is not the case for most American Jews *today.* In the twenty-first century it's illegal for real estate developers to put clauses in contracts that bar Jews from living in certain neighborhoods. It's illegal to fire someone who cannot work on Saturday. It's illegal to tell someone who walks into a public building that he must remove his *kippah*. A qualified Jewish applicant who is repeatedly passed over for promotion at the workplace has legal recourse. Philip Roth has memorably described how his father, who worked for a "Gentile insurance colossus," could never win well-deserved promotions or access more lucrative clients because he was Jewish.[2]

And yet, all is not well. The Mutterer is most likely oblivious to the fact that either a private guard or a police officer is stationed in front of most synagogues in Europe because of concerns about antisemitic attacks. Not long ago, when I tried to attend services at a synagogue in Rome I was turned away, despite the fact that I had my passport and was not carrying a backpack or any other paraphernalia. (This didn't happen when I visited churches, both large and small.) Eventually, a member of the Jewish community who recognized me got me in.

Here in the United States, in March 2015, Rachel Beyda, a well-qualified candidate for a position on the student council's Judicial Board at UCLA, was initially rejected because a majority of council members assumed that as a Jew she would be unable to deal with governance questions in an unbiased way. At the meeting to decide on her nomination, a member of the Undergraduate Students Association Council flat-out asked her, "Given that you are a Jewish student and very active in the Jewish community, how do you see yourself being able to maintain an unbiased view?" After Ms. Beyda left the room, a debate ensued about whether her faith and membership in Jewish organizations would allow her to rule impartially on judicial matters. The oft-stated goal of having a diverse group of voices on college campuses did not appear to include a Jewish voice in this particular instance. Finally, a faculty member who was present pointed out that belonging to a Jewish organization did not in fact constitute a conflict of interest, and a second vote resulted in Ms. Beyda's unanimous election to the board. But a video of the session was uploaded onto YouTube, and after severe expressions of criticism, the four students who had initially opposed Ms. Beyda's nomination publicly apologized, saying that their intentions were "never to attack, insult, or delegitimize any individual or people, [and that they] were sorry for any words used during the meeting that suggested otherwise." It's difficult to believe that had the question been directed to a person of color, a member of the LGBTQ community, or a woman, the students would have had any trouble recognizing the explicit bias in what was being suggested. But I actually don't believe that these students were being disingenuous. Their views reflect a sentiment among many students, including possibly your Mutterer, that Jews are members of the elite and therefore cannot be fair-minded or the victims of discrimination. In doublespeak worthy of George Orwell, for these students, keeping Jews out serves the goal of inclusion.[3]

Thanks to the civil rights movement, overt religious, racial, and ethnic discrimination has become illegal. Covert discrimination persists of course. But prejudice is a hard thing to root out, and racial minorities continue to be subject to overt acts of discrimination. This, however, doesn't mean that Jews are no longer subject to antisemitism. The categories of antisemites we mapped out in our earlier letters were highlighted with examples from *today*, not from fifty years ago.

As recently as September 2017, former CIA operative Valerie Plame tweeted a link to an overtly antisemitic article (that she'd termed "thoughtful") that maintained that Jews were behind efforts to get America involved in wars in the Middle East—including the 2003 war with Iraq. (This ignores the fact that among the main advocates of the war were Vice President Dick Cheney, Defense Secretary Donald Rumsfeld, National Security Advisor Condoleezza Rice, Secretary of State Colin Powell, and President George W. Bush himself.) It also called for Jews publicly commenting on foreign policy to identify themselves as Jews. The Jewish advisers in the White House who strongly supported the war, the article contended, were looking at this foreign policy issue only *as* Jews. When Plame was accused of antisemitism, her initial response was that she was herself "of Jewish decent [*sic*]," a traditional response when someone is caught in this type of situation. That didn't seem to work, and in her eventual apology she claimed that she hadn't in fact read the entire article and had "missed gross undercurrents" in it—a rather strange explanation for an article plainly titled "America's Jews Are Driving America's Wars."[4]

Yes, the Mutterer is right when he says that antisemitism is not the same as some of the acts of extreme physical violence and social discrimination faced by African Americans. But public declarations and acts of antisemitism are still hateful, prejudiced, and wrong. They must be called out for what they are, and anyone who minimizes their intent or impact is either woefully ignorant of history or antisemitic himself. Valerie Plame is not the first person to accuse Jews of advocating for war for their own political or financial gain. In Germany in the 1920s, Jews were accused by Nazis of getting Germany involved in what became World War I for their own personal gain. If the Mutterer considers that piece of information "playing the Holocaust card," that will certainly show everyone else in your seminar where his politics lie. Unfortunately, there's nothing you can do to change his beliefs. But you are correct, Abigail, in your impulse to speak out against his hateful words.

DEL

ANTISEMITISM AND RACISM:
THE SAME YET DIFFERENT

Dear Professor Lipstadt:

Thanks for your letter. I understand that antisemitism and racial prejudice have important things in common but are also, in equally important ways, very different manifestations of hatred. Watching cell phone videos of acts of violence committed against African Americans by police officers makes me sick to my stomach. But does that mean that it's wrong for us to try to point out the commonalities, to try to find common cause with victims of racial prejudice, or to call attention to what Jews face?[1]

Yours,
Abigail

Dear Abigail and Joe:

Abigail, you have zeroed in on an important and much misunderstood question. Today, African American parents live with a gnawing and persistent fear of their children being brutalized at the hands of those who are sworn to protect and to serve. Ta-Nehisi Coates painfully expresses this in *Between the World and Me*, a book of letters to his son. "And I am afraid," he writes. "I feel the fear most acutely whenever you leave me." Coates knows that for a disproportionate number of African Americans "the law has become an excuse for stopping and frisking you, which is to say, for furthering the assault on your body."[2] Though Coates speaks of frisking, there are more ominous possibilities, including physical violence and, in certain cases, even death.[3] The prevalence of this type of violent interaction between law enforcement officers and African Americans has been well documented. A study by John Jay College of Criminal Justice found that while police use force in less than 2 percent of their interactions with white civilians, when those civilians are African Americans the use of force is more than three times as high.[4]

I was recently privy to a conversation between a Jewish parent and her high school–age son that starkly illustrated the differences between the perception white kids and minority kids have of the police. The previous night the young man had attended a party that ended late, in a neighborhood where there is a serious drug problem. The young man told his mother that she needn't have worried because he'd left the party with a group of friends and, more important, a patrol car was nearby. The officer inside the car told the kids he would watch them until they were safely on their way. "So, you see, Mom, all was fine," he said. I couldn't help but wonder if a group of African American kids would have been similarly reassured by the presence of that police car. Not long ago, after a black man was fatally shot by a police officer, his grief-stricken mother stressed in a television interview that she had "always taught him to 'comply' with law enforcement." Does a white mother have to give the same sort of instruction to her son? I was reminded of the fact that what is considered youthful indiscretions for young whites— sneaking into a private pool or playing basketball in a park at night when the park is closed—can be death traps for young blacks.[5] Supreme Court Justice Sonia Sotomayor articulated this in a case involving police officers conducting warrantless searches.

> For generations, black and brown parents have given their children "the talk"—instructing them never to run down the street, always keep your hands where they can be seen, do not even think of talking back to a stranger—all out of fear of how an officer with a gun will react to them.[6]

I am not, by any means, condemning all, or even most, police officers. That would be to engage in the same kind of stereotyping that I have been decrying. Police officers have an important and dangerous job. But in recent times there have been enough incidents to erase any lingering doubts that people of color—both men and women—face a particular liability when confronted by those law enforcement officials who might harbor these stereotypes. It's an institutional racism that makes many people see an African American male as a potential threat. It is not just some police officers who fall prey to these prejudices. In the summer of 2018, a young black woman who was a student at Smith College, an elite school, was sitting in a common room eating lunch. A white college employee saw her there and called the campus police to report a "black male," who looked "out of place." The five-foot-two, 120-pound young woman, the first in her family to attend college, was on campus as a teaching assistant in a chemistry program. She had a teddy bear perched next to her. Sadly, this was not an isolated incident.[7]

Fear of violence at the hands of the police or being declared "out of place" because one wore a kippah or some other Jewish accoutrement is not a current reality for Jewish Americans. It is precisely because of this that Jews bear a special responsibility to speak out against not only this particular type of prejudice but also against all forms of discrimination. As the victims of prejudice ourselves, we know from personal experience how important it is to have the support of other communities when we fight prejudice against us.

I don't think there's any point in playing the "my discrimination is worse than your discrimination" game. Threats against Jewish institutions—which have resulted in the placement of screening machines at most American synagogues, Jewish community centers, and Jewish museums—are real and are scary. In recent years, people have died in this country in attacks on Jewish venues.

Long thought to have been eradicated from American society, antisemitism is back when Jewish college students are reluctant to affiliate with Jewish student organizations because they don't want to spend their university years fighting Israel-bashing or confronting Jew-hatred.[8] Whether it comes from those on the political left or political right, from Christians or, as is the case in many European countries, from Muslims, it is antisemitism when Jews are attacked—verbally or physically—because they are Jews. Antisemitism exists when parents are afraid to enroll their children in a Jewish preschool because they fear for their safety. Is this fear on the same level as that of the African American mother who sends her teenage son off to school in the morning and wonders if he will come back that afternoon? No, but why does this have to be some sort of macabre competition? Why can't they *both* be considered terrible by-products of senseless hatred?

Thus far, I have been giving your Mutterer the benefit of the doubt, assuming that he just got it wrong and didn't understand the nature of antisemitism because it presents so differently from racism against people of color. But there's another possible explanation. The Mutterer's response may not have been a matter of confusion; it may originate in the theory that an act of prejudice or discrimination occurs only if a powerful, privileged Goliath is either literally or figuratively beating up on a David who is a member of a racial or ethnic minority. Let's call this the Corbyn Syndrome. Jews—for the most part white, privileged members of the elite—cannot possibly be considered victims, according to this theory. If anything, they are victimizers. And so when Jews bring up antisemitism in a discussion of discrimination and prejudice, people like the Mutterer not only find their claims illegitimate but also believe that they are "freeloading" on the legacy of the genuine suffering of racial minorities.[9] I believe these people are more than tragically misguided, and I really wonder if it is possible to change their thinking. I hope I am wrong.

Yours,
DEL

A TIME TO PANIC?

Dear Professor Lipstadt:

Thank you. That was helpful, if very discouraging. Here's what may well be described as the "flip side" of this issue. I just spent some time visiting my grandparents. They are terrific people—active, inquisitive, and always interested in me and my work. But they and their friends kept talking about what they called the "explosion of antisemitism" throughout the world today and making comparisons to what the Jews in Germany experienced in the 1930s. They worry about my living on a campus that they refer to as a "hotbed" of antisemitism and insist that Jews everywhere are "under siege." They sound to me far more worked up than I think the situation warrants. Are they oversensitive, or am I blind?

Thanks,
Abigail

Dear Abigail and Joe:

Abigail, your grandparents and their friends are not alone in being worried. The statistics are, indeed, troubling. Antisemitic events have been on the rise—particularly in Europe—since the beginning of the 2000s, with the outbreak of the Second

Intifada and collapse of Middle East peace talks. France's Jewish Community Security Service estimates that the annual incidence of antisemitic acts in the 2000s was seven times higher than in the 1990s. A number of these incidents resulted in serious injuries and even death. In 2006 a young Frenchman, Ilan Halimi, was kidnapped in Paris and brutally tortured; he eventually died of his injuries. His kidnappers, members of a criminal gang, believed that because he was Jewish, his family was rich and would be able to pay a huge ransom to get him back. The French police refused to see this as an antisemitic or terrorist event. In 2012, three children and one adult were killed at the Ozar Hatorah Jewish day school in Toulouse. In May 2014 four visitors to the Brussels Jewish Museum were shot to death.[1] There have also been violent but nonlethal attacks on Jews wearing *kippot* in outdoor public places, such as the 2012 attack on a rabbi in Berlin, whose cheekbone was broken as a result of a beating witnessed by his six-year-old daughter.

Antisemitic incidents proliferated in Europe during the Gaza conflict between Israel and Hamas in July and August of 2014. According to Conseil Représentatif des Institutions Juives de France (CRIF), the umbrella organization of French Jewry, eight synagogues were attacked that July, including one in Sarcelles, which was firebombed by a mob of four hundred people after Jews had sought shelter there. On July 14, Bastille Day, two hundred Parisian Jews were trapped in a synagogue by rioters who chanted "Hitler was right!" and "Jews, get out of France."[2] The chief rabbi of Paris, who happened to be attending the service, was rescued after about an hour by a counterterrorism force, but the rest of the congregants were stuck inside. Using tables and chairs from nearby cafés, members of the Jewish community who have been trained in defense managed to disperse the approximately three hundred protesters outside the synagogue.

It took close to three hours.[3] In Paris, kosher supermarkets and stores owned by Jews have been attacked, most notably in January 2015, when four people were murdered in the Hypercacher supermarket. In July 2014, a synagogue in Wuppertal, Germany (which had been destroyed in 1938 during Kristallnacht and rebuilt after the war), was damaged by Molotov cocktails thrown into it. In June 2014, an elderly Jewish man was beaten at a pro-Israel rally in Berlin. In the summer of 2014, signs were posted in Rome urging a boycott of fifty Jewish-owned business establishments.[4] In July 2014, at a pro-Hamas march in Berlin, a marcher broke away and assaulted an older man who was quietly standing on a corner holding an Israeli flag. The attacker's fellow marchers cheered in approval. There were enough of these incidents that the *Guardian* published an article on the rise of antisemitism with the headline "Worst Since Nazis."[5]

Most of these attacks were committed by European Islamist extremists and their sympathizers. While the majority of antisemitic incidents in Europe are not quite so violent, they are, nonetheless, distressing for European Jews. Particularly unnerving is when an anti-Israel rally is punctuated with calls for "Death to Jews" and "Slit Jews' throats."[6] Some demonstrations include slogans and banners that in some way reference the Holocaust. In Germany, signs at several pro-Palestinian demonstrations read *"Jude, Jude, feiges Schwein!"* ("Jews, Jews, cowardly swine"). In Gelsenkirchen, Dortmund, and Frankfurt protesters chanted, *"Hamas, Hamas, Juden ins gas!"* ("Hamas, Hamas, Jews to the gas!") while marchers in Essen cried, *"Scheiss Juden!"* ("Jewish shit").[7] Other slogans chanted at various demonstrations included: "Jew, Jew, cowardly pig" (Berlin), "Stop the Jewish terror!" (Essen), "Supposedly former victims. Now themselves perpetrators" (Essen), "Child-murderer Israel" (Berlin).[8] While the "Jews to the gas" chant may have originated as a Dutch soccer slogan that, weirdly enough, many soccer fans argue was not really related to Jews, it has clearly migrated to having everything to do with Jews.[9] During a sermon in a mosque in 2014 an imam in Berlin, Sheikh Abu Bilal Ismail, asked Allah to "destroy the Zionist Jews. . . . Count them and kill them, to the very last one."[10]

Jews in Europe have been reacting accordingly. A member of the Belgian parliament publicly acknowledged that she asked her children to remove their Magen David necklaces when they went out into the street. "I felt embarrassed to ask them to do so. But I also felt reassured when they did." After the beating of the Berlin rabbi, the rector of Abraham Geiger College, a liberal rabbinical seminary in Potsdam, suggested that students "not wear their skullcaps on the street. Instead, they should choose an inconspicuous head cover." The rabbi observed that "apparently, a Jew is only safe if he is not visible as such." The notion that a Jew had to go incognito to be safe in Germany was so distasteful to some non-Jewish Germans that they donned *kippot* to march in Berlin.[11]

In April 2018, a week after a nineteen-year-old Syrian refugee attacked two young men wearing *kippot* in Berlin (who, as it happens, were actually Israeli Arabs who donned *kippot* to see for themselves if it was in fact unsafe for *kippah*-wearing people to walk the streets of Berlin), Josef Schuster, the head of Germany's Central Council of Jews, warned Jews against wearing religious symbols in public. The next day, more than two thousand people—Jews, Christians, Muslims, and atheists—rallied in Berlin at a "Berlin Wears Kippa" event, where everyone showed up wearing some type of skullcap. Berlin's mayor, Michael Müller, gave a rousing speech, but a reporter covering the event was quick to point out, at the conclusion of the event, as everyone was leaving the area that had been cordoned off by the police, many were quick to remove their *kippot*. There were similar events in other German cities.[12] .

These heartening gestures of solidarity notwithstanding, many researchers believe that Germany has witnessed a normalization of antisemitism unlike anything since the end of World War II. A 2013 study by the Technical University of Berlin examined the hate-letters, emails, and faxes received over the previous ten years by the Israeli embassy in Berlin and the Central Council of Jews in Germany. They had a very rich body of empirical data on which to draw, including approximately 200,000 Internet texts, 20,000 emails to Jewish institutions, and 150,000 texts related to media coverage of the Middle East conflict. Researchers found that 60 percent of them came from educated, middle-class Germans, including lawyers, scholars, doctors, priests, professors, and university and secondary school students. Irrespective of whether these communiqués came from the Right or the Left—from neo-Nazis, leftists, radicalized Muslims, or "respectable" individuals—they all echoed classic antisemitic stereotypes, including Jews as murderers of little children, shylocks, traitors, liars, and fifth columnists (internal enemies). Jews were described as "vile," "other," and "a threat to mankind." In most of the messages the terms "Jews," "Israelis," and "Israel" were used interchangeably. "Jews are the evil in the world" was recast as "Israel is the evil in the world." Professor Monika Schwarz-Friesel, the lead researcher on this project, believes that more notable than the virulent content was the fact that most of the communiqués' authors provided their names and addresses. This, she contends, is something most Germans would not have done as recently as twenty years ago.[13] A similar lack of inhibition had also been evident in Austria. In February 2018, Oskar Deutsch, president of the Federation of Jewish Communities of Austria, observed that the Vienna-based Nazi hunter Simon Wiesenthal used to receive antisemitic threats all the time. But those letters were anonymous and there was little means of tracing the writers. Today, Deutsch says, "these threats clearly state exactly who they come from. That is the problem— antisemitic statements are becoming ever more normal."[14]

The heads of state of Europe's most vibrant democracies also seemed to consider the surge of antisemitism in Europe at the time of the 2014 Gaza war to be more than a passing phenomenon. On September 10, 2014, Prime Minister David Cameron sent an unprecedented Rosh Hashanah letter to the chief rabbi of the United Hebrew Congregations of the Commonwealth, in advance of his usual videotaped Rosh Hashanah greetings to the Jewish community. "As we enter this time of reflection in marking Rosh Hashanah and Yom Kippur," he wrote, "I hope that your community of rabbis may be able to offer some reassurance to any who need it about the incredible pride that Britain has in its Jewish communities and our continued determination to fight discrimination and to keep Jewish people safe. A Jewish friend once asked me whether it will always be safe for his children and grandchildren to live in Britain. The answer to that question will always be 'yes.' I hope that in years to come we will reach a point where that question will not even need to be asked."[15]

Other European heads of state echoed Cameron's reassurances. Four days later, German chancellor Angela Merkel led a rally against antisemitism at Berlin's Brandenburg Gate. "That people in Germany are threatened and abused because of their Jewish appearance or their support for Israel is an outrageous scandal that we won't accept," she declared. She did more than condemn attacks on Jews. She cast the fight against antisemitism as a national concern: "Anyone who hits someone wearing a skullcap is hitting us all. Anyone who damages a Jewish gravestone is disgracing our culture. Anyone who attacks a synagogue is attacking the foundations of our free society." And four days after that, French prime minister Manuel Valls spoke at a gathering at the Great Synagogue of rue de la Victoire in Paris to an audience of more than a thousand representatives of the French Jewish community. He declared that "the fight against racism and antisemitism [is] a great national cause" and called on all French citizens to "mobilize [and] go out in the street" to fight this prejudice. "It is not possible to deny the right of the State of Israel to exist and avoid being accused of anti-Semitism," he said, and concluded by saying, "Without the Jews of France, France would not be France."[16] The fact that these three prime ministers felt it necessary to reassure their Jewish citizens that they are not alone in their fight against antisemitism indicates how real a threat to the fabric of their societies they felt these incidents to be.

In November 2014, I attended an international conference on antisemitism that was held in Berlin. The government officials present delivered earnest statements attesting to their commitment to fighting this problem. But, as is often the case at conferences, it was the informal chats I had with other delegates in corridors that most stayed with me. During a conversation with members of European Jewish communities, I thought I would hear about the murders in Brussels, Toulouse, Paris, and other cities. A few months later I met with a similar group. Again, I expected to hear about these murders and the one that had just occurred in Copenhagen, where, in February 2015, a Danish-born Muslim attacked a bat mitzvah celebration and killed the volunteer guard outside the building. At both meetings I expected to hear about the murders, violent demonstrations, attacks on synagogues, and antisemitic rhetoric, including "Jews to the gas." The participants acknowledged these incidents, but they were more anxious to talk about the spiritual and psychological effects of what they were experiencing. They told me about changing their daily routine and avoiding certain areas of their cities where they felt under threat. University students spoke of feeling "on guard" and fearing that they would be verbally attacked when the conversation turned to Jewish topics. Jewish institutions have to be protected by armed guards. Parents described feeling reassured when they saw the guards at their children's schools and fearful when they remembered why they were there. Some described being Jewish as having become a negative, a burden, if not for them, then for their friends. "We are continuously on the defensive," they told me. "It gets depressing." Guy, a young Dutchman, recalled that a few months earlier, his Jewish friends had gathered to celebrate his birthday. "What," he asked us with an ironic smile, "do a group of young men talk about when they gather to drink beer and enjoy themselves? The Holocaust, antisemitism, and insecurity." I was told that in certain countries, children who attend Jewish schools are warned not to wear anything that would single them out as Jews: no school insignias on their book bags, no school symbols on their jackets, no *kippot*. In most of these places there have been no serious incidents, but the schools do not want to take a chance.

Even more disheartening was the fact that many of the European students I met were less troubled by those who threaten them than they were by the former allies who have abandoned them. Jewish groups, both on campus and in the broader community, have long participated in coalitions of human rights organizations. "Now," a young Belgian Jew observed, "these human rights groups don't consider Jews to be 'victims.' We may not face job discrimination, but we face violence that is sometimes physical but more often emotional." Even after multiple assaults on Jews in Europe, some European human rights activists dismissed antisemitism as "only words" and of no real importance. Some even suggested that this all happened "because of Israel," which is to say that it was justified because of Israel's treatment of the Palestinians. As one young woman sadly observed, "We feel as if we have no allies." I have heard this repeatedly from students in Europe and increasingly in North America.

Clearly, what I have just described is anecdotal and cannot be used to draw wide-ranging conclusions. But it is a fact that some Jews, unsure that they have a future in Europe, are leaving countries where their families have lived for generations. They head to Israel, the United States, and Canada. The young people I spoke with predicted: "They will never come back." The consensus was that most European Jews will probably stay put. Emigrating is not an easy task. "But," one young person insisted, "some will become 'invisible Jews.'" Nodding her head in assent, another participant described these Jews as "going underground."

Abigail, while I agree with your grandparents about the disturbing reemergence of antisemitism in Europe today, I firmly eschew comparisons to Germany in the 1930s, which was state-sponsored antisemitism in which national and local governmental bodies as well as academic institutions enthusiastically participated. Nothing that we are witnessing today compares in any measure to the kind of endemic hatred and persecution that German and Austrian Jews were subjected to in the years leading up to World War II. But this is not to say that I haven't been alarmed by what European Jews are currently experiencing. I was not so naive as to think that in the aftermath of the Holocaust, European antisemitism had finally been eliminated. I know far better than that, and my research and personal experiences fighting Holocaust denial reaffirmed that fact for me.[17] But I did believe that we had reached a point where antisemitism no longer constituted a personal threat to most Jews living in the West. As has become clear, I was wrong.

On the other hand, I want to be careful not to overstate the negative. In the decades since the Holocaust, there has been an extraordinary resurgence of Jewish life in Europe. And Jewish life in the United States flourishes in a way that would have been inconceivable to Jews living in America before World War II. To ignore these positive developments and focus only on the negative is to do this renaissance and the Jews who are part of it a great disservice. It is to miss out on and even obliterate the good. Most Jewish students on American campuses do not feel besieged or pressured. They can live vibrant Jewish lives as students. People who speak of the campus as a "hotbed" of antisemitism overstate the case and are positing something that is at odds with most students' reality. While things may be hard for students who openly support Israel, they do not feel that they are "under siege."

But what we are seeing, particularly in Europe, does deserve our attention. Note that I say attention, *not* panic. As one American who has lived in Germany for more than thirty years and who has been part of this resurgence of Jewish life recently shared with me, "If this atmosphere continues, it could undo all these good things." She told me how distressed she was when her eleven-year-old daughter, upon seeing a man at a bus stop in Hasidic garb, told her mother that it was not safe for the man to walk around that way. When our children fear there is danger in openly identifying as a Jew, it is indeed something that should concern us all.

Yours,
DEL

· I V ·

"Yes, But": Rationalizing Evil

THE OMINOUS CASE OF SALMAN RUSHDIE

Dear Deborah:

In your catalog of antisemites, I notice you didn't address antisemitism within the Islamic world. I was thinking about this tonight because I just returned from a lecture by Salman Rushdie, whose 1988 novel, *The Satanic Verses,* contained Islam-related material that many Muslims believed was insulting to their religion. As I know you well remember, Ayatollah Khomeini, then Iran's supreme religious authority, issued a fatwa, a religious ruling, declaring the novel blasphemous and calling on "zealous Muslims" to murder Rushdie and "all those involved in [the novel's] publication." Anyone killed in fulfilling this ruling would, he promised, be deemed a religious martyr. The Iranian government put a bounty on Rushdie's head, and he was in hiding for about a decade.[1]

At the lecture, Rushdie spoke of his disappointment at what he felt was a lack of support from some Western intellectuals. What he said had a familiar ring. There may be no connection here to our discussion of antisemitism, but the intolerance and violence that has in recent years been exhibited by some in the Muslim world toward the West makes me wonder if there is in fact some connection. What do you think?

Yours,
Joe

Dear Joe and Abigail:

Joe, you are right. There was a big hole in my taxonomy of the antisemite. Islam has been used by extremists to rationalize the killing and maiming of people throughout the world. Attacks by Islamist extremists, which once were directed mainly at Jews in Israel and throughout the Diaspora, are now aimed at "the West" in general. In Europe, the perpetrators are both citizens who are Muslims and immigrants from North Africa and the Middle East.

Various studies, including one conducted in 2017 by the University of Oslo, have shown that attacks on European Jews, particularly physical assaults, come in the main from radicalized Muslims.[2] Interviews with German Muslims, including well-educated professionals, feature comments about Jews that sound as though they have come directly from the notorious antisemitic forgery, *The Protocols of the Elders of Zion*. They claim that all the major companies in the world are controlled by Jews, that Jews harvest the organs of non-Jews for their own use, and that there are 120 Jewish families who control the world. Much of this animus may be traced back to the Israel/Palestine situation, but no distinction is made between Israelis and Jews.[3]

Too many people in the West—including religious figures, intellectuals, politicians, and journalists—tend to come dangerously close to what can only be described as rationalizing this extremist Islamist terror. We saw this as far back as the Rushdie case and we continue to see it today.

Let's begin with Rushdie: A religious head of state condemned a citizen of another country to death in defiance of even the loosest interpretation of international law. The practical implications were immediate. The Japanese translator of *The Satanic Verses* was murdered. The Italian and Norwegian translators were attacked and seriously wounded. Bookstores throughout the world that stocked the novel were bombed. Dozens of people were killed either during protests that supported the fatwa or at meetings that supported Rushdie.[4]

It was certainly distressing to read that there were British Muslims who publicly supported the fatwa, but I want to focus here on prominent non-Muslims throughout the world who engaged in what I categorize as "yes, but" responses: condemning the death sentence (*yes,* it is horrible) while at the same time trying to rationalize it (*but* he brought this on himself by blaspheming Islam). I do so for two reasons: (1) it gives us some insight into the response by some in the West to Islamist extremists, and (2) this type of rationalization has also become a template for the way in which many prominent individuals in the West have responded to acts of antisemitism.

The archbishop of Canterbury, assuring Muslims that he regarded an offense against other religions to be of the same magnitude as an offense against Christianity, proposed that Britain's much-ignored blasphemy law be expanded to encompass Islam.[5] Despite having not read the book and insisting that he had "no intention of doing so," New York's John Cardinal O'Connor declared Rushdie's novel "insulting and insensitive to the Muslim faith."[6] Britain's then chief rabbi, Lord Immanuel Jakobovits, stated that the book should "not have been published" and accused both Rushdie and the Ayatollah of having "abused freedom of speech, the one by provocatively offending the genuine faith of many millions of devout believers and the other by a public call to murder." He proposed a law that would prohibit the publication of anything "likely to inflame . . .

the feelings or beliefs of any section of society."[7] But it was not only religious leaders who responded this way. Former president Jimmy Carter, writing in the *New York Times,* declared the book a "direct insult to . . . millions of Moslems" and called upon Western leaders to "make it clear" that the police protection Rushdie was receiving did not constitute an "endorsement of an insult to the sacred beliefs of our Moslem friends."[8] Carter did not, of course, endorse the fatwa, but his comments implied that he could understand what the motivating factor for it was, which is just as unacceptable.[9] Some of Rushdie's fellow writers were also notably less than supportive. John le Carré declared that "nobody has a God-given right to insult a great religion." He proposed that Rushdie withdraw the book. Roald Dahl called Rushdie a "dangerous opportunist" who had deliberately decided to arouse among Muslims "deep and violent feelings" as a means of pushing his "indifferent book on to the top of the bestseller list."[10] (This from the man who was famously quoted as saying, "There is a trait in the Jewish character that does provoke animosity; maybe it's a kind of lack of generosity towards non-Jews. I mean there is always a reason why anti-anything crops up anywhere; even a stinker like Hitler didn't just pick on them for no reason."[11]) Paul Gilroy, author of *There Ain't No Black in the Union Jack,* whom Rushdie had once lauded as "the United Kingdom's Cornel West" and a person intent on shedding light on racism, accused Rushdie of having created his own tragedy.[12] The historian Hugh Trevor-Roper declared that he "would not shed a tear if some British Muslim, deploring his manners, should waylay him in some dark street and seek to improve them. If that should cause him thereafter to control his pen, society would benefit, and literature would not suffer."[13]

There were, however, public figures who supported Rushdie. Daniel J. Boorstin, a historian and former Librarian of Congress, declared Khomeini a terrorist and called for the American government to react in "the strongest terms." Boorstin encouraged people to buy *The Satanic Verses* as an act of "affirmation of the freedom of the press in America and our unwillingness to be held hostage in our own country."[14] A similar tone was adopted by the Clinton White House. In 1993, White House director of communications George Stephanopoulos declared: "We unequivocally condemn the fatwa. We do not believe this is a private matter between Mr. Rushdie and Iran. We do not believe people should be killed for writing books. We regard the fatwa as a violation of Mr. Rushdie's basic human rights and therefore as a violation of international law." The *New York Times* put it most succinctly: "So let it be said again: Murder is not an acceptable form of literary criticism."[15]

So, to return to Joe's original question, is there a connection between responses to Rushdie's situation and responses to incidents of contemporary antisemitism? Yes, I believe there is. Jews, together with other religious and ethnic minorities, have always thrived in societies where freedom of speech and religion have been highly valued. They have blossomed in societies that welcome an array of cultures and beliefs. Khomeini's fatwa was a religious attack on freedom of speech. He convicted Rushdie, who does not identify as a religious Muslim, of a religious crime. He insisted that non-Muslims are also bound by Islamic laws regarding blasphemy. And he gave Muslims throughout the world the authority to carry out his religious ruling that "blasphemers," wherever they may be found, be punished.[16]

While most of Rushdie's Western critics did not feel that Khomeini had the right to issue his fatwa, they also blamed Rushdie for doing something that he knew would enrage Muslims who were willing and able to express their anger in acts of violence—as if Muslims are for some reason not expected to adhere to the rules of international law when someone insults them. This is something that has a bitter ring for Jews, as it is often used to rationalize antisemitism. "*Yes,* antisemitic speech and violence are wrong," one version of the argument goes, "*but* how can you expect Muslims to feel and to act when Israel takes actions that oppress Palestinians." The antisemitism manifested by some—and I emphasize some—European Muslims is part of a larger problem of integration. But unless Europeans address the problem strongly, unapologetically, and without "yes, buts," it will sink deep roots, fester, and grow. Ultimately, more than just people wearing *kippot* will disappear from the European landscape. "Yes, but" is the top of the slippery slope of immoral equivalencies. We'll see in my next letter where this has inevitably led.

Fondly,
DEL

PIXILATING THE PROBLEM

Dear Joe and Abigail:

In 2004, Theo van Gogh, a Dutch television and film producer and director, collaborated with Ayaan Hirsi Ali, a Somali-born activist, author, and politician, to produce *Submission,* a twelve-minute film that contended that Islamic law justifies the oppression and abuse of women. In November of that year, after the film was broadcast on Dutch television, Van Gogh was murdered by a Dutch-Moroccan Muslim who linked his action to Van Gogh's film. On the website of the *Index on Censorship,* an organization and journal that had been created in 1972 to fight the censorship imposed by the Soviet Union and by right-wing dictatorships, Rohan Jayasekera, then the associate editor of the *Index,* called Van Gogh a "fundamentalist believer in the right to free expression" who had been on a "martyr-dom operation" and that his film was "furiously provocative." He went on to almost jovially describe Van Gogh's murder as a "marvelous piece of street theatre" that Van Gogh had brought on himself and a wonderful publicity boon for his film. "Bravo, Theo! Bravo!" he exclaimed.[1] Jayasekera's statement was not only heartless but also violated the *Index*'s founding principles.[2] Responding to a storm of criticism of Jayasekera, Ursula Owen, the journal's editor in chief, made the dubious claim that "there was no intent in the article to blame the victim" and that its purpose was, instead, "to tackle the issue of whether rights come with responsibilities."[3]

An equally disturbing event took place in the fall of 2005, when a Danish newspaper, *Jyllands-Posten,* asserted that a popular children's book author was having trouble finding an illustrator for a book he had written on the prophet Muhammed; artists were fearful of incurring the wrath of Muslims because representations of the prophet are forbidden under Islamic law. And so, the newspaper invited forty-two cartoonists to submit drawings of Muhammed for publication. Twelve of them agreed, and their drawings (some quite provocative) were published in the newspaper. A group of Islamic leaders formed a protest group, and a peaceful protest was held in Denmark a few weeks later. Eleven ambassadors from Muslim-majority countries sent letters of protest to the Danish prime minister, who explained that the Danish press is free to publish whatever it wants to. As time passed, tensions began to ratchet up throughout the world. The Danish embassies in Damascus, Beirut, and Teheran were set on fire by protesters, and a consumer boycott was organized by several Middle Eastern countries against Denmark. A political organization in Pakistan put a bounty on the heads of the cartoonists, some of whom went into hiding. Four years later, one of the cartoonists, Kurt Westergaard, encountered an ax- and knife-wielding Somali trying to break into his home. The attack occurred while he was caring for his five-year-old granddaughter.[4]

In their coverage of the situation, some major newspapers (mostly in continental Europe) reprinted the cartoons, but others—including the *Washington Post,* the *New York Times,* the *Times* (London), and *Le Monde*—decided not to. In Britain, the *Sun* and the *Telegraph* displayed the front page of *France-Soir,* which had published one of the cartoons, but obscured the actual image of the cartoon. The *Times* and the *Guardian* posted links to places where the cartoons could be viewed. The *Independent,* a paper that prides itself on championing free speech, declared that, while "there is a right to exercise an uncensored pen . . . the media have responsibilities as well as rights." The *Guardian* contended that "the restraint of most of the British press may be the wiser course—at least for now."[5] Some editors published the cartoons but quickly found out that their editorial boards did not support them. The editor at *France-Soir* was fired and the newspaper apologized for publishing the cartoons.[6] When a student newspaper in Cardiff published three of the cartoons, the editorial board recalled eight thousand copies of the newspaper, fired the editor, and apologized profusely for reprinting the images. The head of the university's Centre for the Study of Islam described the decision to publish as "stupid." Others at the university condemned it as "irresponsible."[7] Appearing on CNN to discuss the cartoons, Christopher Hitchens was horrified when the network pixilated the images. Viewers heard a vigorous discussion about the drawings without ever seeing them.[8] The BBC broadcast fuzzy pictures of newspapers in which the cartoons appeared.[9] Most disappointing of all was the decision of Yale University Press not to include any of the images in Jytte Klausen's *The Cartoons That Shook the World,* an extensively researched scholarly study of the controversy that was published in 2009. In the book's preface the head of the press acknowledged that it was afraid of the "serious risk of instigating violence."[10]

A few Western governments attempted to strike a balance between championing freedom of expression and condemning expressions of religious hatred. The U.S. State Department declared the cartoons to be as "unacceptable as antisemitic images, as anti-Christian images, or as negative images directed against any other religious belief." And then they went on to say, "But it is important that we also support the rights of individuals to express their freely held views."[11] One wonders what they thought they were accomplishing with this let's-try-to-have-it-both-ways statement.

British foreign secretary Jack Straw also attempted to be evenhanded. "There is freedom of speech, we all respect that," he stated, and then added that "we have to be very careful about showing the proper respect."[12] But he also praised those British newspapers that did not publish the cartoons and condemned those few that had. "I believe that the re-publication of these cartoons has been unnecessary, it has been insensitive, it has been disrespectful . . . and it has been wrong."[13] So much for supporting freedom of speech.

The French foreign minister, Philippe Douste-Blazy, echoed his American and British counterparts: "Freedom of expression confers rights, it is true—but it also imposes the duty of responsibility on those who are speaking out."[14] Ultimately, after a series of attacks on Danish embassies throughout the world, some of these governments were a little more outspoken in condemning attacks on freedom of expression. But Christopher Hitchens was having none of this. He observed that governments "have no business at all expressing an opinion" on whether newspapers can insult Islam or any other religion. If governments are to say anything, they are "constitutionally obliged to uphold the right [to freedom of expression] and no more." Fear of Islamist extremism clearly motivated many of the decisions not to publish the cartoons.[15]

Some in the media addressed the issue head-on. *Die Welt* published the cartoons and its editor, Richard Koppel, explained why. "We are living in a secular society where even religion can be subjected to criticism and satire," he said. He then added something that was decidedly different from the "evenhanded" or "yes, but" responses typical of Western commentators and political leaders. "It's not acceptable in a Western country, if you publish a cartoon like this, that the newspaper has to apologize, or even the prime minister has to apologize." The *Salient,* the conservative student newspaper at Harvard, published four of the cartoons. Then, in a biting editorial comment, it also reprinted what the paper described as "even more vile cartoons" from Middle Eastern publications, including those that depicted Jews killing children and drinking their blood.[16]

While many artists and journalists practiced self-censorship, some ultimately moved in the opposite direction. In 2012, British choreographer Lloyd Newson created a dance piece about the Rushdie affair, Van Gogh's murder, the Danish cartoons, and "honor abuse," the practice by some Muslims, including those in the United Kingdom, of killing women who bring "shame" on their families. A reviewer in the *Telegraph* surmised that, unlike Newson, other people in the arts did not tackle these issues "either because they fear being accused of racism, or because simply to raise the matter could expose them to genuine danger from angry Muslims."[17] Newson said that he created the dance piece after a Gallup poll found that zero percent of British Muslims thought homosexuality was acceptable. It was not the poll's results that motivated him, but the response of his decidedly liberal friends. When he mentioned it to them, most expressed concern that in publicizing it he would appear to be Islamophobic. "I'd say, 'Hold on—I'm quoting a statistic. Why is the first thing you gasp at not that statistic but, rather, that I may be Islamophobic for reporting the statistic?'" Newson observed that these same "liberal friends are very happy to criticize Catholicism, Christianity, and Judaism, but when it comes to Islam, it feels as though all their open-minded principles are disregarded."[18] More about this in my next letter.

Yours,
DEL

PARISIAN TRAGEDIES

Dear Joe and Abigail:

The "yes, but" response was also evident after the terrible massacre in Paris of twelve people, including eight staff members of the *Charlie Hebdo* magazine, by Islamist terrorists on January 7, 2015. The Parisian satirical magazine made a point of sticking its finger in the eye of every established institution, including religious ones. Contrary to the general impression, its main target was not Islam. According to *Le Monde*, of the five hundred magazine covers published between 2005 and 2015, only seven ridiculed Islam.[1] Undoubtedly its attacks on Islam were offensive, often extremely so, but, as the *New Yorker* observed, "the magazine was offensive to Jews, offensive to Muslims, offensive to Catholics, offensive to feminists, offensive to the right and to the left, while being aligned with it— offensive to everybody, equally."[2]

But this did not stop the critics. Within a day or so of the *Charlie Hebdo* murders, Jacob Canfield, a young American cartoonist, criticized the notion that the victims were brave souls who suffered a terrible death. He called the editor a "racist asshole," though he acknowledged that calling someone that the day after they were murdered was "a callous thing to do." He defended himself by saying that he didn't "do it lightly." Describing them as "white-guys" (which they were not), he declared that their supporters were "wrong" to defend them and their attacks on Islam.[3]

While Canfield's rantings may have come from a marginal figure, far more notable individuals reacted similarly. Though their words were less distasteful than Canfield's, their position was the same. In June 2015, PEN, a literary organization that has long spearheaded the fight against censorship, gave its annual Freedom of Expression Courage Award to *Charlie Hebdo*. The award was to be accepted by the magazine's two surviving editors, both of whom were late to work on the morning of the murder. Six authors, members of PEN, protested and announced that they would neither serve as literary hosts nor attend the dinner. Suggesting that poverty and lack of political power motivated the murderers, one of the boycotters condemned "PEN's seeming blindness to the cultural arrogance of the French nation, which does not recognize its moral obligation to a large and disempowered segment of their population." Another inaccurately castigated *Charlie Hebdo* for promotion of "a kind of forced secular view." Unsurprisingly, Salman Rushdie pointedly disagreed. "If PEN as a free speech organization can't defend and celebrate people who have been murdered for drawing pictures," he stated, "then frankly the organization is not worth the name."[4] One of the surviving editors said it best at the PEN gathering when he declared, "Being shocked is part of democratic debate. . . . Being shot is not."

In a tragically ironic coda, Stéphane Charbonnier, the editorial director of *Charlie Hebdo*, had completed, only two days before his murder, the manuscript for a book about what he termed the "disgusting white, left-wing bourgeois paternalism" that fanned the flames of Islamist terrorism. According to Charbonnier, when "the media decided that republishing the Muhammad caricatures could only trigger the fury of Muslims . . . it triggered the anger of a few Muslim associations."[5] By accusing Rushdie, Van Gogh, and the *Charlie Hebdo* cartoonists of inciting Islamist extremists, their critics come very close to making excuses for the subsequent violence and murders. The "yes, but" message is particularly painful because it comes precisely from those who should have fiercely defended freedom of expression. As Theodor Holman, a journalist and one of Van Gogh's best friends, argued, "Tolerance has been transformed into cowardice." He admitted that he was frightened of writing about the murder in his column in a leading Dutch newspaper. "I'm afraid, because a friend was . . . slaughtered because of what he was saying."[6]

In the end, there is only one acceptable response when freedom of expression is met with terrorism and murder: a plain and unequivocal declaration that this is wrong. Nothing—not poverty, anger, disenfranchisement, religious belief, or anything else—can justify it.

Now let's go back to Joe's original question: How does all this connect to antisemitism? A leftist school of thought holds that one of the reasons for the anger of Muslims toward the West is nineteenth- and twentieth-century Western political imperialism in Muslim lands. And contemporary Western critiques of Islam (whether they come from "crusaders" or secularists is completely immaterial) only fan the flames of this anger. From there, it's just a short journey for some leftists to regard Islamic terrorists as fellow "anti-imperialists." And it's an equally short journey for some to regard Jews—for centuries concentrated in Europe (in addition to their centuries-long second-class treatment in Islamic lands)—as Western imperialists when they seek to return to their ancient homeland, which was for centuries part of the Islamic empire. Islamic antisemitism and anti-Zionism therefore become rationalized as a legitimate response to Western imperialism. And so, we are confronted with another disgraceful "yes, but" argument.

Yours,
DEL

Dear Joe and Abigail:

In the aftermath of the *Charlie Hebdo* and Hypercacher attacks, I exchanged emails with my friend Jean, a Frenchman in his forties. He has many other Jewish friends, and he is fascinated by Jewish history and tradition. A businessman, he would probably describe himself as slightly left of center. In light of our most recent change, I thought this might resonate with you.

Yours,
DEL

Dear Jean:

It was good to speak to you right after the massacres at *Charlie Hebdo* and, two days later, Hypercacher. The sadness in your voice about these events was palpable. When you called again after the massive protest marches in France on January 10 and 11 you sounded better. Participating with the millions of people who attended the marches had clearly lifted your spirits.

I was touched by your quiet pride that you, as a non-Jew, had carried a "Je Suis Juif" sign at the Paris march. You were heartened by the way the march commemorated all the victims—cartoonists, shoppers, and police officers—as one. I tried to share your enthusiasm, but I think you heard in my voice that I could not. I owe you an explanation. I don't want to be one of those Jews who "can never take yes for an answer," which is to say, who can't seem to accept that good things are happening. But as I watched the television coverage of masses of people at the protest march, I found one thing troubling. Though the demonstration honored all the victims of all the recent attacks, in fact there were fundamental differences among them. The *Charlie Hebdo* editorial staff was murdered for something that they *did*. (Which is, of course, no justification for their murder.) The police officers (one of whom was a Muslim) were murdered in the line of duty. (Which is, of course, just as unconscionable.) But the victims in the kosher supermarket were killed because of who they *were* (or who the terrorist assumed they were). It's hard to believe that within living memory of World War II, Jews are once again being murdered on French soil just because they are Jews. The first violent attack on a Jewish institution in France since World War II was the October 1980 bombing directed against a synagogue on rue Copernic in Paris in which four people were killed and forty-six injured, most of them on the street outside the synagogue. The French prime minister at the time, Raymond Barre, infamously commented, "This odious bombing wanted to strike Jews who were going to the synagogue and it hit innocent French people who crossed the Copernic street." His repugnant distinction between "Jews" and "innocent French people" did not go unnoticed, and he was eventually condemned by the French parliament.[7]

Jews constitute no more than 1 percent of the French population, yet in recent years close to half the racist attacks in the country have been directed against them.[8] The president of one of the synagogues in France has noted that whenever there is some sort of special event at the synagogue, he alerts the police. Living on the defensive has become the new normal for many French Jews. As one young Frenchwoman told me, "When I bring my children to their Jewish school and see the guards with submachine guns, I feel relieved. Then I wonder, Why am I sending my children to a school where they have to be protected by armed guards? But if I send them to a 'French' school, they are harassed, particularly by the Muslim students."

The initial reluctance to see an antisemitic attack for what it is continues to be troubling. When CNN's Wolf Blitzer asked a reporter on the scene at Hypercacher whether there was "anything to indicate that this was an antisemitic act," the reporter's response was that because Muslims shop at the store, too, it wasn't necessarily antisemitic. It took the killer's proclamation that he had chosen the kosher supermarket in order to kill Jews to end that line of reasoning.[9] Equally myopic is the attempt by some in the media to downplay the role of Islamist extremists in these attacks. The day after the supermarket massacre, MSNBC host Melissa Harris-Perry asked *Forward* columnist J. J. Goldberg to assure viewers that the "antisemitism problem in France is not primarily a problem of antisemitism from French Muslims."

"I'm afraid I let her down," Goldberg recounted in his column in the *Forward*. "I cited Ilan Halimi, the school in Toulouse, the Jewish Museum in Brussels, the mob attack on the synagogue in Paris last summer—all perpetrated by Muslims . . . I was intending to expand on it and talk about the increasing presence of pure, old-fashioned Jew-hatred in various strains of radical Islamism, especially since the 1998 merger of Al Qaeda with Ayman al-Zawahiri's Egyptian Islamic Jihad. But the segment ended sort of abruptly and I was told I was done, so I never had the chance to finish the answer."[10]

Fortunately, there are those in France who do seem to get it. In an emotional speech at France's National Assembly following the funerals of seven of the victims of the terror attacks, Prime Minister Manuel Valls eloquently condemned France's failure to take antisemitism seriously:

> I say to the people in general who perhaps have not reacted sufficiently up to now, and to our Jewish compatriots, that this time [antisemitism] cannot be accepted. . . . How can we accept that cries of "death to the Jews" can be heard on the streets? . . . History has taught us that the awakening of antisemitism is the symptom of a crisis for democracy and of a crisis for the Republic. That is why we must respond with force. . . . There is also a new antisemitism that is born in our neighborhoods, coming through the internet, satellite dishes, against the backdrop of loathing of the State of Israel, which advocates hatred of the Jews and of all the Jews. . . . It has to be spelled out—the right words must be used to fight this unacceptable antisemitism. When the Jews of France are attacked, France is attacked, the conscience of humanity is attacked. Let us never forget that.[11]

But there are others who tried to rationalize these anti-semitic attacks by suggesting that they are a response to Israel's actions in the Middle East. The BBC's Tim Willcox did precisely that when, during an interview with a Jewish woman at the Paris march, he interrupted her comments about the tragedy to say that "many critics of Israel's policy would suggest that the Palestinians suffer hugely at Jewish hands as well."[12] British film director Ken Loach contended that an increase in antisemitism is "perfectly understandable because Israel feeds feelings of antisemitism."[13] One wonders what their response would be to a children's program broadcast by Hamas's al-Aqsa television channel in May 2014 in which its young viewers were urged to kill Jewish children. When a young girl announced her intention to kill "all of them," the smiling host responded "good."[14]

And then there are the individuals who defend themselves against accusations of antisemitism by insisting that it's actually Zionism to which they are opposed. In Brooklyn, on the eve of Yom Kippur in 2014, the proprietor of a coffeehouse posted a virulent antisemitic rant on Instagram about greedy Jews, which went viral.[15] When he was criticized, he insisted that he had been misunderstood; he was not antisemitic but "anti-Zionist." Then in a rather incoherent gloss (or perhaps a very coherent one), he added, "It's about greed."[16] In June 2009, the Reverend Jeremiah Wright, a pastor emeritus of Trinity United Church of Christ in Chicago, which Barack and Michelle Obama had attended when they lived there, told the Newport News *Daily Press* that "them Jews aren't going to let him [President Obama] talk to me." When a firestorm of criticism erupted, he insisted that he had been misunderstood. "I misspoke. Let me just say: Zionists . . . I'm not talking about all Jews, all people of the Jewish faith, I'm talking about Zionists."[17]

I'm with Prime Minister Valls on this one. There are ways of disagreeing with the policies of the Israeli government without sounding antisemitic. And blaming all Jews for something wrong that Israel has done—that's antisemitic.

No one who offers the "yes, but" rationalization actually engages in racist violence or even thinks that they are condoning it. But they are virtually guaranteeing that it will continue because what they *are* doing is facilitating it.

Jean, I know I have wandered a bit afield from the topic of the march. I apologize for that and for putting a damper on your upbeat feelings. But if ever there was a moment that demanded the airing of some painful truths, this is it.

Yours,
DEL

Dear Joe and Abigail:

I wrote the preceding letter right after the 2015 Paris attacks. There have been more than a few incidents since then, one of the most notorious in April 2017, when Sarah Halimi, a retired doctor in her mid-sixties, was murdered in Paris by Kobili Traoré, a twenty-eight-year-old Muslim neighbor, who shouted *Allahu Akbar* and referred to her as Satan as he beat her, fracturing multiple bones in her body. He then threw her from a third-floor window in her apartment onto the street, where she was found dead. French officials initially refused to classify this as an antisemitic assault and held Traoré for months in a psychiatric hospital, although he had no history of mental illness.[18] Almost a year after the murder, and after much public protest and an appeal from the Paris Prosecutor's Office, the French magistrate amended the indictment against Traoré to "murder with antisemitism as an aggravating factor."[19] The initial police reaction to this horrendous crime seemed to many people, including a group of prominent French intellectuals, a "denial of reality."[20]

In the past, French police often failed to see the antisemitic nature of crimes committed by Muslims against Jews, treating them instead as ordinary criminal acts. Such was the case in Paris in February 2006 with the kidnapping and horrific torture and murder of twenty-three-year-old Ilan Halimi. Some French Jews reported being told by police that as long as they lived in the same neighborhoods as Muslims, little could be done to prevent these attacks.[21]

But we are also beginning to see some hopeful signs. On March 1, 2018, a young boy wearing a *kippah* was beaten outside a synagogue by four teenagers believed to be of North African descent, who called him and his sister "dirty Jews." This time the police responded with alacrity, and the assault was immediately classified as an antisemitic incident.[22]

That same month, Mireille Knoll, an eighty-five-year-old Holocaust survivor who as a child had escaped the notorious roundup of Jews in Paris in 1942, was murdered by a Muslim neighbor and his friend. After stabbing her eleven times, they set fire to her apartment in an apparent effort to cover up the murder. One of the suspects was reported to have cried *Allahu Akbar* as he stabbed Mrs. Knoll, and one of the suspects was reported to have told the other, "She's a Jew. She must have money." While the murder bore tragic similarities to the killing of Sarah Halimi, this time French officials responded differently. The Paris prosecutor immediately asked that the suspects be charged with "premeditated murder of a vulnerable person for antisemitic motives."[23]

A few days after the murder, thousands of people participated in a march in Paris organized by the Jewish community in Mrs. Knoll's memory.[24] French president Emmanuel Macron attended her funeral, after attending that morning a state ceremony honoring a gendarme who had been murdered by an Islamist extremist in an attack on a supermarket in southern France in which two other hostages had also been killed. In a speech at the ceremony, Macron connected the two crimes, one committed by a "terrorist in Trèbe" and the other by murderers "who assassinated an innocent and vulnerable woman because she was Jewish."[25]

At last, some recognition that terrorist acts may at first be directed at Jews, but they never end with Jews.

Yours,
DEL

· V ·

Holocaust Denial: From Hard-core to Soft-core

A MATTER OF ANTISEMITISM,
NOT HISTORY

Dear Professor Lipstadt:

Thank you for that sobering and thought-provoking series of letters. I'd like to move our conversation in a slightly different direction. I know that fighting Holocaust denial has long been a central focus of your professional life and that you have persistently confronted deniers and their historical distortions.

Please don't think I'm minimizing your accomplishments in this area, but aren't deniers the equivalent of flat-earth theorists who are peddling an utterly bogus and thoroughly discredited version of history? Why should we take them seriously and give their perverted and unquestionably false view of history the dignity of a response? How much of an impact do they really have?

Yours,
Abigail

Dear Abigail and Joe:

Abigail, you're not the first person to ask me this question. Sometimes I ask it of myself. When I first began researching

and writing on this topic, colleagues would frequently tell me
I was wasting my time. "These people are dolts," they would
insist. "Forget about them." In truth, I thought the same thing
when I first heard of Holocaust deniers. I, too, dismissed them
as not worthy of serious analysis. Then I looked more closely,
and I changed my mind.

Denial flies in the face of basic logic. The Holocaust has the
dubious distinction of being the best documented genocide in
the world. For deniers to be right, all survivors would have to
be wrong.[1] Who else would have to be wrong? The bystanders,
those non-Jews who lived in the cities, towns, and villages in
eastern and western Europe and watched as their Jewish neighbors were being marched away, to be put on trains to concentration camps or to be shot in the woods and left to die in ditches.[2]
The scores of historians who have studied and written about the
Holocaust over the past seventy years would either have to be
part of this massive conspiracy or have been completely duped.

But, above all, the perpetrators themselves—those who
actually admitted their guilt—would have to be wrong. Survivors say, "This was done to me." Perpetrators say, "I did it."[3] In
criminal cases, the perpetrator's admission of guilt has more
clout than the victim's accusation. How can deniers explain
that in not one war-crimes trial since the end of World War II
has a perpetrator of any nationality denied that these events
occurred? They may have said, "I was forced to kill," but not one
asserted that the killing did not happen. Finally, why has Germany shouldered the enormous moral and financial responsibility for the crimes committed in the Holocaust, if it did not
happen?[4] Of course, according to the deniers, the answer to
this question is quite simple: German officials were forced into
a false admission of guilt by "the Jews," who threatened to pre-

vent Germany's reentry into the family of nations. But this, too, makes little sense. German leaders had to know that admitting to a genocide of such proportions would impose upon the nation a horrific legacy that would become an integral part of its national identity. Why would a country take on such a historical burden if it were innocent? Moreover, seventy years after the end of the war, with Germany now a global political and economic leader, it could have proclaimed that "it's not true; the Jews made us say this back in 1945." Instead, the German government created a massive memorial in Berlin to the murdered Jews.

There is yet another bit of illogic on which deniers depend. They demand to be shown the one specific piece of evidence that would prove to them there was a Holocaust: Hitler's written order authorizing the murder of all of Europe's Jews. In all likelihood, Hitler realized the folly of affixing his signature to such an order, which, had it become public, many might not have accepted. More important, historians are not troubled by the absence of such a document. They never rest their conclusions on one document, particularly in this instance, when the Third Reich left a vast cache of evidence attesting to a government-directed program whose goal was the annihilation of the Jewish people. Deniers, of course, will insist that "the Jews" have forged these documents. But if that were the case, why didn't the Jews also forge the all-important document from Hitler himself?

The list of illogical arguments goes on. Deniers contend that had the Third Reich, a regime they describe as the epitome of efficiency and power, wished to murder all the Jews, it would have ensured that no witnesses remained alive to testify about the death camps. Therefore, the fact that there were survivors alive at the war's end constitutes proof that there was no genocide and that the survivors' testimonies are lies. One need not be familiar with any documentary evidence to recognize the fallacious nature of this argument. The Third Reich was also intent on winning the war, which it did not do. Therefore, the assumption that the Third Reich succeeded at all it set out to do is false. Anything based on that premise is equally false.

Struck by the complete lack of logic in any of their claims, I initially dismissed the Holocaust deniers and their theories out of hand. Then two respected historians suggested that I take a closer, more systematic look. They wondered how deniers—given the implausibility of their arguments—had been able to attract any adherents at all. Though still skeptical, I took up their challenge and thought this would be, at most, a two-year project before I moved on to other matters. I was wrong.

It soon became apparent to me that deniers were a new type of neo-Nazi. Unlike previous generations of neo-Nazis—people who celebrated Hitler's birthday, sported SS-like uniforms, and hung swastikas at meetings where they would give the *Sieg Heil* salute—this group eschewed all that.[5] They were wolves in sheep's clothing. They didn't bother with the physical trappings of Nazism—salutes, songs, and banners—but proclaimed themselves "revisionists"—serious scholars who simply wished to revise "mistakes" in the historical record, to which end they established an impressive-sounding organization—the Institute for Historical Review—and created a benign-sounding publication—the *Journal for Historical Review*.[6] Nothing in these names suggested the revisionists' real agenda. They held conferences that, at first blush, seemed to be the most mundane academic confabs. But a close inspection of their publications and conference programs revealed the same extremism, adulation of the Third Reich, antisemitism, and racism as the swastika-waving neo-Nazis. This was extremism posing as rational discourse.

Abigail, in your letter you compliment me for consistently confronting deniers. While I have spent time exposing their lies and inconsistencies, I have not entered into debate with them. They will tell you that I am afraid to. The truth is that they are liars, and one cannot debate a liar. It is akin to trying to nail a blob of jelly to the wall. Generally speaking, people differentiate between facts and opinions—you can have your own opinions, but not your own facts. But in the case of deniers, there are facts, opinions, and *lies*. In 2000, when I was on trial in London for libel, having been sued by David Irving—then one of the world's leading Holocaust deniers—for having called him a denier, my defense team and I tracked all of his "proofs" back to their sources and found that embedded in the claims he made about the Holocaust were falsifications, inventions, distortions, changes of dates, or some other form of untruth. Once these lies were exposed, his arguments collapsed.

Among the leading purveyors of Holocaust denial arguments are far-right, neo-Nazi, and white power groups. Their adulation of Nazi ideology, "Aryan" superiority, and, above all, Adolf Hitler make them perfect candidates for denial. They are masters of inconsistency. They argue that murdering the Jews would have been entirely justified but that it never happened. I suppose you could call this the "no, but" argument: "No, it didn't happen. But it should have."

It should be obvious that Holocaust denial is, quite plainly, a form of antisemitism. It's not about history. It's about attacking, discrediting, and demonizing Jews. The claims of the deniers— that the Jews planted evidence, got German prisoners of war to admit to crimes they did not commit, and forced Germany to shoulder a tremendous financial and moral burden when the war ended—are predicated on the notion of the mythical power of the Jews, which, they firmly believe, was extensive enough to realize this vast conspiracy. Unconcerned about how their actions would affect millions of people and with only their own political and financial benefit in mind, the Jews created the myth of the Holocaust in order to obtain a state of their own and extract vast amounts of money from Germany. Then, according to this so-called "theory," they proceeded to displace another people from their land in order to gain sovereignty for themselves. These assertions rely on classic antisemitic tropes, the same ones found throughout two thousand years of antisemitic accusations. Just as the Jews persuaded the Roman Empire, then the rulers of Palestine and much of the rest of the world, to do their bidding and crucify Jesus, so, too, they persuaded the Allies to create evidence of a genocide for their own financial and political gain.

Now back to your question: Should we be worried about these people? To be honest, while I don't think they are an imminent threat, I do believe that there is room for concern. Deniers have learned to use social media to their advantage. On Holocaust Remembrance Day in 2017, a survivor was interviewed on a BBC radio program. The producers were "shocked" by the "staggering" number of "brazen" Holocaust denial and antisemitic phone calls and social media posts they received. Though they had previously broadcast programs on the Holocaust and had received some antisemitic and denial comments, this response, one producer told me, was "unprecedented . . . unlike anything we have seen before." They were so deeply unsettled that they invited me to appear on a subsequent program that addressed Holocaust denial.[7] But denial is not something engaged in only by the Far Right. In many segments of the Muslim community, including among European Muslims, there is also an inclination to deny this historical reality. There are schools in Europe where teachers find it difficult to teach about the Holocaust because the students insist that it never happened, and the material the teachers present is dismissed by the students as false.[8] As has become evident in recent years, there are those on the far left who also engage in denial. During a BBC interview in September 2017 on leftist antisemitism within Britain's Labour Party, Ken Loach was asked to comment on a session at the party's annual conference where a participant called for a "yes or no" discussion of the Holocaust. Loach's rather ambiguous response: "I think history is for us all to discuss, wouldn't you?"[9]

Ultimately, it's hard to gauge whether deniers have increased in number or are just good at using social media to make themselves seem more numerous than they actually are. While either alternative is disturbing, the deniers clearly feel more emboldened than ever before.

Deniers are not the equivalents of flat-earth theorists, nor are they just plain loonies. Theirs is not a cognitive error that can be rectified by showing them documentation or evidence. They are, pure and simple, antisemites, and their agenda is to reinforce and spread the very antisemitism that produced the Holocaust. They can't be completely discounted.

Yours,
DEL

INVERTING VICTIMS AND PERPETRATORS

Dear Professor Lipstadt:

Thanks for that explanation. While I haven't run into the kind of Holocaust denial you initially wrote about or faced in court, I have encountered something else that gives me pause. It doesn't fit into any of the categories of denial that you just described. These people do not deny that the Holocaust happened; instead, they use it to create a moral equivalency with other events. Is this just legitimate political expression? Does using the Holocaust in this way diminish its significance? Or does it depend upon *what* particular event it is being compared to?

Let me give you a few examples. I often hear Israelis described as the equivalent of Nazis. I have seen protestors on the streets of London and New York, and in other cities in Europe and North America, carrying placards with the image of Israeli leaders in Nazi dress. Sometimes the signs read "Israelis = Nazis." At a rally in Berlin in July 2014, during one of Israel's wars with Hamas in Gaza, people chanted, "Jews to the gas." At a meeting of the United Nations Security Council in May 2016, the Venezuelan ambassador asked, "What does Israel plan to do with the Palestinians? Will they disappear? Does Israel seek probably to wage a final solution? The sort of solution that was perpetrated against the Jews?"

This linkage between Israel and the Nazis leaves me deeply

disturbed. Quite frankly, it sounds to me like some form of Holocaust denial or, more to the point, like a particularly virulent form of antisemitism. Am I wrong?

Yours,
Abigail

Dear Abigail and Joe:

Abigail, you're not wrong. What you are describing is what many scholars call "genocide inversion," turning the victims of genocide into perpetrators. In most cases, it is Israelis, and not Jews in general, who are equated with Nazis. This tactic can be traced to the Soviet Union, which, within a week of the conclusion of the Six-Day War, was calling then Israeli defense minister Moshe Dayan a "pupil of Hitler and a darling of the Nazis all over the world."[1] This Holocaust inversion is a form of soft-core Holocaust denial, in which the event to which it is being compared shares none of the characteristics of the Holocaust. It often presents itself, as you noted, in the "yes, but" context. "Yes, what happened to the Jews was awful. But look at what the Israelis (i.e., Jews) are doing today to the Palestinians." Soft-core deniers speak of a "genocide of the Palestinians" or of the "Nazi-like tactics of the Israeli Army." You mentioned the Venezuelan ambassador's comments at the United Nations. In fact, after some criticism, he subsequently apologized "*if* he had offended Jewish people (emphasis added)."[2] (It is hard to imagine how he could possibly think that his remarks might *not* offend Jews, since they seemed designed to do precisely that.)

In 2013, a British member of Parliament used the opportunity of Holocaust Remembrance Day to link Israel with the Nazis. After signing the House of Parliament's Book of Remembrance he said: "Having visited Auschwitz twice . . . I am saddened that the Jews, who suffered unbelievable levels of persecution during the Holocaust, could within a few years of liberation from the death camps be inflicting atrocities on Palestinians in the new State of Israel and continue to do so on a daily basis in the West Bank and Gaza." When he was accused of Holocaust inversion and antisemitism, he defended himself by saying that he was only attacking those Jews who did these things. "So, if you're a Jew and you did not do it, then I'm not accusing you. I'm saying that those Jews who did that and continue to do it have not learned those lessons."[3] He was still, of course, equating what the Nazis did with what the Israelis were doing. As I've stressed earlier, one can *totally* disagree with Israel's policies vis-à-vis the Palestinians, as many Israelis do, but to equate this with a genocide is beyond the pale.

A similar attack was mounted by Oxford professor Tom Paulin in an interview with *Al-Ahram,* the Egyptian newspaper. He described Jewish settlers in the West Bank as "Nazis and racists," recommended that they be "shot," and then stated that "I feel nothing but hatred for them." Even though his comments were made on the same day that a suicide bomber in Jerusalem killed six people and injured sixty, he not only stood by his remarks but also added words of empathy for Palestinian suicide bombers. His only critique of the bombers was of the efficaciousness of their actions. "I can understand how suicide bombers feel," he said. "I think, though, it is better to resort to conventional guerrilla warfare. I think attacks on civilians in fact boost morale."[4] Some of his colleagues dismissed his remarks as "'Tom being Tom'—a loose cannon whose thinking is so erratic it is not worth dignifying with a response."[5] I wonder if they would have been so understanding had he made these comments about someone who opened fire on an abortion clinic because he sincerely believed that the people inside were murdering babies.

Many of the people who make these accusations contend that their remarks are not antisemitic because they concern Israel specifically and not Jews in general. But their accusations against Israelis hearken back to classic medieval antisemitic accusations—murdering non-Jews to achieve world domination. Some observers posit that these comparisons are used precisely because by upsetting people—Jews in particular—they draw immediate attention. In other words, they constitute a kind of "Jew-baiting."[6]

This desire to garner attention may have been what motivated Rutgers University professor Jasbir Puar, who, in a talk at Vassar College, accused Israel of creating a state that "debilitate[s] Palestinian bodies and environments as a form of bio-political control," collected "body parts" for medical "experimentation," and "dismantled and dismembered [Palestinian] bodies" for "gendering," "ungendering," and "epigenetic deterioration." She went on to assert that because of its desire to engage in biological "hacking," Israel chose not to kill Palestinians but "maim[ed]" them so that they could be used for medical experimentation. According to Puar, Israel controlled the Palestinians' "infrastructure" and "modulate[d] calories . . . to provide a bare minimum for survival," resulting in their "stunting."[7] Puar claimed that Israel was subjecting Palestinians to medical "experimentation" by providing them with "the bare minimum for survival" and was using dead Palestinians to "mine for organs for scientific research." Anyone with the most basic knowledge of the Nazi atrocities against the Jews will immediately recognize in her evidence-free accusations deliberate echoes of the Nazi treatment of Jews in ghettos, slave-labor camps, and concentration camps. Puar's point was immediately understood. When she was specifically asked if the Israeli treatment of the Palestinians was the equivalent of genocide, she agreed that it was. Then she added that she objected to the use of the term "genocide" because it was too "tethered to the Holocaust."[8]

Puar's presentation created a firestorm of controversy. Vassar's president issued a rather tepid response. Although she described the talk as "objectionable," she gave it credibility by announcing that Vassar would organize a series of lectures that provided "*other* viewpoints" on Israel—as if this were a legitimate viewpoint instead of a collection of antisemitic falsehoods. In a *Wall Street Journal* editorial, former president of the University of California Mark Yudof and professor emeritus of history at Michigan State University Kenneth Waltzer "respectfully call[ed]" on Vassar's president to speak out "in the face of such venom" and urged faculty and administrators at the college to "confront this wave of antisemitism with the primary tools at their disposal: free speech and rigorous academic inquiry."[9]

Their critique was subjected to intense criticism from Puar's supporters. They charged that she was being "silenced" and subjected to a right-wing smear campaign. Faculty linked with the United States Campaign for the Academic and Cultural Boycott of Israel (USACBI) described the Yudof and Waltzer article as part of a "campaign of intimidation and harassment" against Professor Puar. Despite the fact that their article made no mention of political orientation, either left or right, Jason

Stanley, a professor of philosophy at Yale, claimed that they had urged Vassar's leadership to condemn "leftist ideology." Stanley accused Yudof and Waltzer of promulgating an "anti-free-speech message" when they maintained that "hatred of Israel and Jews should not implicitly be characterized as merely another perspective to be debated."[10] What he appears to be saying is that Jew-hatred is a legitimate subject for debate because, in the interests of free speech, arguments can be made both for and against it.

Abigail, you knew antisemitism when you saw it and, sadly, you were absolutely correct.

Yours,
DEL

BRANDING VICTIMS AS COLLABORATORS

Dear Professor Lipstadt:

Thanks for that explanation. I hope you don't mind a follow-up question. During a visit I made to England last year, the media was awash with stories about Ken Livingstone, the former mayor of London, who had recently claimed:

> During the 1930s, Hitler collaborated with the Zionists and supported them because he believed that a possible solution to his problem—the Jews—was that they should all move to Palestine. Then in the 1940s that changed, and he decided on genocide.[1]

Unlike white supremacists who might defend Hitler, Livingstone condemned him as "a monster from start to finish." But then he made it sound as if the Zionists were in cahoots with him. "It's simply the historical fact. His policy was originally to send all of Germany's Jews to Israel, and there were private meetings between the Zionist movement and Hitler's government which were kept confidential; they only became apparent after the war."[2]

Livingstone's remarks were the lead story on almost every news broadcast in England that day. I was left a bit baffled by it all. Is he flat-out lying? Is there any truth to this?

Yours,
Abigail

Dear Abigail and Joe:

In my opinion, Ken Livingstone can be described as a soft-core denier or soft-core denier-enabler—someone who provides the ammunition for the deniers. What Livingstone did was take a limited agreement between an organization of German Zionists and the Third Reich and misrepresent it to fit his own political agenda. Here are the facts: In August 1933, the Zionist Federation of Germany and the Economics Ministry of the German government reached an agreement—which became known as the Transfer Agreement—that allowed German Jews who wanted to emigrate to Palestine to turn some of their assets into funds that they would use to buy goods in Germany, which they could then export to their new home in Mandatory Palestine. These funds would have otherwise been frozen and confiscated by the Nazis. The agreement took three months to negotiate, but it was *not* a secret deal that "only became apparent after the war." Because there was at the time an unofficial international boycott of German-made goods, Jews living outside Germany condemned it, as did by both the United States leadership of the World Zionist Congress and the Revisionist Zionist movement. There were also Nazis who opposed it. It was in place from 1933 until the German invasion of Poland in 1939.

Livingstone also falsely claimed that "the SS set up training camps so that German Jews who were going to go there [i.e., Palestine] could be trained to cope with a very different sort of country when they got there." In fact, these camps to prepare German Jews for life in Palestine were actually set up by German Zionists before the Nazis came to power. Livingstone was sort of right on one point regarding Nazi involvement in the Zionist camps: When the Nazis came to power in 1933, the SS prohibited any singing and dancing at the camps.

The best refutation to Livingstone's claims that Hitler thought his "Jewish problem" would be solved if all Jews moved to Palestine comes from Hitler himself, in this excerpt from *Mein Kampf,* which was published in 1925, fifteen years before, according to Livingstone, Hitler "went mad" in 1940 and decided to annihilate the world's Jews.

> For while the Zionists try to make the rest of the world believe that the national consciousness of the Jew finds its satisfaction in the creation of a Palestinian state, the Jews again slyly dupe the dumb Goyim. It doesn't even enter their heads to build up a Jewish state in Palestine for the purpose of living there; all they want is a central organization for their international world swindle, endowed with its own sovereign rights and removed from the intervention of other states: a haven for convicted scoundrels and a university for budding crooks.[3]

Hitler's plans for the Jews of Palestine became part of the historical record during his meeting with the Grand Mufti of Jerusalem, Haj Amin al-Husseini, on November 28, 1941, in Berlin, during which he reassured the Mufti of his "active opposition to the Jewish national home in Palestine. . . . Germany was resolved, step by step, to ask one European nation after the other to solve its Jewish problem and at the proper time to direct a similar appeal to non-European nations as well." And when the German army eventually reached the Middle East from Caucasia, "Germany's objective would then be solely the destruction of the Jewish element residing in the Arab sphere under the protection of British power."[4]

Critics such as Livingstone who claim there was a collaboration between Nazis and Zionists do so for one repugnant reason only: to imply that the Jews themselves were complicit in the Nazis' horrendous crimes. Livingstone's argument is rooted in an immoral equivalency that treats Nazis and Zionists as ideological soulmates.[5]

While not an exterminationist antisemite, Livingstone is an antisemitic enabler who provokes in others contempt for Jews.[6] When criticized for antisemitic remarks, he reflexively casts himself as the victim of pro-Israel hacks. "There's been a very well-orchestrated campaign by the Israel lobby to smear anybody who criticizes Israeli policy as antisemitic. I had to put up with thirty-five years of this."[7] He relies on this rhetorical device so frequently that sociologist David Hirsh has branded it the Livingstone Formulation: "Accuse me of antisemitism and I will accuse you of smearing me in the name of Israel."[8] This Holocaust inversion of victims with perpetrators and "Holocaust-Zionist collaboration" plays politics with the Holocaust by accusing Jews of playing politics with the Holocaust. "It engages in victim competition by accusing Jews of engaging in victim competition. It obscures the actual relationship between Israel and the Holocaust by proposing all sorts of tangential, exaggerated and invented relationships between Israel and the Holocaust."[9]

Abigail, what you encountered on your trip to England is one of the more sophisticated and slippery forms of Holocaust denial. To be perfectly honest, I fear this type of denial far more than the kind I confronted in court when defending myself against David Irving.

Yours,
DEL

DE-JUDAIZING THE HOLOCAUST

Dear Professor Lipstadt:

I've noticed that in recent times some eastern European governments (i.e., former Soviet bloc countries) have been attempting to refashion their World War II history. But this seems to be more about politics than history. Is this considered denial? It also appears to come with some latent antisemitism. Is this accurate, or am I beginning to see Jew-hatred in too many places?

Thanks,
Abigail

Dear Deborah:

I've also been following the events in eastern Europe with some trepidation. I worry not just about the rewriting of history but also about the attack on democracy that seems to come with it. And I've watched with concern the concurrent proliferation of antisemitic sentiment. Is this simply a coincidence or are we, once again, looking at an interlocking directorate of sorts: trampling on historical accuracy, feeding the antisemitic beast, and attacking democracy and its institutions?

Yours,
Joe

Dear Abigail and Joe:

You are both quite right. In eastern Europe today we are witnessing soft-core denial on a national level. What is taking place
in a number of former Soviet bloc countries—particularly those
governed by parties with strong nationalist orientations—is
serious. These countries are currently engaged in blatant and
conscious efforts to rewrite their histories. They may not be
motivated by antisemitism, but that is one of the end products
of what they are doing.

Strongly anti-Communist, these governments are often the
ideological and political heirs of the nationalist groups that collaborated with the Nazis during the war against the hated Soviet
Communists. Thirty years after the collapse of the Soviet Union,
their hatred of it and of communism persists. And who was
behind the Communists? The Jews, of course. Some of these
countries have even gone so far as to designate soldiers who collaborated with the Nazis and, in some instances, participated in
the murder of Jews, as national heroes. At the same time, these
governments have labeled as traitors those who fought with
the Soviet-backed anti-Nazi partisan groups, which included
many Jews. In Lithuania in the early 1990s, one of the first acts
of the post-Communist government was the exoneration of
Lithuanian nationalists who participated in the Holocaust. In
2004, after Lithuania had already qualified for membership in
the EU and NATO, the government began to prosecute Jewish partisans as pro-Soviet collaborators who "paved the way
for postwar Soviet 'genocide.'"[1] An academic paper posted on
the website of the Lithuanian governmental body responsible
for investigating war crimes questioned whether the Holocaust
even constituted genocide. This paper argued that "although an
impressive percentage of the Jews were killed by the Nazis, their

ethnic group survived" and subsequently thrived. In contrast, the paper pointed out that the Lithuanian intelligentsia that was exterminated under Stalin has never been replaced.[2]

In Poland, the newly elected far-right nationalist Law and Justice party (PiS) has attempted to rewrite Poland's World War II historical record. Any person or institution that casts aspersions on Poland's wartime record of battling the Nazis is attacked. Museum curators who have tried to present an accurate portrait of Poland's behavior during the war have been fired.[3] Exhibits at various government-sponsored museums have been reconfigured to stress Polish battlefield heroics and erase any evidence of complicity with the Germans.[4] The situation escalated in the winter of 2018 when, after extended deliberation, both houses of the Polish parliament adopted legislation that made it a crime to publicly claim that the Polish nation bears any responsibility for crimes committed by the Third Reich during the Holocaust. It was signed into law by the president of Poland in February 2018. Norman Davies, a professor and historian specializing in Polish history, described the law's effort to paint Poles purely as victims as "a part of the present government's attempt to rewrite history. It's one of the pillars of every authoritarian or totalitarian regime, that they want to reorder the past to their own fantasies."[5] There were certainly Poles who helped Jews during the war. (More than sixty-seven hundred of them have been recognized as Righteous Among the Nations by the Yad Vashem museum in Jerusalem.) But there were also Poles—probably many more— who betrayed Jews. And there were Poles who murdered Jews on their own, without any instigation by the Germans.[6]

Even though, after an international outcry, the Poles changed the punishment from criminal to civil punishment, this law does more than just fly in the face of historical accuracy and scholarly freedom. It constitutes an attempt to obscure Poland's long history of antisemitism, one that persisted even after World War II. A recently declassified 1946 State Department report assessed the situation of surviving Jews in postwar Poland. It described Jews "fleeing" Poland in "panic" because of the attacks on them, some of which were facilitated by Polish police. The report took particular note of the fact that Jews—whom the Germans had tried to annihilate—would now rather live in Germany than in Poland. Polish Jews were experiencing, the report contended, the continuation of prewar Polish nationalist antisemitism.[7]

With the 2018 law, PiS intended to satisfy its rural and nationalist electoral base and to demonstrate to them "that Poland has risen from its knees and won't be humiliated."[8] While this may have been the intent, the law did something else as well: It helped dredge up antisemitic sentiment. Suddenly, antisemitism seemed to be everywhere: throughout social media, on television, and in the press that supported the government. The PiS-controlled media contended that outside forces—"Jews in particular—want to prevent Poland from telling the truth about its own history."[9]

Responding to strong international criticism, Polish prime minister Mateusz Morawiecki justified the law by arguing that "there were Polish perpetrators, as there were Jewish perpetrators, as there were Ukrainian; not only German perpetrators." While there were Jews who served on the ghetto police forces or as members of the *Judenräte*, the ghetto councils established by the Germans, their actions could in no way be equated with the genocidal activities of the Nazis and their collaborators— which included many Poles. Jews who agreed to serve as ghetto police or in leadership positions in the ghettos generally did so to save themselves and their families from certain death. Poles who collaborated with the Nazis did so, by and large, for either antisemitic or financial reasons.[10]

Regrettably, the Trump administration missed an opportunity to confront the Polish government about this new law. When President Trump visited Warsaw in July 2017, the law was under discussion but had not yet been enacted into law. He gave a vigorously nationalistic speech at Warsaw's war memorial, calling for protection of borders and urging Poles to join Americans in fighting forces, "whether they come from inside or out," that threaten the shared "values ... of culture, faith and tradition."[11] Many in Poland saw this as a clear expression of support for PiS's nationalistic tendencies. The Polish government was delighted with Trump's speech, and he neither publicly nor privately said anything about the then pending legislation. Then he became the first American president to visit Poland since the fall of the Soviet Union in 1989 and not make a stop at the Warsaw Ghetto Memorial, the site of the first armed uprising against the Germans anywhere in Europe during World War II. Though the Republican Jewish Coalition tried to blame this on time constraints, Poland's Jewish community was not mollified and expressed its "deep regret" at this "break with that laudable tradition."

In Hungary there has been a consistent effort by the government of Prime Minister Viktor Orbán to diminish, if not deny, the role of Hungarians in the murder of the Jews during the war. As Germany's wartime ally, the Hungarian government persecuted its Jews severely but resisted German attempts to deport them. In March 1944, upon discovering that the Hungarian government was considering armistice negotiations with Britain and the United States, the German army invaded Hungary and established a puppet government. Most Hungarian government officials remained in place and enthusiastically carried out German orders. That spelled the end for Hungarian Jews. Adolf Eichmann, who was in charge of deporting Hungary's Jews to death camps, had only a few hundred SS officers under his command, hardly enough to destroy the substantial Hungarian Jewish community. But he was energetically assisted by Hungarian police, militia, railway officials, and private citizens. With their help, over the course of approximately seven weeks, Eichmann organized the deportation of more than half a million Hungarian Jews to Auschwitz-Birkenau, where more than four hundred thousand were murdered.

In an effort to strengthen Hungarian nationalism and erase an inconvenient history of collaboration and complicity, Orbán depicts Hungary as a victim, not a perpetrator, of war crimes during World War II.[12] Any attempt to challenge this view and insist that Hungary own up to its past crimes is interpreted by the government and its supporters as an attempt to blacken the country's good name and reputation.

Western Europe is not immune to this type of historical reconfiguration. On April 9, 2017, Marine Le Pen, president of the National Front (a far-right political party in France) and a member of France's National Assembly, contended that France bore no responsibility for the notorious Vél d'Hiv roundup of more than thirteen thousand Jews (including approximately four thousand children) in July 1942. Jews were held at a stadium near the Eiffel Tower in Paris for five days in searing heat and horrific conditions—little food, water, or facilities—until they were deported to death camps and murdered.[13] This roundup was planned by the Gestapo and members of France's collaborationist government, conducted by French police, and supervised by French officials. But for decades after the war the French government steadfastly denied any complicity in the affair. That changed in July 1995 when then president Jacques Chirac unequivocally declared, "France, the homeland of the Enlightenment and of the rights of man, a land of welcome and asylum—France, on that day, committed the irreparable. Breaking its word, it handed those who were under its protection over to their executioners." Every subsequent French president and leading politician has reaffirmed that statement. But in 2017 Le Pen attacked France's willingness to own up to its blemished historical record. She condemned the teaching of the July 1942 roundup in French schools. "I want them to be proud to be French again," she stated. And in July 2017, Jean-Luc Melenchon, a left-wing member of the National Assembly, echoed Le Pen's comments, declaring it "totally unacceptable" to say that "France, as a people, as a nation, is responsible for this crime [of the deportation of the Jews]."[14]

But this kind of historical obfuscation does not come only from those at the more extreme ends of the political spectrum. *Le Livre des Commemorations Nationales* (Book of National Commemorations) is an annual publication by the French government to recall notable events and people and, in the words of the French minister of culture, to bring French citizens "great pleasure and beautiful emotions." In the 2018 edition, notice was made of the 150th anniversary of the birth of Charles Maurras. Maurras, an author, politician, poet, and critic, was also the editor of the antisemitic and antidemocratic newspaper *L'Action Française,* and wrote many vitriolic articles about Jews. A supporter of Vichy during World War II, he described French collaboration with the Nazis as a "divine surprise." After the war, he was sentenced to life imprisonment for his collaboration with the Nazis and for "betraying French resistance workers to the Nazis."[15] As a result of the public outcry against Maurras's inclusion in the Book of National Commemorations, all copies were recalled and the book was reprinted without his entry. Many wondered how a man whose principal claim to fame was his opposition to the French Revolution, his antisemitism, and his pro-Nazism had merited inclusion in the first place.

We will in the future continue to witness instances of soft-core denial. On some level, this is much harder to fight than the hard-core deniers, but fight it we must. You're right, Joe, about the connections among the rewriting of history, attacks on democracy, and expressions of antisemitism. As I've said before, these things never happen in isolation. And what starts with attacks on Jews rarely ends there.

Yours,
DEL

· VI ·

The Campus and Beyond

TOXIFYING ISRAEL

Dear Professor Lipstadt:

I didn't plan on writing to you so soon after our exchange about Holocaust denial. But something disturbing happened to me recently that seems to exemplify much of what you have been saying, and now it's up close and personal. I don't want to sound melodramatic, but I am a bit shaken by what I experienced.

I was visiting a friend at a large public university. The campus was astir. The previous night a lecture on Israel had been canceled or, more properly put, shut down. The Israeli lecturer—a professor at Hebrew University—never got to speak. He was shouted down by students from various groups, including Students for Justice in Palestine. These students could not have disagreed with what he said because he never got to say anything. He was Israeli, and that was reason enough to deny him the right to speak. The next night my friend and I went to what we anticipated would be a pleasant party. Most of the people there were social activists involved in various progressive causes—including environmental and women's issues—that I'm passionate about, too. I was hanging out with a small group consisting of both Jews and non-Jews, students whom I knew from previous visits to this campus. I was probably the most strongly identifying Jew in this rather congenial group, where the conversation flowed freely.

Someone brought up the incident with the Israeli lecturer,

and I responded by criticizing the protesters' behavior and their failure to adhere to the fundamental notion of civil discourse. I suppose that in a democracy people have a "right" to shout at a speaker, but the university, I argued, should be a venue for the free exchange of ideas. These protesters, I contended, were not interested in that exchange. The other students seemed taken aback that I was in favor of the Israeli speaking on campus. Not only were they highly critical of Israel's treatment of Palestinians, which was certainly their right, but they also began to say some disturbing things, such as "Israel is an illegitimate, non-democratic country. A state should not be founded on religious identity. It's an anachronism. It's racist." Then something even more disturbing happened. The loudest person among them, a guy I hardly know, began to move from trashing Israel's policies to associating *me* with them. "You Jews don't belong there, running everything. Zionism is what's at the heart of the problem. You Zionists have got to recognize that Israel is a colonizing state." Most painful was when he said, "If you can't accept the truth about Israel and Zionism, you're not a progressive."

In his eyes, I, as a Jew, was directly responsible for whatever Israel did. He used the terms "Israelis," "Jews," and "Zionists" interchangeably. Moreover, he seemed to have only the foggiest notion of what Zionism was and of the history of the Jews in the region. He had no trouble concluding that because Israel was a Jewish state, it was ipso facto racist and colonial. I was so taken aback by what he was saying, I was unable to pull my thoughts together to reply to him. Then things got worse. A few other students chimed in with statements like, "Of course we'll never have a real conversation about Israel in this country because you-all have such control of the media, Congress, and American foreign policy. The Jewish lobby decides what it wants and gets it." They went on like that for a while, mentioning AIPAC and wealthy pro-Israel American Jews. These were not people situated at the far left of the political spectrum, from whom I might have expected this. They were just ordinary college kids who seemed to be echoing what they had heard elsewhere, which made what they were saying even more frightening. What should I have done?

Yours,
Abigail

Dear Abigail and Joe:

It seems that in the space of a few days, Abigail, you have actually lived much of what we have been writing about in these letters. I wish there was something I could say that would ease your discomfort, but you have encountered some attitudes that are very real and very disturbing. Sadly, the rhetoric that you encountered is not just a university-based phenomenon.

That verbal assault on the Israeli speaker is not unique. In 2016, protesters at London's King's College disrupted a talk by Ami Ayalon, the former head of Shin Bet, Israel's version of our FBI. Students from a pro-Palestinian group chanted, threw chairs, smashed windows, and repeatedly set off the fire alarm in the room where Ayalon was speaking about the two-state solution to the Israel/Palestine situation, which is something he strongly supports. In 2015, representatives from the Palestinian Solidarity Committee of University of Texas–Austin entered an event sponsored by the university's Institute for Israel Studies. They refused to sit, listen, or leave and stood there chanting "Long live intifada."[1] That same year Moshe Halbertal, a distinguished Israeli law professor and world-renowned philosopher, was scheduled to speak at the University of Minnesota on the moral challenge an army faces when it is engaged in fighting "asymmetric wars," which are defined as conflicts between professional armies and resistance or insurgent movements. Halbertal is known for his position that the army must always "err on the side of protecting" civilian insurgents, even if this threatens its soldiers' well-being. As his lecture began, protesters stood up and began to shout him down. When the police finally ejected them from the room, they situated themselves outside the building in a place where their chanting could be heard, making it difficult for those in the hall to listen to the lecture.[2]

These tactics are not new. They have been used against Israeli speakers in the past and are part of the broader effort known as the Boycott, Divestment, and Sanctions movement, or BDS. Founded in 2005 by Palestinian organizations, it advocates for the following: (1) boycotting Israeli-made products and services, as well as public events in which Israelis participate; (2) the divestment by governments and private institutions of investments in Israeli companies; and (3) the establishment of international sanctions against Israel. Its goal is to punish Israel for what it terms Israel's "apartheid" policies toward Israeli and Palestinian Arabs. But Arab-sponsored boycotts against Israel go back decades, to the pre-state Jewish community in Palestine, international supporters of the Zionist movement, and Jews in general. In 1945, before the United Nations vote on the partition of Palestine, before the establishment of the Jewish state, the Arab League prohibited its members from doing any business with "Zionists/Jews" and with companies that did business with Zionists. Eventually they expanded the boycott to encompass "anything Jewish." In the 1950s the Saudi Arabian government established a boycott of all businesses throughout the world that were owned by Jews, did business with Jews, or employed Jews.[3] After the establishment of the State of Israel in 1948, the Arab League prevented anyone whose passport bore an Israeli stamp from entering most Arab and Muslim-majority nations. When I was a student at Hebrew University in 1967, I had to have a "clean" American passport—one without any Israeli visa stamps—in order to visit Lebanon, Syria, and Jordan. When I hesitatingly explained to the clerk at the American embassy in Athens what I needed, he replied, rather matter-of-factly, "Oh, we get that request all the time."

The boycott in the academic world today against Israelis has its roots, in some measure, in the 2001 United Nations–sponsored Durban World Conference Against Racism, Racial Discrimination, Xenophobia, and Related Intolerance. There were actually two gatherings in Durban—the official United Nations conference and one sponsored by a group of about three thousand nongovernmental organizations (NGOs). The discussion about Israel at both meetings was vituperative and overshadowed all other issues on the meetings' agendas. The final declaration adopted by the NGO forum laid the groundwork for the BDS movement by equating Zionism with racism and calling for a boycott of Israel.

One of the stated goals of the BDS movement is establishing a right of return for Palestinians throughout the world, which in practical terms would result in Jews being in the minority in Israel, and its end as a Jewish state.[4] The statements that form the foundation of the BDS movement are, as some critics have noted, "the antithesis of a call for peace and reconciliation between two people in a compromise situation."[5] One of the founders of the BDS movement, Omar Barghouti, has explicitly stated, "We definitely oppose a Jewish state in any part of Palestine."[6] He told the *Electronic Intifada,* "I am completely and categorically against bi-nationalism because it assumes that there are two nations with equal moral claims to the land."[7] Ignoring these statements and his call for the "right of return to 1948 lands," he nonetheless insists that BDS has "consistently avoided taking any position regarding the one-state/two-state debate."[8] But some BDS organizers do call for the creation of "one secular and democratic state for all those living in historic Palestine."[9]

BDS-inspired academic and cultural boycotts can be inconsistent and capricious. Some BDS advocates argue that only Israeli academic institutions should be boycotted and not individual Israeli scholars.[10] If Israeli academics attend a conference without institutional support and their research has been done independent of their institution, they are welcome. But this is a false distinction, designed to make BDS appear reasonable and to give the impression that it is not a blacklist. Scholars generally attend academic conferences with their institution's financial support. Even if they were to pay their own expenses, their research has been conducted as part of their university work. Restrictions against scholars who have been supported by Israeli institutions would a priori eliminate all scientists who conduct laboratory research in Israel. It would also eliminate those who use university libraries or university-issued computers. And what about Israeli Muslim, Christian, or Druze scholars who teach at Israeli institutions? Are they included in the boycott? Or Israelis who teach at American institutions with branches in Israel, such as New York University?

In 2006, some BDS organizers proposed that only those Israeli academics who support their government's "apartheid" policies be boycotted. Unsurprisingly, no official protocol for creating this loyalty test was ever established. But that didn't stop individual academics from implementing this policy on their own. At the 2012 South African Sociological Association convention, an Israeli who was about to participate in a panel discussion was asked by a professor from a South African university to "denounce Israeli apartheid" as a precondition of his participation. When the Israeli declined to do so, an association board member invited the other panelists and the audience to leave the room and reassemble at a different venue, so that the Israeli was free to exercise his freedom of speech and present his paper—to an empty room.[11]

In 2015 the American Jewish pop star Matisyahu was disinvited from appearing at Rototom Sunsplash, an annual international reggae music festival held in Spain that was, ironically, devoted to "the promotion of peace, equality, human rights and social justice."[12] He was told by festival organizers that the pressure to disinvite him came from BDS members, and that if he made a public statement in support of Palestinian statehood and against Israeli "war crimes," he would be able to perform.[13] When he refused to do so, his performance was canceled and Rototom Sunsplash issued the following statement:

> Rototom Sunsplash, after having repeatedly sought dialogue in the face of the artist's unavailability to give a clear statement against war and on the right of the Palestinian people to their own state, has decided to cancel [his] concert.

Even though Rototom Sunsplash's other goals included examining the "rise in Islamophobia in Western countries, as well as the situation of the prisoners in Guantánamo," no European performers were required to denounce expressions of Islamophobia in their countries, and American performers were not required to share their views on the United States policy toward prisoners in Guantánamo. After an international outcry at the festival's assertion that an American Jewish musician was answerable for Israeli government policy, the invitation was reinstated. Rototom Sunsplash apologized for the disinvitation and stated that it "rejects antisemitism and any form of discrimination towards the Jewish community."[14]

But it's not only Jewish performers who have been subjected to such pressure. When Taylor Swift expressed interest in performing in Israel, Ramah Kudaimi of the U.S. Campaign for Palestinian Rights told the *Daily Beast* that if she did so, it would "help Israel whitewash its denial of Palestinian rights" and would threaten her career. Other artists have been subjected to similar threats.[15]

In 2002, Mona Baker, a professor of translation studies at the University of Manchester Institute of Science and Technology and the publisher of two scholarly journals—*Translator* and *Translation Studies Abstracts*—dismissed Gideon Toury, a professor at Tel Aviv University, from the advisory board of *Translator.* She also dismissed Miriam Shlesinger, a lecturer in translation studies at Bar-Ilan University, from the advisory board of *Translation Studies Abstracts.* Ironically, both Toury and Shlesinger oppose the Israeli government's policies vis-à-vis the Palestinians.[16] The late British physicist Stephen Hawking, who had previously visited Israel on several occasions, canceled a planned appearance at the President's Conference in Israel in 2013 because he had "come under heavy pressure from activists who favor an academic boycott of Israel, both within Britain and outside it, [and] decided to listen to his Palestinian colleagues and stay home."[17]

But BDS has not only targeted those visiting Israel. In 2009, the Melbourne International Film Festival scheduled a screening of *Looking for Eric,* a film by British director Ken Loach. When Loach learned that the Israeli embassy was a sponsor of the festival, he canceled the screening in protest of Israel's "illegal occupation of Palestinian land, destruction of homes and livelihoods."[18] In 2012, American author Alice Walker refused to allow a new Hebrew translation of her novel *The Color Purple* to be published in Israel, "which is guilty of apartheid and persecution of the Palestinian people."[19]

There are, of course, academics, filmmakers, artists, and intellectuals who continue to participate in events in Israel. But the growing list of those joining this boycott effort is disturbing. There are artists and scholars who, without making any public statements, simply decline invitations to appear in Israel. In the academic world, BDS often operates in a covert, unofficial fashion. A particular graduate student may not be accepted, a job applicant not considered, a paper rejected, or a conference invitation not issued because the person in question is Israeli.

A particularly cruel irony inherent in the targeting of Israeli academics, artists, and intellectuals is that a disproportionate number of them publicly oppose many of Israel's settlement policies. Instead of encouraging their efforts, BDS lumps them in with the very people and policies that they oppose. All this does is bar Israeli advocates for change from participating in the larger conversation with like-minded Palestinian individuals, and instead empower extremists on both sides. British sociologist David Hirsh rightly observes that "much of the important communication between Palestinians and Israelis has been conducted via academic engagement." If one wants to resolve this political situation, efforts should be made to "facilitate communication, not exclusion, [to] listen, not close down voices."[20]

Ultimately, however, the personal politics of those affected by BDS are irrelevant. Law professor Martha Nussbaum notes that nobody should be fired for a political position, left or right. Boycotts are "blunt instruments." They assume that all those associated with an institution hold a singular view.[21] A central tenet of academic freedom is that a scholar's academic work and politics are separate and distinct from each other. In America in the 1940s and 1950s, men and women who were fired or blacklisted from jobs in academia and entertainment because they had in the past been members of the Communist Party were victims of the same type of discrimination. How ironic it is that leftist BDS supporters have adopted the tactics of right-wing McCarthyites.

A boycott strikes at the free exchange of ideas, which is why the American Association of University Professors (AAUP) firmly opposes it.[22] The BDS movement is a direct descendant of Marxist antisemitism and anti-Zionism. BDS activism on the college campus is a deliberate challenge to the liberal Jews—students and academics—who may strongly disagree with Israeli government policies but who oppose the idea of a boycott on ethical and political grounds. They often feel their only option is silence. I hope that won't be your response.

Yours,
DEL

BDS: ANTISEMITISM OR POLITICS?

Dear Deborah:

This is all very enlightening—and very disturbing. But one question remains. However antithetical to academic freedom BDS may be, can it truly be called antisemitic? Whether its proponents publicly advocate for a "two-state solution" or a single "bi-national" Jewish and Arab state (putting aside for the moment the question of how viable that option may be), do they truly fit into any of our previously established categories of antisemites?

Yours,
Joe

Dear Joe and Abigail:

I begin with a deeply unsatisfying answer to Joe's question: It depends.

First, I separate the BDS movement from many of its followers. Though that is generally a false dichotomy, in this case I believe it applies. BDS supporters who are critics of specific Israeli government policies believe this protest movement will result in Israel's relinquishing control of the West Bank, which will then (together with Gaza) become the State of Palestine, which will peacefully exist alongside the State of Israel, and everyone will live happily ever after. But if they were to seriously examine BDS's founding documents or some of the statements made by its founders (such as those of Omar Barghouti that I quoted in a previous letter), they would find that its objective is in fact the dissolution of Israel as a Jewish state, which is what would occur if the more than seven million Palestinians currently living outside of Israel were granted Israeli citizenship and permitted to exercise their right of return.[1]

There are anti-Israel activists who take matters further by propagating the Arab and Marxist charge that Zionism is a form of racism. In actual fact, Zionism is the national liberation movement of Jews. To argue that only Jews, among all the peoples in the world, are not to be permitted to have a national home (or, more precisely, to return to their national home) is to deny Jewish peoplehood. The negation of Jewish nationhood is a form of antisemitism, if not in intent, then certainly in effect. This is particularly so today, when the State of Israel, which was created by a United Nations resolution in 1947, exists. To have debated the efficacy of a Jewish state prior to its establishment was one thing. To advocate for the dissolution of a state that is now home to seven million inhabitants is something else entirely. Policies that will lead to the end of Israel as a Jewish state constitute, in the words of progressive essayist Ellen Willis, "an unprecedented demand" for an existing democratic state, "one that has a popularly elected government, to not simply change its policies but to disappear."[2] This may explain why people such as Ken Livingstone always talk about their opposition to Zionism rather than to the existence of Israel: It's easier to oppose a movement than it is to call for the end to a nation-state.

Many anti-Israel advocates contend that the fact that Israel is a country with an established state religion renders it archaic, and this justifies its dissolution. They are strangely silent on the validity of the nondemocratic Islamic theocracies in the same neighborhood. And the fact that Great Britain, Denmark, Greece, and Monaco have official state religions doesn't seem to bother them, either.

Ultimately, however, the BDS campaign is not about divestment. As one Stanford University professor observed when the issue was debated on that campus in 2015, even the proponents of the effort knew it was not going to happen. Why, then, bother to fight for it? Because "the actual goal" is not "the stated goal."[3] BDS supporters aim to convince students that Israel is the sole impediment to peace in the Middle East, if not the world. Nussbaum describes BDS as a "symbolic" boycott that is intended to make a "public statement" about opposition to Israel's policies.[4] It's another example of the attempt to toxify Israel.

In response to an attempt in 2016 by the American Anthropological Association to sign on to the BDS initiative, the Harvard professor Steven Pinker issued a public statement that eloquently sums up the situation:

> [Are Israel's] policies really so atrocious, so beyond the pale of acceptable behavior of nation-states, that they call for a unique symbolic statement that abrogates personal fairness and academic freedom? It helps to put the Israel-Palestine conflict in global and historical perspective—something that anthropologists, of all people, might be expected to do. . . . Why no boycotts against academics from China, India, Russia, or Pakistan, to take a few examples, which have also been

embroiled in occupations and violent conflicts, and which, unlike Israel, face no existential threat or enemies with genocidal statements in their charters? In a world of repressive governments and ongoing conflicts, isn't there something unsavory about singling the citizens of one of these countries for unique vilification and punishment?[5]

Nor do these critics of Israel acknowledge that there is virtually no Muslim state that treats its minority populations—Christians, Jews, Buddhists, Yazidis, or any other religious group—with equality.[6]

When BDS was hotly debated by students at Stanford, more than one hundred and fifty faculty members issued a statement decrying the "one-sided condemnation of Israel" and the "single minded ferocity" of the BDS campaign. (Rarely do faculty members criticize a student resolution.) Professor of history Steven Zipperstein observed that in his thirty years at Stanford, "no issue has captured as much attention" at the school. Zipperstein put it bluntly: "That's bizarre."[7] It is bizarre unless one acknowledges that something else is hovering beneath the surface. Equally bizarre were the responses given by those professors who led their academic associations in support of BDS resolutions. After the American Studies Association (ASA) voted in 2013 to adopt BDS and boycott Israeli academic institutions, the president of the organization was asked why it had done so, given that it had never before called for an academic boycott of any other country, "including many of Israel's neighbors, which are generally judged to have human rights records that are worse than Israel's, or comparable." His stunningly simplistic answer: "One has to start somewhere." Equally strange was the answer given by University of Texas professor Barbara Harlow when she was asked why she was advocating an academic boycott of Israel and not any other country accused of human-rights abuses. Her response: "Why not?"[8]

The proponents of these campaigns would vigorously deny that their singling out of Israel in this way is antisemitic. But their myopic focus on Israel is antisemitic in consequence, if not in intent. There are those who use traditional antisemitic stereotypes to demonize Israel, as Mark Yudof, president emeritus of the University of California writes:

> [T]heir rhetoric corrupts the language of human rights and expropriates the words historically used to demean the Jew, focusing instead on the Jewish state. . . . For example, at the University of California at Berkeley, a professor who attended the BDS debate reported to me that Israeli soldiers were accused of deliberately killing women and poisoning wells. In an age of exquisite sensitivity on some campuses to microaggression, or language that subtly offends underrepresented groups, the ironic toleration of microaggression against Jews often goes unnoted.[9]

But it seems to me that this response doesn't typify most of those engaged in this debate. There are supporters of pro-Palestinian causes who do not wish to see the destruction of Israel and who believe that their participation in movements such as BDS may genuinely lead to Israel changing those policies that adversely affect Palestinians. It seems unnecessary to point out that many Israeli citizens also oppose some of these policies. While some BDS supporters may not *knowingly* engage in the demonization of Israel I described above, the movement they support, with its singular and imbalanced view of Israel and its support of the dissolution of a Jewish state, does.[10]

The impact of BDS on Jewish students is quite real. Jewish students running for office in student government have also been uniquely targeted by Israel-bashers. Jewish candidates have been asked by other students to sign pledges not to travel to Israel or affiliate with student groups considered pro-Israel. A candidate for Stanford's student government, a Latina Jew, sought the endorsement of the university's Students of Color Coalition. During her interview, she responded without incident to a multiplicity of questions concerning campus issues. She was then asked: "Given your Jewish identity, how would you vote on divestment?" The student, "taken aback by the question," inquired about what the students interviewing her were "really asking." According to this student candidate, her questioners told her that they saw "that I had a strong Jewish identity, and [wondered] how that would impact my decision." When the student candidate said she opposed divestment, there was "an awkward silence, and the interview ended a minute later." She did not receive the endorsement. (The student group claims this exchange never happened, but it's hard to believe the student would have fabricated such an exchange.) Equally revealing of the atmosphere on campus is that prior to her campaign, this candidate had felt compelled to remove all her pro-Israel posts from her Facebook page. Her campaign manager explained, "We did it, not because she isn't proud [to support Israel]—she is—but the campus climate has been pretty hostile, and it would not be politically expedient to take a public stance. She didn't want that to be a main facet of her platform. Of course, she was going to be honest if she was asked about her stance on divestment."[11]

I often hear the argument that the BDS movement can't be considered antisemitic because many of its supporters are Jews. And, just as often, I hear the counterargument that these people are, simply, "self-hating" Jews—a term that I find unhelpful and inaccurate. It is sadly true that one of the most pernicious results of prejudice is when members of a persecuted group accept the ugly stereotypes used to characterize them. As Anthony Julius has observed, "contempt *for* Jews, when sufficiently widespread, can foster self-contempt *among* Jews." It can convince Jews that unfounded, inaccurate accusations leveled against them or, by extension, against the Jewish state, are true.[12] Anti-Zionist Jews who are opposed to Israel's existence believe that they are expressing universalistic Jewish "values," such as support for the downtrodden and for victims of injustice. It's unfortunate that they have bought into the anti-Israel narrative and are proud of the fact that they have the "courage" to counter what they feel is a deluded, omnipotent, organized Jewry. I feel sad and frustrated that these people have internalized these antisemitic motifs. They may not personally be antisemites, but they facilitate it. On the other hand, I wouldn't consider them antisemitic. But organizations such as BDS that negate the existence of a Jewish state most definitely are.

Yours,
DEL

CAMPUS GROUPTHINK:
NOT-SO-SAFE ZONES

Dear Deborah:

While we're on the subject of on-campus activity, there's another recent development that I find troubling and would like to discuss with you. It may seem a bit off our topic, but in my gut, I feel that it is in some way related to it.

In a speech Salman Rushdie gave at Emory in 2015, he remarked that "these are not good days for liberty. . . . Freedom seems everywhere in retreat."[1] Given his personal experience, one might have expected that he was referring to Islamist extremists. He was, but he was also referring to the North American university campus, which he described as becoming an "insult-free zone." He condemned the fact that threats to freedom of expression in America

> [are] beginning to be the greatest where they should be the most defended, that is to say within the walls of the academy. . . . And the people most willing to sacrifice, or limit, this fundamental right are young people. . . . To equate social good manners, the way we interact with each other, with the liberty to say what one thinks, even if people don't like it, is to make a false comparison. . . . Ideas are not people. Being rude about an idea is not the same thing as being rude about your aunt. . . .

What you don't have is the right to use your alleged offended-ness as a reason to stop other people from speaking.

Students on American college campuses seem to have taken notions of political correctness, as well as ideas about "inclusivity," "exclusivity," and "safe space," to a point where they trump freedom of speech. In 2015, a student theater group at Mount Holyoke, after seeking student feedback, canceled their annual production of Eve Ensler's groundbreaking play, *The Vagina Monologues*, because transgender women do not have vaginas, and the play therefore "offers an extremely narrow perspective on what it means to be a woman." Responding in *Time* magazine, Ensler pointed out that "inclusion doesn't come from refusing to acknowledge our distinctive experiences, and trying to erase them, in an attempt to pretend they do not exist. Inclusion comes from listening to our differences and honoring the right of everyone to talk about their reality, free from oppression and bigotry and silencing."[2] (She also noted that she has in recent years made available an optional monologue based on interviews she'd conducted with transgender women.)

Am I wrong to see a connection between these trends and the silencing of pro-Israel speakers on campus?

Yours,

Joe

Dear Joe and Abigail:

No, Joe, you're not wrong. Before the Free Speech Movement of the mid-1960s, it was campus administrators who decided what constituted "acceptable" public speech for students and faculty. How ironic it is that nowadays, it's left-wing student groups who are attempting to establish rules delineating what types of public speech are permissible.[3] As the chancellor of the University of California at Berkeley observed, "Free speech has become controversial."[4] In 2017, students there objected to appearances by Milo Yiannopoulos and Ann Coulter, both of whom hold a decidedly right-wing perspective on world events. The students—assisted by Antifa groups from outside the university—rioted until the events were canceled, ostensibly because the university could not guarantee the guests' safety. That was wrong. However reprehensible their pronouncements are, if Yiannopoulos or Coulter have been invited to speak on campus, their right to do so must be respected (unless, of course, they are inciting violence). As Berkeley professor Robert Reich observed, "How can students understand the vapidity of Coulter's arguments without being allowed to hear her make them, and question her about them?"[5] I am convinced that if the students who object to her so-called "ideology" were to listen to her for two minutes, they would understand she has none, just a series of well-honed insults.

Even more disturbing is how some faculty members have been responding to free-speech controversies. In 2017, Wellesley faculty who are part of the college's Commission on Race, Ethnicity, and Equity issued a statement, in the aftermath of an appearance by a professor who maintains controversial views on sexual violence on campus. They expressed concern over "the impact of speakers' presentations on Wellesley students who often feel the injury most acutely and invest time and energy in rebutting the speakers' arguments."[6] Students, they seemed to be suggesting, should not be exposed to ideas that might challenge their comfort zone. But isn't the university experience all about challenging one's comfort zone? And how long would it be before a speech about technology developments in the State of Israel would be placed in this discomfort zone by Israel's opponents?

For several decades, Evergreen College in Olympia, Washington, had been observing a "Day of Absence" each April, during which students and faculty of color did not come to campus, to demonstrate what an all-white society would look like. In 2017, the organizers decided that, instead, "white students, staff, and faculty [were] invited to leave campus for the day's activities."[7] Biology professor Bret Weinstein expressed his objections in an email to faculty and staff:

> There is a huge difference between a group or coalition deciding to voluntarily absent themselves from a shared space in order to highlight their vital and underappreciated roles, and a group or coalition encouraging another group to go away. . . . On a college campus, one's right to speak—or to be—must never be based on skin color.[8]

During a subsequent student protest, Weinstein was surrounded and verbally assaulted by students outside his classroom. When he was threatened with violence, the university administration told him that the campus police could not protect him. He and his wife resigned their faculty positions in September of that year and left the area.[9]

There are, however, times when university administrations take the necessary and appropriate action in these situations. In 2017, the American Enterprise Club, a conservative student group at Middlebury College, invited Charles Murray to speak on campus. His controversial 1994 book, *The Bell Curve,* implied that innate intelligence differences between the races, rather than discrimination, explained the disparity in the socioeconomic achievements of blacks and whites in America. When the book was published many people objected, myself included, to its implied racism. In all likelihood, I would not have invited Murray to speak at my campus. But the American Enterprise Club did, and, to its credit, it created a program in which a left-leaning professor would engage Murray in conversation after his lecture, for a potentially hard-hitting exchange. Nonetheless, some students, together with off-campus protesters, prevented the program from proceeding.

Prepared for this contingency, Middlebury had arranged for a backup site from which the conversation between Murray and the professor would be broadcast. The protesters learned of the site's location and physically attacked Murray and the professor, who ended up in the emergency room. But in this case, Middlebury's president, Laurie Patton, unequivocally condemned the protesters and subsequently called for an "embrace of freedom of expression and inquiry as an educational value for everyone, regardless of their background or political views." She acknowledged that "controversial speech is especially difficult" but considered it imperative that we "move beyond the false dichotomy between free speech and inclusiveness." In her view, "an educational institution does not become more inclusive by limiting freedom of expression. Nor does it achieve greater freedom by reducing its commitment to building an inclusive, robust, brave public square where all students are equally welcomed and valued."[10]

The University of Chicago took an equally strong stance. In 2014, president Robert J. Zimmer and provost Eric D. Isaacs tasked a faculty committee on freedom of expression with drafting a statement "articulating the University's overarching commitment to free, robust, and uninhibited debate and deliberation." The committee acknowledged that there will be ideas that members of the campus community might find disturbing; nonetheless, the university's commitment was to open and free inquiry. The committee cited the observation of a past president of the university, Hanna Holborn Gray: "Education should not be intended to make people comfortable, it is meant to make them think. Universities should be expected to provide the conditions within which hard thought, and therefore strong disagreement, independent judgment, and the questioning of stubborn assumptions, can flourish in an environment of the greatest freedom."[11] (When I read that statement, I couldn't help but be reminded that Gray's family fled Nazi Germany in 1933.) Jay Ellison, dean of students at the College at the University of Chicago, subsequently made this position very real in his letter welcoming the class of 2020. Addressing the infamous "trigger warnings" now prevalent on so many campuses, which require faculty to warn students if anything in their lectures or the readings might make students feel "unsafe" or "excluded," Ellison wrote, "Our commitment to academic freedom means that we do not support so-called 'trigger warnings,' we do not cancel invited speakers because their topics might prove controversial, and we do not condone the creation of intellectual 'safe spaces' where individuals can retreat from ideas and perspectives at odds with their own."[12]

So, going back to your question, Joe, how is all this related to what we have been discussing? First of all, throughout history, Jews have thrived in societies with robust freedom of expression and strong democratic institutions. They have faced far less felicitous conditions in societies that curtailed free speech. This has been true of both right-wing and left-wing governments, the best examples being Nazi Germany and the Soviet Union. Second, authorizing any institution or group of people—be they government officials or fellow academics—to decide what is and is not acceptable speech, whether that refers to speech that is antisemitic, anti-Islamic, racist, homophobic, sexist, etc., is dangerous. What troubles me even more is that there are today some Jewish organizations that believe legislative bodies, including the United States Congress, should pass legislation defining antisemitism and determining when anti-Israel speech crosses the line into antisemitism. If such laws are passed, pro-Israel Jewish students will be further marginalized, as they will now be associated with suppressing, rather than answering, speech they don't like.

The irony is, of course, that most pro-Israel students on campus probably don't agree with an approach that would repress freedom of expression. But the pro-Israel students don't yell as loudly as the off-campus Jewish groups fighting "for" them.[13] If those who oppose the right of Israel to exist were to be labeled antisemitic, would that mean that anti-Zionist ultra-Orthodox groups such as Satmar Hasidim would be included in such a definition? These proposals open a Pandora's box of absurdities and orthodoxies. Some of what we are currently seeing on campus—shouting down of speakers, faculty calls for invitations only to speakers who do not make students feel uncomfortable, and physical attacks on speakers—are of a piece with the attacks we have been seeing on Israeli speakers.[14] I have no doubt that, should these restrictions on "offensive" speech be formally enacted on college campuses, those who speak on

Israel's behalf would soon find themselves disinvited because they might make some students "uncomfortable."

Using the law as a means of silencing those with whom we disagree is misguided and dangerous. I say this from not just a professional but also a personal perspective. David Irving tried to use the law to silence me when he sued me for libel in the British courts. Antisemitism must be fought, but that fight must be strategic. Many of the more militant off-campus advocacy groups that have taken up this fight against "offensive" speech call for the defeat of the "other side" and insist that there be no exchange of ideas with them. For them it's a zero-sum game. There are, of course, groups with whom an exchange of ideas is impossible. (I would include in this category deniers, who, as we demonstrated in court, are liars and falsifiers of history.) But it's in the free exchange of ideas that extremists are revealed to be what they are. And it's in the free exchange of ideas that the truth is brought to light and prejudice and intolerance are revealed for what they are. How sad it is that on some college campuses today, there does not appear to be room for that conversation.

Yours,
DEL

PROGRESSIVISM AND ZIONISM: ANTISEMITISM BY SUBTERFUGE?

Dear Professor Lipstadt:

I hope you're having a good break. I'm home for a few days, and this past Friday night I was hanging out with friends with whom I attended Hebrew school. Some of us are at small private colleges and others attend large public universities. When we began to compare the Jewish aspect of our campus experiences we found a common and disturbing thread, and I thought it would be appropriate to explore it with you.

But before I begin, let me tell you a bit about us. My hometown friends and I are all from middle-class, suburban Jewish families. Our parents instilled in us a strong sense of Jewish identity and Jewish values, including devotion to family and community, love of Israel, and a commitment to working for social justice and equality. As a result of our upbringing, when we arrived at college many of us gravitated toward campus groups that support progressive causes, including racial justice, women's rights, and LGBTQ rights.

And here's where our troubles began. Increasingly, we find that at meetings of these progressive groups—irrespective of the agenda of the meeting—opposition to Israeli government policies, or to the very existence of the State of Israel, is almost certain to figure into the conversation. We are not naive. We had been warned and knew to expect that some courses on Middle East history and politics would have an anti-Israel bias.

Some courses are structured to present both sides of the Israel/Palestine issue, but others just flat out claim that the State of Israel is a racist, colonialist occupier of land to which it has no legitimate claim. What surprises and disturbs us is when this becomes part of the conversation in courses and at meetings that have nothing to do with the Middle East.

And, sometimes, it's not what's said about Israel that makes us feel uncomfortable; what alarms us are the assumptions that are made about Jews in general. In discussions about bigotry and prejudice, our attempts to bring antisemitism into the conversation are shot down by some faculty and students with the comment that because Jews are a "privileged" group, the connections we are trying to make are irrelevant and invalid. They contend that for something to be racist or prejudicial it must be composed of "prejudice plus power." As per this construct, those without power or privilege cannot be guilty of racism or any form of prejudice and those with power cannot be victims of prejudice.

These problems exist on an organizational level as well. Some of us who are active in Hillel often find ourselves seeking partners for programming on social-justice issues. We know that many members of the Black Student Union, of sexual assault awareness groups, of LGBTQ groups, and of other progressive campus organizations have signed on to pro-BDS and anti-Israel campaigns. But we would still like to partner with these organizations on issues such as racism, sexism, hunger, ecology, and gay rights because we feel that our differing stances vis-à-vis Israel should not keep us from working together for these other issues, which are not related to the Middle East and are of great importance to all of us. But many of these groups are refusing to work with Hillel groups on social-justice programs because Hillel supports Israel.

At the University of Illinois, during a rally sponsored by the campus chapter of the Students for Justice in Palestine (SJP), one of the speakers proclaimed that there was "no room for fascists, white supremacists, or Zionists at UIUC." Speakers repeatedly stressed the notion of the "confluence of fascism and Zionism." Both were described as "forms of racial supremacy" that are merging "seamlessly." During the protest, the participants chanted: "No justice! No peace! No war in the Middle East! No Zionists, no KKK, resisting fascists all the way."[1] In April 2017 at the University of Michigan, a group of students associated with Black Lives Matter hung posters on campus decrying an array of prejudices. There was no mention of antisemitism. This absence was not lost on Jewish students, who had been targeted by antisemitic incidents earlier that year. In a sad bit of irony, that night a local (probably nonstudent) white nationalist, alt-right group tagged the posters with Happy Merchant stickers. They implied that liberal Jews were behind the hanging of the anti-bias posters. So the Jewish students on campus found themselves simultaneously facing a refusal to recognize antisemitic bias from the left and antisemitic bias from the right.[2]

Initially, we thought that if, at gatherings of these progressive groups, we kept our pro-Israel beliefs to ourselves, we would be able to participate. But some of these groups have become so aggressive in their hostility to Israel—and, by extension, to anyone who they assume has a connection to Israel—that they now demand of Jewish participants what we refer to among ourselves as a "disloyalty oath," an affirmation that we are opposed to "Israeli racism," or "Israeli fascism," or "the Israeli occupation of Arab lands." (They rarely specify what they define as "Arab lands.")

We are all sad and frustrated about this. We went off to college eager for intellectual and social exploration. We wanted to try new things, develop new friendships, and become involved with new ideas and causes. We never assumed that, instead, we would find ourselves engaging in self-censorship about essential aspects of our identity. I don't mean to suggest that this is the sum total of our college experience. It's not. But it is disconcerting. I've told my friends about the correspondence we've been conducting, and they encouraged me to write to you.

Yours,
Abigail

Dear Abigail and friends, and Joe:

If it's any consolation, know that others are facing the same problem—on campus and beyond. Many Jews involved with progressive causes are increasingly feeling this tug, if not outright war, between their Jewish and political identities. The anti-Israel campaign in general and the BDS campaign in particular have partnered with progressive causes that have no connection to Israel/Palestine. Using a language of shared oppression, progressive groups have made Israel part of the matrix of their concerns.

No place is this more evident than on the college campus. In 2015, students at the University of Massachusetts at Amherst participating in the nationwide Million Student March protested high tuition costs, advocated for racial diversity on campus and for support for victims of on-campus sexual violence—and also called for the university to divest from investments in Israeli companies and for Israel to end the occupation of Palestinian territories.[3]

In November 2015, Assi Azar, an Israeli television person-

ality and LGBTQ activist, appeared at a screening of his film
about how Israeli parents deal with their children's coming out
that was sponsored by Hillel at Goucher College. Members
of Goucher's queer organization circulated a petition to have
the event "shut down" to protest "Israel's participation in the
apartheid, colonialism and genocide that affects queer Palestinians."[4] Fifteen protesters then showed up at the screening and
disrupted the public conversation Azar held with the audience
at its conclusion.

At Columbia University, No Red Tape (NRT), a campus
advocacy and support group for victims of sexual assault, has
partnered with Students for Justice in Palestine, promoting, in
2015, an event that discussed "the intersections of sexual violence activism at Columbia and Palestine solidarity. We'll examine the ways in which settler colonialism has led to the invasion
and violation of Palestinian bodies. We will explore the current
and historical use of sexual violence in the ethnic cleansing of
Palestine since 1948 as both a tool of dispossession, domination,
and brutality towards women and as an attempt to mute the
voices of Palestinians."[5]

A Columbia student, herself a rape survivor, poignantly
commented:

> I felt this [NRT] was a safe space to talk about campus
> sexual assault issues. There is so much on this campus
> that is about Israel and Palestine, but this was finally a
> place that wasn't. But then it was. My speaking about
> being a survivor in Hillel would never elicit something
> about Israel, Palestine, or any other political issue. It
> would only elicit someone talking to me about being a
> survivor.[6]

In the fall of 2017, a "Disorientation Guide," published by Tuft University students as an alternative to the university's official orientation guide, referred to the campus Hillel as a "Zionist place at Tufts . . . that promotes a white supremacist state." A particularly heinous action appears to have been Hillel's inviting Trayvon Martin's parents to speak on campus in 2015 about gun violence and race, which, according to the Guide, "exploit[ed] black voices for their own pro-Israel agenda."[7]

In November 2015, Students for Justice in Palestine chapters at colleges throughout the City University of New York protested planned tuition increases by what it referred to as a "Zionist administration [that] invests in Israeli companies, companies that support the Israeli occupation, hosts birthright programs and study abroad programs in occupied Palestine and reproduces settler-colonial ideology throughout CUNY through Zionist content of education. While CUNY aims to produce the next generation of professional Zionists, SJP aims to change the university to fight for all peoples [*sic*] liberation."[8] Oberlin students have observed that to be a Zionist on their campus, one "which prides itself on accept[ing]" a broad swatch of opinion, is to have an opinion that is "condemned to illegitimacy."[9] Winston Shi, student editor at the *Stanford Daily* and a non-Jew, echoed this view: "There is an *expectation* these days that university campuses are havens for anti-Israel sentiment." In July 2016, when two unarmed black men were killed by police in one week, the New York University chapter of Students for Justice in Palestine blamed Israel "because we must remember that many US police departments train with the #IsraeliDefenceForces. The same forces behind the genocide of black people in America are behind the genocide of Palestinians."[10]

Abigail, it's probably small consolation to you and your

friends that faculty members also feel the need to downplay their
Jewish identity and/or support of Israel, even when that support
is highly qualified. Some feel almost an obligation to be publicly critical of Israel because they want to preserve their "progressive Jewish" bona fides. After the National Women's Studies
Association voted to support BDS in the fall of 2015, one faculty
member shared what has become a familiar refrain: "I have long
been involved in the NWSA. . . . While I can convey my progressive politics in Jewish groups, increasingly, I do not feel I can
express my Jewish voice within the progressive community."[11]
This is particularly so for nontenured faculty, who fear that support of Israel might jeopardize their chances for advancement.
Many faculty members seem to have chosen simply to remain
silent about the issue, because "anti-Zionism becomes the necessary precondition of all other progressive commitments."[12]

More on this in my next letter.

Yours,
DEL

Dear Abigail and friends, and Joe:

The way in which some progressives have turned their ire on
anyone who is "suspected" of being pro-Israel was in startlingly
sharp evidence during the 2017 Chicago Dyke March. At the
rally and community picnic following the march, three women,
who were carrying rainbow flags emblazoned with the Star of
David, were told by one of the organizers to leave because their
flags looked like Israeli flags and were therefore unacceptable.
When one of the women replied that their flags displayed Jew-

ish pride and had nothing to do with Israel or Zionism, she was told that the Star of David was "too triggering" and made other participants feel "unsafe." Another woman, who told organizers that she was a Zionist who supported both Israeli and Palestinian statehood, was told that she "can't believe both ways."[13]

At the National LGBTQ Task Force's 2016 Creating Change Conference in Chicago, a Shabbat dinner was scheduled to be hosted by A Wider Bridge, an organization that advocates strengthening the relationship between the LGBTQ communities of North America and Israel. Conference organizers had initially canceled it but, after intense public criticism, reinstated it. The event had just begun when a crowd of protesters, carrying signs reading "Zionism Sucks" and chanting "No Justice, No Peace," stormed the room. The Israelis who were attending the dinner were hustled out a back door. Some of the participants were pushed and shoved as they left the room. "Pinkwashing" is the term used by some anti-Zionist progressives to condemn efforts by the Israeli government and pro-Israel LGBTQ activists to showcase Israel as a particularly gay-friendly country. What was especially ironic was that the Israelis were attending the conference in large measure to discuss the aftermath of the murder of a young girl at the 2015 Jerusalem gay pride parade.

One of the people who tried to attend the Shabbat gathering was a former student of mine, now a successful businessman in his late thirties, who takes his Jewish and gay identity very seriously. He described his experience that night: "I couldn't find the room because the location had been changed for security reasons. The atmosphere was so toxic that I was afraid to ask for directions." I found what he said sadly ironic, too. He was more than willing to openly identify as a gay person—something that would have been impossible not long ago—but afraid to identify as a Jew.[14]

There are, however, students who aren't afraid to call out antisemitic speech when they hear it. In April 2016, during a debate at a meeting of the Stanford University Student Senate about a resolution that would commit the university's student government to combating antisemitism, one student senator questioned whether the statement "Jews control the media, economy, government and other societal institutions" should be considered antisemitic. The student contended that "questioning these potential power dynamics, I think, is not anti-Semitism." Rather, it was a matter for "a very valid discussion."[15] In light of this statement, the *Stanford Daily,* the student newspaper, decided to withdraw its support for this student's reelection. An article by one of its editors, Winston Shi, began by noting that "antisemitism, though stupid, is not the sole provenance of stupid people." Shi went on to say:

> People who have faced death for the crime of being Jewish will be more than happy to tell you that 'Jews run the world,' is the oldest trick in the book. . . . As long as Jews have been minorities in the world around them, they have been dealing with this garbage. I cannot phrase this strongly enough. What Mr. Knight described as a "very valid discussion" are words that have launched pogroms and genocide, destroyed communities for generations and left a tragic stain on the human conscience. Do I think Mr. Knight intends to recreate the Holocaust? No. Do I think Mr. Knight is responsible for the words he says? Absolutely. . . . As a half-Palestinian, it would not be terribly surprising if Mr. Knight had a low opinion of the State of Israel; but to go from the quarrel over the Palestinian crisis to "Jews control the media" makes a mockery of logic.

Ignorance is not an excuse. Apparently, Mr. Knight did not get the memo.[16]

As we have seen, a familiar argument in these settings is that Jews' concerns about antisemitism are just a means of camouflaging Israel's wrongs. British film director Loach asserted that reports about the increase of antisemitism across Europe are intended merely to "distract attention" from Israel's military crimes.[17] David Clark, a former Labour MP, described charges of antisemitism as "poisonous intellectual thuggery" and a kind of "blackmail."[18] The British Pakistani writer Tariq Ali described reports of antisemitism as "a cynical ploy on the part of the Israeli Government to seal off the Zionist state from any criticism of its regular and consistent brutality against the Palestinians."[19] By accusing Jews of instrumentalizing antisemitism, some on the progressive left are denying Jews something they enthusiastically accord to other minority groups. As Jonathan Freedland aptly described it:

> When Jews call out something as antisemitic, leftist non-Jews feel curiously entitled to tell Jews they're wrong, that they are exaggerating or lying or using it as a decoy tactic—and to then treat them to a long lecture on what anti-Jewish racism really is. The left would call it misogynist "mansplaining" if a man talked that way to a woman. They'd be mortified if they were caught doing that to LGBT people or Muslims. But to Jews, they feel no such restraint.[20]

But leftist antisemitism persists. Linda Sarsour, a Palestinian American activist and former executive director of the Arab American Association of New York, who was also a co-chair of the 2017 Women's March, infamously tweeted in 2012, "Nothing is creepier than Zionism," to which she appended, "Challenge racism," embracing the canard that Zionism is racism. In April 2017, she admonished those who "call themselves Zionists . . . we will not change who we are to make anybody feel comfortable. If you ain't all in, then this ain't the movement for you." She confirmed her position in the fall of 2017 when she attacked attendees at the March for Racial Justice who had brought signs proclaiming that they were both Zionists and progressives. She declared that they were not welcome because they adhered to a racist ideology. Despite the fact that these people were greatly outnumbered by other participants, Sarsour declared that they made her feel "unsafe."[21]

While Sarsour was made uncomfortable by the presence of women with pro-Israel signs, she and some of her colleagues did not seem to be similarly troubled by expressions of overt antisemitism and homophobia when they came from Minister Louis Farrakhan, leader of the Nation of Islam (NOI), which has been described by the Southern Poverty Law Center (SPLC) as "deeply racist, antisemitic, and anti-LGBT."[22] In March 2018, Tamika D. Mallory, who was a co-leader of the Women's March, attended the annual NOI Saviours' Day, at which Farrakhan described "the powerful Jews" as "my enemy," and "the mother and father of apartheid." He declared that "the Jews" control the government and are responsible for "degenerate behavior in Hollywood, turning men into women and women into men." After the speech, Mallory posted videos and pictures of herself with Farrakhan and even received a shout-out from him during his speech. When she was criticized for her attendance at this gathering and her failure to condemn Farrakhan's overtly antisemitic statements, she tweeted: "If your leader does not have the same enemies as Jesus, they may not be THE leader!

Study the Bible and u will find the similarities." This reference to Jesus's enemies ("the Jews") rankled many people who condemned its unmistakable antisemitic references.[23] When the criticism did not abate, Mallory reverted to the familiar tactic of turning on her critics and tweeted about how she was being "bullied."[24]

Carmen Perez, another Women's March leader, posted photos of her holding hands with Farrakhan and rhapsodized about her encounter with him. "There are many times when I sit with elders or inspirational individuals where I think, 'I just wish I could package this and share this moment with others.'"[25] Sarsour has also participated in NOI events. In 2015, at a large NOI gathering, she declared that "the same people who justify the massacres of Palestinian people and call it collateral damage are the same people who justify the murder of young black men and women." She went on to assert that the "common enemy" faced by black people and Palestinians is "white supremacy."[26]

In the wake of the controversy, Women's March leaders belatedly issued a statement insisting, "We will not tolerate anti-Semitism, racism, misogyny, homophobia, and transphobia and we condemn these expressions of hatred in all forms. . . . Minister Farrakhan's statements about Jewish, queer, and trans people are not aligned with the Women's March Unity principles." Then, instead of a straightforward condemnation of Farrakhan and the NOI, they declared that they do not "shy away from the fact that intersectional movement building is difficult and often painful."[27] I suppose it is, particularly when you are trying to intersect with an antisemitic homophobe who stigmatizes trans people.

The situation shows no signs of changing. In April 2018, two African American men entered a Philadelphia Starbucks to wait for a third man. When they asked to use the bathroom, they were told that it was available only to paying customers (the men had not ordered anything). Shortly thereafter, police arrived in response to a 911 call made by a Starbucks employee. They arrested the men for trespassing and took them away in handcuffs. A video of the incident went viral on Twitter, with other patrons' exclamations that "they didn't do anything" clearly heard in the background. The men were released about eight hours later, and Starbucks issued a public apology to them five days afterward. Starbucks' press release also mentioned that the company would be closing its more than eight thousand company-owned stores in the United States on Tuesday, May 29, to conduct racial-bias education for its nearly 175,000 employees geared toward preventing discrimination in their stores. The curriculum would be developed with the guidance of experts on confronting racial bias, including, among others, the president and director of the NAACP Legal Defense and Education Fund, former U.S. attorney general Eric Holder, and the CEO of the Anti-Defamation League. Tamika Mallory tweeted a response that attacked Starbucks for including the ADL, an organization that "is CONSTANTLY attacking black and brown people." (The ADL has often been critical of Farrakhan for his racism, homophobia, and antisemitism.) Linda Sarsour echoed Mallory's critique.[28] Sadly, Starbucks buckled and dropped the ADL from the program.

Abigail, what you and your friends are experiencing is very real and, sadly, not unique. In my next letter, I will try to make some suggestions for action.

Yours,
DEL

RESPONDING TO THE PROGRESSIVE "CRITIQUE"

Dear Abigail and friends, and Joe:

How does one most effectively address the subtle—and sometimes not-so-subtle—antisemitic attitudes and behaviors that one encounters in groups that are connected with progressive causes?

It's probably pointless to ask these groups where their protests are against human rights abuses in countries such as Russia, China, Syria, Saudi Arabia, Turkey, North Korea, Sudan, and Zimbabwe, although it would certainly be interesting to hear.

There is another step we can take, even though it will roil many Jews in the pro-Israel community. There's nothing wrong in acknowledging that the current situation in the West Bank is untenable, and in explaining that the most reasonable solution would be two states—a Jewish state and a Palestinian state— side by side, with secure and defensible borders. This idea will be rejected by those who deny the legitimacy of a Jewish state anywhere in Mandatory Palestine, or those who claim that Israel will never be a good-faith negotiator. Discussing anything with them is, indeed, pointless. At the same time, we must carefully differentiate between campaigns that disagree with Israeli policy and those that essentially call for the elimination of the Jewish state. There is a vast difference between being opposed to the policies of the Israeli government and being an antisemite. Those of us who want to fight this scourge do ourselves no favor if we automatically brand ideas with which we disagree "antisemitic." Too often, some Jewish organizations and their leaders reflexively fall back on this accusation.

We must not think of fighting antisemitism or anti-Israel animus as a one-size-fits-all process. Tactics that may succeed in the halls of Congress may well fail, if not backfire, on the campus. American Jewish communal leaders have boasted that, as of spring 2017, seventeen states have passed legislation against boycotts of Israel. They also made mention of the fact that at "the federal level, Congress passed a law that opposes politically motivated actions that penalize or otherwise limit commercial relations with Israel, such as BDS." And they called attention to the losses suffered by BDS in Canada, the United Kingdom, France, and Spain.[1] While efforts to stop commercial boycotts may well succeed (as they absolutely should), these kinds of antiboycott tactics are doomed to fail on the campus. Some off-campus groups have pressured university administrations to ban BDS groups and their affiliates, such as Students for Justice in Palestine. They have insisted that the universities and their trustees declare that they will reject any student-supported pro-BDS resolution. Efforts to ban anti-Israel groups from the campus are not only sure to fail but, even more significantly, they will be a boon for the pro-BDS forces. University officials cannot ban a student organization that is legally sanctioned by the student government. This is not how a university functions. They cannot control whom the students choose to invite to campus. Moreover, these kinds of actions play right into the hands of BDS's proponents. As I have argued, BDS's real objective is not boycotts or divestiture, but the toxification of Israel. And they are succeeding at that, as Israeli speakers at various campuses (regardless of their own personal politics) find their lectures disrupted. What we cannot assess, of course, is how many Israeli speakers are simply not invited to campuses because the problems this creates are too overwhelming. Banning anti-Israel or pro-Palestinian groups from campus will only increase this toxification and buttress the narrative propounded by many progressive groups, who argue that Israel's criminality is being defended by "white, privileged, and powerful" Jews.

Some Jewish organizations have compiled lists of professors who have signed BDS resolutions and have urged Jewish students to boycott the classes of these teachers. This non-nuanced and often mistake-laden effort assumes that professors are unable to separate what they teach from their personal politics.[2] (Some cannot. Many can.) These organizations have included on their lists the names and pictures of those faculty members they have deemed to be pro-BDS or anti-Israel. By advocating what is essentially a blacklist, these Jewish organizations are practically mimicking the tactics of the pro-BDS campaign. Mistakes easily creep into such lists. A number of years ago a list of "anti-Israel" Emory instructors was circulated by one of these groups. It was riddled with errors and incorrect accusations. Included on the list were people who had left Emory years earlier. Even pro-Israel and anti-BDS faculty members found the idea of such a list, as well as the list itself, to be outrageous and counterproductive. Some Jewish communal organizations have even gone after Israelis who are themselves victims of BDS. Such was the case with the singer Achinoam Nini, known professionally as Noa. They have demanded that their communities not invite her to perform because, they wrongly claim, she supports BDS. The irony is that, despite being a firm opponent of the current Israeli government, Noa has been prevented by BDS supporters from performing in the United States. Nonetheless, pro-Israel advocates who do not live in Israel have demanded that, even if she is not a BDS supporter, she not participate in communal events because she is a severe critic of Israeli foreign policy. Talk about eating your own.[3]

There was a similar disproportionate, if not absurd, reaction to the decision by the actress Natalie Portman to decline to travel to Israel to accept the 2018 Genesis Prize, an annual award cosponsored by private philanthropists and the Israeli government that honors individuals who they deem to have attained excellence and international renown in their chosen professional fields, and who they feel inspire others through their dedication to the Jewish community and Jewish values. Portman's representative said that Portman had been distressed by recent events in Israel and did not feel comfortable participating in any public events there, particularly one at which Prime Minister Netanyahu (whom she has criticized in the past) would be speaking. In response, one Israeli cabinet member accused her of being a BDS supporter (which Portman immediately denied) and another accused her of acting in a way that bordered on antisemitism.[4] It was a ludicrous and unfair attack, not to mention counterproductive. Not only did this accusation bear no relationship to reality, it also buttressed the arguments of those who claim that any criticism of Israel is unfairly categorized as antisemitism.

Israel has, on occasion, taken other counterproductive steps to fight BDS. Such was the case with a bill passed by the Knesset in 2017 that bars entry to the country to anyone "who knowingly issues a public call for boycotting Israel."[5] Some of the harshest criticism of this effort came from the heads of Israeli universities and the Diaspora leaders of the anti-BDS movement. They described the law as a "clear erosion of the principles of academic freedom and free scholarly exchange" and argued that rather than trying to silence BDS voices or bar them from the campus, these people should be directly confronted because, as they so powerfully put it, "we believe we have a more compelling narrative to share." This law not only violates the principles of academic freedom, it also—like the lists of pro-BDS professors compiled by the Jewish organizations—is a classic shoot-oneself-in-the-foot strategy.[6]

Speaking of shoot-oneself-in-the-foot, during the summer of 2018 Israel seemed to be engaged in precisely that. It detained longtime supporters of Israel trying to enter the country because they have opposed Israel's presence in the West Bank. Some were subjected to questioning by Shin Bet representatives. They were accused of doing no wrongs, except for belonging to organizations that are critical of current Israeli policy. Among them were a prominent journalist, who was in Israel for his nephew's bar mitzvah. His treatment garnered headlines in many places, including Israel. Though the Shin Bet acknowledged that some of its actions, including this one, were "errors in judgment," the attorney general's office decided to investigate. In another case, a longtime supporter of Israeli philanthropies, who has donated millions of dollars to Israeli causes, among them schools and hospitals, was stopped upon leaving Israel. He had visited his sister, who lives in a town on the West Bank, and some of the philanthropies he supports. He had also participated in an encounter program with Palestinians. While on the program he was handed a document that he considered propaganda. He set it aside to examine more closely later. Security officials found it in his luggage and subjected him to an extended interview prior to allowing him to board his flight. Israeli officials subsequently apologized.[7]

Some of Israel's defenders use rhetorical weapons. Such was

the case when a Los Angeles rabbi declared that "BDS is no different than the Nazis of the 1920s and 1930s who created a myth that all Jews were guilty of insidious crimes against the international community and were intent on world domination."[8] These comparisons distort history and contemporary reality. They use charges of antisemitism as a cudgel and give validity to those who accuse Jews of citing the Holocaust "too much." The only thing these lists and hyperbolic comments accomplish is to give those who make them a self-satisfied feeling.

A number of Israeli and American organizations have pointed to their legislative achievements and these "name and shame" lists and declared victory. At a 2017 World Jewish Congress–sponsored anti-BDS student gathering at the United Nations, Israeli and American speakers repeatedly stressed, "We are winning." While the number of on-campus BDS activities may be down, the touted "achievements" of anti-BDS activists are at best false or pyrrhic victories. They come at the cost of alienating many potential allies and supporters and, more important, these efforts nullify the most potent argument against boycotts. In the recent past, increasing numbers of academics, including critics of Israel's policies, have come to recognize that BDS is antithetical to the foundation stones of higher education. On campus, "boycotting the boycotters" will do more than just fail. By urging boycotts of anti-Israel groups, the anti-BDS advocates surrender the academic moral high ground—support of academic freedom and freedom of inquiry—to their opponents.

Yours,
DEL

MYOPIA: SEEING ANTISEMITISM
ONLY ON THE OTHER SIDE

Dear Abigail and Joe:

Over the past few years, as Jews have become increasingly concerned about rising expressions of antisemitism, I have witnessed a disturbing development. I've alluded to it earlier in our exchange. I want to explore it more extensively here. There is a growing tendency among those who fight antisemitism to see it as a problem that exists only on the "other" side of the political spectrum. Those on the left see Jew-hatred only on the right. Those on the right see it only on the left. Both are correct in what they see. But they are blind or rather willfully blind themselves to the antisemitism in their midst.

Consider the response to Linda Sarsour's comments about Zionism and women who are Zionists. More than one hundred and fifty progressive Jews, among them many rabbis, denounced Sarsour's critics. Some among them contended that she was opposed only to right-wing Zionism, without supplying supporting evidence. This does nothing but embolden anti-Zionists.[1]

Less forgiving was Rabbi Sharon Brouse, a prominent progressive rabbi. "There is no room in a multi-faith, multi-ethnic coalitional movement for antisemitism, homophobia, or transphobia," she said. "Full stop. You can't fight racism but excuse antisemitism, just as you cannot fight antisemitism while excus-

212 THE CAMPUS AND BEYOND

ing and justifying racism or Islamophobia."² Subsequently, additional information about meetings of some leaders of the Democratic Party with Farrakhan have come to light. Here, too, the outrage has been strikingly muted.³

Progressives are not, of course, the only ones who have a less-than-stellar record of addressing racism in their midst. In the fall of 2017, details emerged regarding the far-right leanings of Steve Bannon and Breitbart News. There is no credible evidence that Bannon is himself an antisemite, but it is extremely distressing that right-wing Jewish groups that trumpet his support for Israel ignored the racism, anti-immigrant, and white nationalist views promulgated by Breitbart News when he ran it.⁴ He helped galvanize the emerging white nationalist movement. Nonetheless, some Jewish organizations embraced and continue to embrace him.

When the *GQ* reporter who wrote the critical profile of Melania Trump was being aggressively trolled by the *Daily Stormer* and other pro-Trump antisemites, *New York Times* editor Jonathan Weisman repeatedly pressed the Republican Jewish Coalition for a response. Finally, after great equivocation, it released a statement: "We abhor any abuse of journalists, commentators, and writers, whether it be from Sanders, Clinton, or Trump supporters." Weisman marveled at the fact that the RJC could equate with "a straight face" the trollers who issued overtly antisemitic statements, threatened reporters with rape and death, and depicted them being pushed into gas chambers with members of pro-Clinton and pro-Sanders groups who had done no such things.⁵

A particularly bizarre phenomenon is antisemitic white supremacists who express fervent admiration for Israel. At an appearance at the University of Florida in October 2017, alt-right leader and white nationalist Richard Spencer depicted Israel as an example of the "ethno-state" he would like to create in the United States—a state in which non-whites (which include, in his determination, Jews) would be ghettoized away from white people.[6] He hates Jews but loves Israel.

Being simultaneously antisemitic and pro-Israel seems to be possible in several European countries as well. In the summer of 2017, Hungarian prime minister Orbán began a concerted attack on George Soros, a billionaire Hungarian American Jew and Holocaust survivor who has funded pro-democracy and human rights groups in many former Soviet-bloc countries, including Hungary. The Hungarian government erected billboards throughout the country with a picture of a grinning Soros and the caption: "Let's not allow George Soros to have the last laugh." The Federation of Hungarian Jewish Communities denounced this campaign, noting that "while [it was] not openly antisemitic, [it] clearly has the potential to ignite uncontrolled emotions, including antisemitism." The Israeli ambassador to Hungary initially also forcefully condemned the posters. But then, in an unprecedented move, Israel's Foreign Ministry ordered him to retract his criticism. It seems that Israeli leaders feared that such criticisms might impede Israel's efforts to forge closer ties with Orbán, who is not only ardently anti-Muslim but also one of the few European leaders who supports Israel in the European Union. Soros, by contrast, has funded groups that are virulently critical of Israel's policies. The formal end of this aspect of the campaign against Soros coincided with a visit by Benjamin Netanyahu to Hungary, during which Orbán assured Israel's prime minister that the country will never again tolerate antisemitism. Netanyahu declared that he was "reassured" and expressed his conviction that the Hungarian government stood with the Jewish people. The Hungarian Jewish community was not as easily mollified. And, it turns out, their skepticism was justified. A few months later, the Hungarian government conducted a national survey that was ostensibly designed to assess the Hungarian people's positions on immigration and refugees. All seven questions on the survey dealt with something it called the Soros Plan, which was supposedly secretly created by Soros in cahoots with the EU leadership. (That there was no evidence of anything like the Soros Plan was inconsequential to the government officials who wrote the survey questions.) According to the government, Soros intended to compel all EU members to "take down border protection fences and open the border for immigrants." EU countries would be forced to accept immigrants on a "mandatory basis." The supposed goal of this alleged plan was "to diminish the importance of the language and culture of European countries." This unmistakably echoed the classic twentieth-century antisemitic accusation against the "cosmopolitan" European Jew (nowadays, the "globalist" Jew) who has no national roots or loyalties. Then a Hungarian government official gave a speech in Hungary's parliament titled "The Christian Duty to Fight against the Satan/Soros Plan," in which he described Soros as "Satan" with an agenda that "from its heart hates Christian Europe's traditions and civilization."[7] It was classic conspiracy theory. So much for Orbán's assurances to Netanyahu of his commitment to fighting antisemitism.

Despite all this, in February 2018, the Israeli government invited the governments of Hungary, Poland, Slovakia, and the Czech Republic, who have formed a cultural and political alliance known as the Visegrad Group, to hold their next meeting in Israel.[8] Such a gathering would give Hungary and Poland an opportunity to slough off charges of antisemitism and Holocaust denial. (After all, would Israel host them if they were engaging in Jew-hatred?) At around the same time, an adviser to Poland's president told reporters that the reason Israel opposed the new Polish law outlawing any assertions that Poles collaborated with Nazis during World War II was that Israel felt "shame at the passivity of the Jews during the Holocaust" and was "fighting to keep the monopoly on the Holocaust."[9]

But Hungary's Orbán did not have to wait for a Visegrad meeting in Israel to get a "clean bill of health." In summer 2018 he visited Israel, where Netanyahu praised him as a "true friend of Israel," and someone committed to "the need to combat antisemitism." The Israeli prime minister said this, despite the severe opposition of the Hungarian Jewish community, Orbán's overtly antisemitic campaign against Soros, and his denial of Hungary's role in the decimation of the Jewish community in 1944. Orbán had praised Hungary's World War II leader Admiral Horthy. Horthy not only passed severe antisemitic legislation that forced Jews into labor camps but also cooperated with the Germans in the deportation and annihilation of the last major wartime Jewish community in continental Europe.[10]

Nor did Poland have to wait for such a gathering to get a reprieve on its attempt to rewrite the history of the Holocaust. After earnestly attacking the Polish 2018 law regarding the Holocaust, Netanyahu's government suddenly reversed course in July 2018. Poland made virtually no substantive changes in the bill, other than changing the criminal punishment to a civil crime. The leaders of the two countries signed a highly controversial joint statement stipulating that the Polish underground and wartime government in exile offered a mechanism of systematic help and support to Jewish people." The joint statement admitted that there were cases in which Poles committed cruelties against Jews, but balanced that by noting that "numerous Poles" risked their lives to rescue Jews. It decried anti-Polonism and antisemitism.

Israel's leading historians, including those at Yad Vashem, were infuriated. They described the statement and the revised law as full of "grave errors and deceptions." Regarding the supposed help of the Polish government in exile to Jews, they declared that decades of research provide a "totally different picture." Poles' aid to Jews was "relatively rare" and attacks, even murder, of Jews "widespread." The joint statement left all the wrongs of the original law in place. The historians decried the statement's juxtaposition of antisemitism with so-called "anti-Polonism," calling the latter, "fundamentally anachronistic and [having] nothing whatsoever to do with antisemitism." The unsparing criticism of the statement by Yad Vashem took on extra power given that the institution is a government-sponsored entity. One of the world's leading Holocaust historians, Yehuda Bauer, declared the statement a "betrayal" that "hurt the Jewish people and the memory of the Holocaust." He explained the Israeli government's decision to issue this statement as entirely political. Its goal was to strengthen "the diplomatic, political, and economic ties between the Israeli government and the government of Poland."[11]

When Austria's far-right populist and anti-immigrant Freedom Party (FPO) joined the government's ruling coalition in 2000, Israel temporarily recalled its ambassador in protest. But in recent years the FPO has touted its admiration for Zionism, supported the building of settlements in the West Bank, and advocated moving Austria's embassy to Jerusalem. And in 2018, after scoring significant electoral victories, FPO leaders began to woo Israel in an effort "to improve relations between our [Austrian] people and the Jewish people." In response, a Likud MP traveled to Vienna to meet with party leaders, some of whom then visited Israel. The protests of the Austrian Jewish community to the Israeli government were to no avail.[12] What makes these strange alignments even more upsetting is the fact that the Polish and Hungarian governments, as well as Austria's FPO, are all on record as having expressed strongly anti-Muslim sentiments and have made it clear to Muslim refugees that they are not welcome in their countries.[13]

These strange alignments can be explained in part by the shared sense of nationalism that characterizes all these governments. Poland, Hungary, and Austria have all shown themselves willing to support Israel in the UN and the EU, something the other democracies have been less than willing to do. In essence, Netanyahu has made a decision based on realpolitik, apparently willing to live with their legacy of antisemitism, Holocaust denial, and contemporary expressions of Jew-hatred in exchange for their support today. The problem is that it is a pact made with dubious partners. If they can engage in such pure expressions of antisemitism and rewriting of history today, what will they attack tomorrow? Will Hungarian children be taught a fictional account of the Holocaust, that their country was a victim of the Nazis and that it tried to save its Jews? Will the guides at Auschwitz-Birkenau be compelled to tell a fanciful history about how Poles suffered equally with Jews and, nonetheless, tried to save them? Moreover, this pact raises serious questions about Netanyahu's claim that Israel is the primary protector of Jews worldwide against antisemitism and persecution.

Back in the United States, a meeting was held at the United Nations in March 2017 for two thousand students and pro-Israel advocates hosted by the Permanent Mission of Israel to the United Nations and the World Jewish Congress to strategize about combating BDS activity on college campuses and in social media. While most of the speakers at the conference as well as its organizational sponsors were right-of-center, the student participants represented a broad political spectrum, including members of the left-of-center J Street U and the New Israel Fund, who strongly advocate for the creation of a Palestinian state on the West Bank (the "two-state solution"). When two J Street U students, one from Barnard and one from Princeton, identified themselves and asked what they should say to fellow students who oppose the occupation of the West Bank to convince them that BDS was wrong, "hisses" were heard in the large auditorium. One of the speakers, Alan Clemmons, a Republican serving in the South Carolina House of Representatives, responded with what one reporter described as "the most popular line of the day." He told them that he personally believed that J Street was "an antisemitic organization that chooses to ignore the law and reality to push back on Israel and the Jewish nation." His statement was met with "whoops of support," and many in the audience rose to give him a standing ovation.[14] Not one of the organizers or sponsors, including those from some of the more centrist Jewish groups, publicly condemned Clemmons's appalling comments and the reaction to them. (They did so only in media interviews after the meeting.) Israeli government representatives who were present at the meeting declined to comment, possibly because Clemmons has been so supportive of antiboycott legislation.[15]

The J Street U students, who all wore identifying T-shirts, were taken aback at being labeled antisemites by fellow pro-Israel Jews, and they were also puzzled when, according to one of them, "we were asked by a security guard and one of the event organizers to cover [the J Street logos] up when we tried to take a photo. It's unclear exactly why."[16]

Even more distressing was the fact that one of the speakers at the event is a Messianic Jew—a born Jew who converted to Christianity through Jews for Jesus. He was not publicly identified as such at the gathering, and he was most likely invited because he is a lawyer who is active in the anti-BDS movement. (The fact that he is one of President Trump's personal lawyers might have also been a factor in the invitation.) But one wonders how the organizers (who knew of his religious affiliation) were in good conscience able to reconcile among themselves the cheers he received after his rousing address with the hoots showered upon the J Street U kids.

I'm sure this all sounds pretty depressing to you. But it's important not to give in to despair. There are positive steps that we can take. One of the most important is simply to *be present*. Abigail, you and your friends cannot abandon the various progressive groups with which you have been involved. You must be present as the Zionists and lovers of Israel—with all its faults—that you are. Progressive organizations cannot be convinced to descend into antisemitism by the few Jew-haters in their midst. Your continued presence among them will make it harder for them to claim victory. And you must challenge the overt antisemitism that comes from within these groups. This will not be pleasant or easy for you, but it's important to stand up for what you believe in. I've watched friends in the United Kingdom who are longtime Labour Party members fully acknowledge their party's willingness to abide the antisemitism in its midst. But they don't leave, and instead keep jumping into the fray, uncomfortable as it may be for them.

Joe, this goes for you and me as well. We, too, must speak

up, especially to colleagues who have silently—and sometimes not so silently—acquiesced to policies that are riddled
with antisemitism and antithetical to the principles for which
the university stands. We must be willing to fight back when
we become aware of colleagues who reject Israeli students and
job applicants because of their national origin. We must insist
that antisemitism be treated with the same seriousness as racism, sexism, homophobia, and Islamophobia. We must call out
both friends and foes. If Abigail and her friends are going to put
themselves on the line, we must do the same. As uncomfortable
as it may be, we must also recognize that within sectors of the
Muslim community, particularly in Europe, there is endemic
antisemitism. We cannot ignore, rationalize, or brush it off as
a consequence of events in the Middle East, as something that
will disappear once the Israel/Palestine conflict is settled. We
cannot dismiss it as the beliefs of misguided immigrants who
don't fully grasp the nature of Western democracy. It comes
from individuals who have been raised to hate Jews. But it's
much more than an attack on Jews; it's an attack on the broad-
est reaches of Western society. At the same time, we must be on
guard that this not turn into a demonization of Muslims. We
cannot fight hatred of Jews with hatred of other groups.

And most important, we must make people aware that antisemitism is not solely a problem of the Right or the Left, but
that it exists in both arenas. It might be more institutionalized
on the left, but we are also seeing it as an element in the rise of
right-wing nationalism both in the United States and abroad.
We cannot let those on the left—progressive people who are
dedicated to righting long-standing wrongs—blind themselves
to the antisemitism that has tragically insinuated itself into
some areas of the political Left.

Similarly, we must forthrightly acknowledge those on the right who say they are merely trying to protect "European culture" as the antisemites and racists that they are. It was not by chance that those who gathered in Charlottesville in 2017 to protest the removal of a statue of Robert E. Lee also chanted "Jews will not replace us," or that when Richard Spencer ended a speech at an alt-right conference in Washington, D.C., shortly after the 2016 presidential election with the cry "Hail Trump, hail our people, hail victory," some of those in attendance responded with the Nazi salute. Just as you, Abigail, must call out the antisemites among those with whom you are politically aligned, so must you make sure you are heard when right-wing antisemites appear on campus. This is something that the organized Jewish community, which has responded with such vigor to the threat posed by the BDS movement, Jeremy Corbyn, and other left-wing sources must do as well. With the exception of singular events, such as Charlottesville, it has in recent years too often reacted strongly to the attacks from the left but not from the right. There has been little communal outcry about Poland, where the prime minister (the same one who signed the joint statement) told a child of Holocaust survivors that there were "Jewish perpetrators" of the Holocaust. There has been relative silence about the Ukraine, where individuals with neo-Nazi ties have gained political clout, or in this country, where people with white supremacist affiliations have increased access to government officials.

There are Jewish leaders on both the right and the left who have argued that in the realm of public advocacy you cannot agree with your allies on everything. I concede that this is a reality and that politics does, indeed, sometimes make for strange bedfellows. But I cannot make common cause with putative allies who, deep down, harbor contempt for me and my group—or for any other racial, religious, or identity group, for that matter. My self-respect, my abhorrence of prejudice, and my recognition of their attempts to dismantle the democratic institutions that I love preclude any alliances with them.

This will be a lonely and unpleasant fight, especially when it entails taking issue with those whom we have long called allies. But if we continue to speak the truth, not just to those with whom we disagree, but to our compatriots as well, we will emerge with our values and our self-respect intact, our voices heard, and—we must continue to hope—our goals achieved.

Yours,
DEL

·VII·

Oy versus Joy:
Rejecting Victimhood

MISSING THE FOREST FOR THE TREES:
A DENTAL SCHOOL AND A FRATERNITY

Dear Professor Lipstadt:

I know that our conversation is winding down, but I had a strange encounter on a plane flying back to school after the break and felt I had to share it with you. I got into a conversation with my seatmate, a Jewish woman who saw me reading some books for one of your Jewish history courses. We talked about the class and about Emory. I sensed that there was something she wanted to ask and, finally, she did: "How can you, a committed Jew, go to Emory, given what's happened there?" When I looked surprised, she responded that she had heard that Emory had some serious problems with antisemitism. I was quite taken aback. Nothing I have encountered on campus would rise to the level of "serious problems." With the exception of my Mutterer, most of what I have encountered would not even rise to the level of "problems." When I asked her to elaborate, she was fuzzy on the details but remembered something about the Emory dental school and about a Jewish fraternity at Emory. A quick Internet search revealed information about the incidents to which she was referring. In 2014, large swastikas and overtly antisemitic slogans were painted on the Alpha Epsilon Pi (AEPi) fraternity house at Emory. Parents posted some rather distraught comments about the incident. They stressed that they had sent their children to Emory because it was an intellectually challenging institution with solid moral and ethical standards, and that they had believed it was a university that would allow their kids to be fully comfortable as Jews—especially in a historically Jewish fraternity such as AEPi. As one parent put it, we thought this campus was a "safe place for Jews." Some parents mentioned working the phones and social media to make sure that this incident got maximum publicity.

Then I went looking for the dental school story. That was more disturbing. My search revealed that, over the course of the 1950s and into the 1960s, Jewish students had been intentionally and groundlessly flunked out of the dental school. Unlike the AEPi incident, this unfair practice was not a "one off" but seemed like a secret policy to keep Jews from graduating from the dental school. I know that you weren't here during those years, but you were here when the fraternity house was vandalized. What's the story? Is this something Jewish students at Emory should be worried about today?

Yours,
Abigail

Dear Abigail and Joe:

As it happens, Abigail, your experience on the plane leads me to something that has been nagging at me throughout our conversations. Though I share this letter with Joe, my words here are directed at you, Abigail, and our fellow Jews. But first some background about both of these stories.

Regarding the AEPi incident: Having swastikas and antisemitic slogans painted on your home—which is what a fraternity house becomes to its members—would be disconcerting enough whenever it happens. It was particularly painful in this case, because it came but a few hours after the conclusion of Yom Kippur. Within a short while, the fraternity house was swarming with police, investigators, deans, and other concerned folks. Some parents called me and I tried to calm them down, but without much success. This was probably my fault, as I told them they might be overreacting to what was essentially a small act.

"A *small* act!" one of them exploded. "You've spent your professional life studying antisemitism and antisemites. You are an outspoken critic of antisemites. Now *you* are telling *me* not to overreact? And what exactly is a *small* act of antisemitism? Shouldn't there be a zero-tolerance policy for *any* act of antisemitism?"

The parents with whom I spoke were right to be confused. As I have said in our exchanges, genocide begins with words and not with acts of violence. But these words are often the precursors to violence. How then can I speak of overreactions? Moreover, *is* there such a thing as *over*sensitivity to prejudice and hatred? In the passions of the moment, I had failed to explain properly that I was taking into consideration context and proportionality in this particular incident. Even as we seethe with anger, we must act strategically, not passionately. The stakes are too high to do otherwise. We must assess each "assault" and ask, Is this just a prank by high school kids who don't really know the meaning of the swastika that they are painting on a synagogue or a Jewish fraternity house? Will a strong reaction by the media produce copycats who also want to have their handiwork appear on the evening news? The AEPi incident was clearly not part of a concerted attack by extremists with the potential to do long-term harm. I'm not sure if the graffitists were "influencers" who embolden haters, or just ignorant, sorry souls who don't really know what the symbols they painted represent. It was, however, critical that the identities of the perpetrators be determined and that they not only be punished but also be made to understand the severity of their actions. Even if they had not fully appreciated the significance of the swastika as a symbol, their vandalism could not be excused. If, however, it had been determined that the vandals were part of a group that was motivated by ideology, then a very different response would be in order.

But there's a second chapter to this story, one that your seatmate clearly did not know. Less than twenty-four hours after the incident, two important emails showed up in my mailbox. The first was an eloquent and passionate condemnation of the vandalization from the university's president. It had been sent to every person with an Emory mailbox—tens of thousands of people. He described this act as the antithesis of all that Emory stood for. I wasn't surprised that he wrote this; I would have expected no less. What I didn't expect was the second email. Short and direct, it came from the president of the Student Council:

> The Student Government Association Executive Board condemns the reprehensible act of bigotry carried out against the Alpha Epsilon Pi fraternity, the Jewish community, and the entire Emory community. The individuals responsible have sickened us.
>
> Emory students engage in conversations about our differences. . . . We affirm each other's identities. In everything we do, we strive for courageous inquiry. Used in this way, the swastika represents the systematic silencing and murder of human beings because of their iden-

tities. In this context, there is nothing courageous about a swastika.

We are committed to making sure that this moment of anger is a springboard for action. . . . We invite you to wear blue on Monday in support of Emory's Jewish community and the rights of all people to live freely and safely.

Though I wasn't scheduled to teach until late that Monday afternoon, my curiosity got the best of me. So, early in the day, I headed off to campus. Undergraduates, graduate students, professors, administrators, and secretaries were all wearing blue. The campus was awash in blue. Some students even hung navy blue bedsheets out of their windows. Just to make sure I wasn't imagining things or mistaking someone's fashion choice for an ideological statement, I asked people why they were wearing blue. Invariably, their answers were variations on the same theme: "We are showing the swastika-drawers that they don't speak for us." "We are not standing silently by." "The bad guys lost. The good guys won."

Why do I stress this part of the story? Because too often, when the details of the antisemitic vandalism at AEPi are recounted, this chapter falls by the wayside. Yet it's the heart of the story. I am repeatedly told by people that Emory must have a significant antisemitism problem. When I request specifics, I am invariably told about the AEPi swastika incident. I then ask if the person knows the rest of the story. And, just as invariably, they don't. What's important is not that a couple of kids decided to do something that was hateful and repulsive, but that an entire campus community stood up and said: not in our name. The perpetrators were indeed punished. But the real story—the response of the Emory community—should have been given just as much prominence.

What about the charges of discriminatory behavior at the dental school? For almost twenty years after World War II, Emory University's dental school, along with many of the most selective schools in the nation, operated under a *numerus clausus* (literally, "closed number," or quota) system. This was designed to prevent "too many" non-WASPS (which is to say, Jews) from being admitted.[1] (That blacks were to be kept out went without saying.) The schools knew that if they accepted applicants based solely on their academic records, more Jews than they considered "desirable" would be admitted. Bigotry trumped merit.

From 1948 to 1961, a small number of young Jewish men would be accepted to the Emory dental school each year. The school's dean, John Buhler, believed that Jews did not "have it in the hands" for dentistry, but he did not control the admissions process. Before the end of each school year Buhler would see to it that the few Jewish students who had been admitted were either flunked out or forced to repeat the year. Their lives were, in the words of one student, "a living hell." The students who had flunked out then had the humiliating task of informing their astonished parents, many of whom were immigrants who were heavily invested in their children's education and took great pride in their accomplishments. To this day, the expelled students still recall their parents' responses: "Couldn't you have worked harder? Studied more?" Many of these men went on to other dental schools and had stellar careers in dentistry. Some went to medical school. One became a cardiac surgeon. But, continuing to bear their humiliation privately, most never told their spouses and children about their "failure."

The situation at Emory changed in 1961, when some of the

victimized students tried to make their case for antisemitism on the part of the dental school to local Jewish organizations. Told that they were simply trying to make excuses for their failures, the students then approached Art Levin, who was a regional director of the Anti-Defamation League and who proceeded to compile statistics showing that, from 1948 to 1961, while 65 percent of the Jewish students at the dental school were either flunking out or being forced to repeat the year, only 4 percent of the Jewish students in the medical school met the same fate. When university administrators were presented with this data, and with the fact that the dental school application form included a space where the applicant had to check "Caucasian," "Jew," or "Other," they denied that antisemitism was involved— but also said that it wouldn't happen anymore. Dean Buhler resigned—unrelated to the charges of antisemitism, insisted the university leaders—and the issue faded away.

The story might have ended there but for an exhibit in 2006 on the history of Jewish life at Emory that included the ADL's chart from 1961 that demonstrated the extent of the discrimination at the dental school beginning in 1948. Dr. Perry Brickman, a prominent Atlanta oral surgeon who was one of the Jews who had been flunked out of the dental school in 1952, attended the opening of the exhibit, and I was standing next to him when he saw the chart. He knew of Dean Buhler's antisemitism, but he had no idea of the more than decadelong pattern of discrimination. Shocked at this statistic, Dr. Brickman proceeded to spend the next four years finding and conducting filmed interviews with other Jewish students who had been expelled from the dental school during the period in question. Their work, even if it was far better than that of their non-Jewish classmates, was never considered good enough. Many of these septuagenarians emotionally recounted their experiences and their parents' shame. After compiling his information, Dr. Brickman brought it and his film to the university. Remembering his dental school experience, he fully expected to be rebuffed. Much to Dr. Brickman's surprise (but not to the surprise of current faculty members), the chairman of the board of trustees, the president, and the provost all agreed that Emory had to acknowledge this wrong publicly.

As a result, in October 2012 a few dozen of the expelled Jewish dental students were invited to a special event at Emory. They came from all corners of the United States, with spouses, children, grandchildren, and colleagues in tow. After a private meeting with the president and university trustees, they entered a large auditorium for a screening of the documentary film Dr. Brickman and Emory professor Eric Goldstein had created from the videotaped interviews. They were amazed to find a standing-room-only crowd. University president James Wagner stepped up to the podium, looked down at the former students and their families seated before him, and—departing from his prepared text—said, "I am sorry. We are sorry." There were tears in the eyes of many of the men. Wagner did not say, in the all-too-familiar manner of so many public figures who have been caught doing wrong, "if anyone was hurt, I am sorry," or "it didn't happen on my watch but, nonetheless, I am sorry." Rather, he acknowledged that such behavior diminished the university, and he bemoaned the fact that it took so long for this apology to come.

What happened at the Emory dental school is not unique. For many years, American institutions of higher learning were rife with prejudice and discrimination. In recent times, many schools, Emory included, have acknowledged and apologized for the fact that slave labor was used to construct their buildings in the eighteenth and nineteenth centuries. Sadly, of course, these apologies did not come while any of the slaves were alive to hear them.

What your seatmate recalled was only part of the story of antisemitism at Emory. The more important part of the story is how the current university administration responded when they learned of the wrongs that had been committed. Not only was their response appropriate and admirable, it also illustrated how much America has changed. The terrible history of discrimination in America's universities cannot be ignored. But when proper amends are made or sincere apologies are offered, we must include them as an essential part of the story. If we don't do this, we run the risk of casting ourselves as perennial victims, and we also diminish those who have come forward to acknowledge with sincere contrition the wrongs committed by their institutions. We must allow ourselves to be reassured and encouraged by the fact that the same schools that openly maintained quotas against Jews in the past now have extensive campus Jewish studies programs and Jewish student life, and, in some cases, have or have had a Jewish president.

The swastika incident and the dental school story were causes for "oy." Emory's responses were causes for "joy" and a reminder that we Jews do not stand alone, but have many allies who are acting not just out of solidarity with the Jews in their midst but also because these incidents represent assaults on the society of which they are part. Isn't that an—if not *the*—essential part of this story?

Yours,
DEL

SPEAKING TRUTH TO FRIENDS:
BEYOND VICTIMHOOD

Dear Deborah:

I want to thank you for spending so much time in correspondence with me and with Abigail. Given that in your most
recent letters you've focused on what we should *not* do, I want
to raise one last topic. I admit to having been a bit reluctant to
bring this up, but I must because for me it is the elephant sitting
in the middle of the room.

In recent years, when the subject of Israel has come up and
I am with my Jewish friends, I have found myself behaving like
some of the Jewish students you have described in your letters:
self-censoring. The Israeli government has taken some actions
that have troubled me greatly. Yet I'm reluctant to share my feelings with my Jewish friends, who might be hurt by what I say,
and with some of my non-Jewish friends, who might take this
as license to launch their own, less tempered attacks on Israel.
And so I don't speak up because I fear that my criticisms—
which I think are valid—will be misinterpreted as unfair and
even as antisemitic. If anything has become crystal clear to me
as a result of our exchanges, it's how much—though absolutely
not all—of the criticism of Israel relies on antisemitic motifs or
is simply a cover for antisemitism.

I've visited Israel a number of times and have enjoyed those
trips tremendously. It's an impressive place. I host scholars from

Israeli law schools at our law school. But I continue to keep silent. I know that what I have to say has the potential to cause pain and offense. And if I cause pain, I know I will not be heard. Your honesty in your letters has given me the courage to admit this. How do I, as a non-Jew, speak critically about policies of the Israeli government that I may find troubling without being misunderstood? Is this even possible?

Your friend,
Joe

Dear Joe:

Your voice is greatly respected both on and off the campus. You have a long record of speaking truth to all, and you have repeatedly shown your support of and solidarity with Jews. You, above all, must not be afraid to speak out when you feel that the Israeli government is deserving of criticism. If Israel's advocates want your support, they must be prepared to hear your critique. You will not be branded an antisemite, except by those who automatically categorize any negative comment about Israel as antisemitism—and you know what I think of them. In fact, you will be heard by the very people who are desperate to find a solution to the problems that plague Israel today.

Up to this point in our correspondence I've tried to speak analytically and professorially. But now I'd like to speak more as a Jew. This may sound strange, after our extended exchange about antisemitism, but in my opinion, antisemitism is not the greatest threat facing Jews today. Don't get me wrong: I wouldn't spend my time teaching and writing about this subject if I didn't think it posed a threat today to both Jews in particular and the world as a whole. But if antisemitism becomes the sole focus of our concerns, we run the risk of seeing the entire Jewish experience through the eyes of the people who hate us.

I am hardly the first person to caution against this danger. More than eight decades ago, one of the great historians of the Jewish people, Columbia University professor Salo Wittmayer Baron (the first person in the United States to hold a named professorship in Jewish history at a secular university) cautioned against succumbing to "the lachrymose conception of Jewish history." Writing in the mid-1930s, as the Third Reich was beginning to cast its shadow over Europe, Baron pointed to the prevailing perception of the Jewish experience as a "sheer succession of miseries and persecutions." These bad experiences loomed so large in the Jewish people's collective memory that they eclipsed the multitude of positive and noteworthy accomplishments that fill Jewish history. Baron was hardly an unrealistic optimist. He was born in Tarnów, Galicia, which before World War II had a large, thriving Jewish community with schools, synagogues, and a host of charitable and cultural institutions. When he returned after the war he found that his community had been obliterated. But he understood that focusing only on what has been lost negates centuries of extraordinary economic, intellectual, and communal achievements. It allows the "oy" rather than "joy" to become the prism through which our view of the Jewish past is refracted.

In his 1948 essay "Israel: The Ever-Dying People," the philosopher and historian Simon Rawidowicz addressed this phenomenon of Jewish pessimism. "The world makes many images of Israel," he wrote. "But Israel makes only one image of itself: that of being constantly on the verge of ceasing to be, of disappearing." With good historical reason, Jews have long been inclined to assume that some sort of catastrophe was just around the bend. This, of course, fits my earlier description of the Jewish optimist as someone who thinks things cannot get any worse. The pessimist is certain they can and will get worse, but is not sure precisely how soon. Both traditionalists and secularists have frequently expressed pessimism about the future of the Jewish people. From the earliest rabbinic writings in the first and second centuries of the Common Era to the twentieth-century Zionist poets, our literature is filled with predictions that this generation might well constitute the "final link in Israel's chain." Some feared that the end would come through physical destruction at the hands of an enemy. Others were convinced that it would be caused by internal apathy or too great a faith in the promise of emancipation and enlightenment.

For Rawidowicz, this Jewish view of itself as "ever-dying" is in fact a psychological coping mechanism, a kind of "protective individual and collective emotion." By anticipating the worst, Jews protect themselves from being blindsided by bad turns of events. In anticipating a cataclysmic end, they prepare themselves for it and "become its master." No disaster could take Israel "by surprise . . . put it off its balance . . . obliterate it."[1] The upside is that this teaches us to be on guard in a legitimately dangerous world. The downside is that this worldview could become the sum total of our identity.

I tell you all this because I don't want you to see Jews as perennial victims who must be coddled. We are not. Do not fear speaking truth to us because you worry that it might hurt or offend us. We cherish people like you who have stood by our side not out of pity or guilt, but because hatred in all its forms is something you cannot abide and because you recognize that antisemitism is a threat to the well-being of any just and democratic society.

Despite the fact that only seven decades ago one out of every three Jews on the face of the earth was murdered, the Jewish people thrive today as a culture, a community, and a nation. There are many explanations for this, and one of them is that good friends like you stand with us. And good friends speak truth—not just to power, but to one another.

Your appreciative colleague,
DEL

CELEBRATING THE GOOD
IN THE FACE OF THE BAD

Dear Professor Lipstadt:

I write to thank you very much for the time you've spent these past few months in dialogue with Professor Wilson and me. Our exchanges have helped me put a painful phenomenon into perspective and to understand its conspiratorial and delusional qualities. I feel that I'll be able to fight it more effectively now. I'm also committed to battling against other forms of discrimination, for moral as well as strategic reasons. In my metaphorical toolbox are both a scalpel and an ax. I will be careful to discern when to use one and when to use the other. Thank you for giving me the information and the courage to proceed.

Your student,
Abigail

Dear Abigail:

Thank you so much for your kind words. I'm particularly gratified that you feel so committed to this fight. But, as usual, something is gnawing at me. And so knowing that but a few months ago you were handed your diploma, and now are about to go out into the real world and become my former student, let me leave you with one more thought.

Thus far, I've tried to avoid making our exchange a cri de coeur and to speak instead as dispassionately as possible. But now I'm speaking to you from my heart, not about what the antisemite might do to us, but about what we are in danger of doing to *ourselves.*

Most Jews will immediately step forward when Jews anywhere are being attacked by antisemites. This is of course as it should be. What is regrettable, however, is that for some Jews, the fight against antisemitism becomes the sum total of their Jewish identity. Recently, a much-respected Jewish communal leader lamented to me that he regretted not having educated his children about Jewish traditions and culture. He was, however, very proud of the fact that he had embedded within them a total intolerance of antisemitism. His kids were prepared to be at the barricades to do battle against this hatred, and many others as well. His comments made me sad. Antisemitism has become the drummer to which his family's Jewish identity marches. They know of Jew as object, not subject. In other words, what is done *to* Jews becomes far more significant than what Jews *do.* This well-intentioned Jewish father has deprived his children of a rich and multifaceted legacy. They have been taught to see themselves mainly as perennial victims. This cedes to the oppressor control over one's destiny. It leaves many Jews, including this man's children, aware of what to be *against* but not what to be *for.*

I have repeatedly stressed that antisemitism is a delusional form of hatred. It conjures a malign image of the Jew that does not in fact exist, and then it proceeds to find it everywhere. But we cannot allow this delusion to lead to another delusion—

that because this hatred is, unfortunately, ever present, we must make fighting it the fulcrum upon which our identity pivots.

What is necessary for Jews to survive and flourish as a people is neither dark pessimism nor cockeyed optimism, but realism. It would be ludicrous to dismiss as paranoid the concerns of those who react strongly to the escalating acts of antisemitism in recent times. In countries throughout the world, armed guards are now regularly stationed in front of synagogues, and Jewish communal organizations have had to institute tight security measures. In some parts of the world, Jews intentionally avoid carrying or wearing anything that identifies them as Jews. But at the same time, it would be folly for Jews to make this the organizing principle of their lives.

Although I have devoted most of my professional life to the study of the persecution of the Jews, that has never been what has driven me personally as a Jew. I value and celebrate my tradition and its teachings. My awareness of the many grievous wrongs that have been perpetrated against Jews throughout history is not the foundation of my Jewish identity. Jewish culture and Jewish history constitute the foundation of who I am. This dichotomy was starkly illustrated during a recent Jewish holiday, as I entered my synagogue along with two friends—a five-year-old girl and her mother. The mom smiled at the security guard stationed at the door, turned to her daughter, and said, "Let's say hi and thank you to the guard for keeping us safe." A look of puzzlement swept across my little friend's face. From the many books we have read together, she knows about "safe" places and "dangerous" places, and in her mind a synagogue did not fall under the latter category. It's a joyful place where she runs around with the other kids in the playground, attends a children's service that is filled with singing, and then wends her way into the main sanctuary, where she and her play-mates help conclude the services and receive lollipops from the rabbi. Why would she need someone to help keep her safe in such a place? Yet we know that she does, indeed, need protection there. My hope for my little friend is that as she grows up, her awareness of the dangers that may threaten her well-being at the synagogue or any other Jewish venue will never over-shadow the joys she finds there.

And my hope for you, Abigail, is not dissimilar. Should you choose to, you can participate in a vibrant Jewish future. You will encounter antisemitism along the way, but I entreat you to avoid letting this "longest hatred" become the linchpin of your identity. Jewish tradition in all its manifestations—religious, secular, intellectual, communal, artistic, and so much more—is far too valuable to be tossed aside and replaced with a singular concentration on the fight against hatred.

This need for Jews to balance the "oy" with the "joy" is an exhortation that could well be shared with many other groups that have become the objects of discrimination and prejudice. To you and all your peers whom I have had the good fortune to have taught, and whose questions have inspired me to explore this topic from a variety of perspectives, I say, in the words of the Hebrew Scriptures, "be strong and of good courage."[1] Never stop fighting the good fight, even as you rejoice in who you are.

Your grateful teacher,
DEL

ACKNOWLEDGMENTS

I am appreciative of the support I have received from Emory's Tam Institute for Jewish Studies Judith London Evans Director Fund, and TIJS chair Eric L. Goldstein. My other academic home at Emory, the Department of Religion, and its chair, Gary Laderman, have consistently been generous in their support of my work. I am grateful to the myriad people who, over the course of my many years of thinking about this issue, have helped to make this a better book. They have contributed in countless ways: challenging my ideas, expanding my vision, strongly rejecting or affirming my arguments and conclusions. I have listened carefully to their comments—to those that supported what I wrote and, even more carefully, to those that did not. Their fingerprints are on all that is good in this book. Its shortcomings and mistakes are entirely my own.

To my editor, Altie Karper, and her team at Schocken, my thanks for your careful attention to the manuscript. I am deeply grateful for the care with which you have treated this work and the enthusiasm you have expressed about it. My agent, Gary Morris, was the first one to urge me to write a book on this topic. I demurred. He insisted. I am glad he did. My thanks to him and his colleagues at David Black Agency. My thanks also to Ben Ogden, who helped with research and checking citations.

Elka Abrahamson, Jon Boyd, Perry Brickman, Erica Brown, Michael Broyde, Jonathan Freedland, Eric Goldstein, Natalie Grazin, Anthony Julius, Jonathan Rosen, Chaim Seidler-Feller, Judith Shulevitz, Kenneth S. Stern, Kenneth Waltzer, Myra Weiss, and Mark Yudof read the manuscript in its entirety or portions thereof (sometimes more than once). They offered their insights and their critiques with a generosity of spirit that far outstripped any obligations of friendship or collegiality. I am very grateful. For many years, Leslie Wexner has been my frequent and treasured interlocutor on this painful topic. Without the innumerable conversations and email exchanges I have had with my students at Emory and the various programs of the Wexner Foundation, this book would not have come to be.

How good and pleasant it is to have such friends, students, and conversation partners.

NOTES

A NOTE TO THE READER

1. L. Daniel Staetsky, *Antisemitism in Contemporary Great Britain: A Study of Attitudes towards Jews and Israel* (London: Institute for Jewish Policy Research, 2017), pp. 3–5.

A DELUSION

1. Chip Berlet and Matthew Nemiroff Lyons, *Right-Wing Populism in America: Too Close for Comfort* (New York: Guilford Press, 2000), p. 9.
2. Cass R. Sunstein and Adrian Vermeule, "Conspiracy Theories" (working paper, Public Law & Legal Theory Working Paper No. 199, University of Chicago, 2008), pp. 6, 7.

A DEFINITION

1. 378 U.S. at 197 (Stewart, J., concurring) (emphasis added).
2. Jane O'Reilly, "The Housewife's Moment of Truth," *New York* magazine, December 20, 1971 (*Ms.* originally appeared as a forty-page insert in *New York* magazine).
3. Joshua Cherniss and Henry Hardy, "Isaiah Berlin," *Stanford Encyclopedia of Philosophy,* September 21, 2016.
4. European Forum on Antisemitism, "Working Definition on Antisemitism," http://european-forum-on-antisemitism.org/.
5. Arthur Miller, *Focus* (New York: Arbor House, 1984).
6. Italics in original. Helen Fein, "Dimensions of Antisemitism: Attitudes, Collective Accusations, and Actions," in Helen Fein, ed., *The Persisting: Sociological Perspectives and Social Contexts of Modern Antisemitism* (Berlin and New York: De Gruyter, 1987), p. 67.
7. Review of Arthur Hertzberg, *The Chosen People,* in *New York Review of Books,* October 24, 1968.
8. Kathleen Belew, *Bring the War Home: The White Power Movement and Paramilitary America* (Cambridge, MA: Harvard University Press, 2018), pp. ix–x.

9. Monika Schwarz-Friesel and Jehuda Reinharz, *Inside the Antisemitic Mind: The Language of Jew-Hatred in Contemporary Germany* (Waltham, MA: Brandeis University Press, 2017), pp. 29, 32.

10. Charles Y. Glock and Rodney Stark, *Christian Belief and Anti-Semitism* (New York: Harper & Row, 1966), p. 102.

11. Joseph Sungolowsky, "Criticism of Anti-Semite and Jew," *Yale French Studies* 30 (1963): 68–72.

12. Anthony Julius, *Trials of the Diaspora* (London: Oxford University Press, 2010), p. xliii.

13. Jean-Paul Sartre, *Anti-Semite and Jew* (Paris: Schocken Books, 1948), pp. 10–11.

14. I thank Anthony Julius for this approach to fighting not just antisemitism but the antisemite as well. It is how he understood my legal defense against David Irving, whom the court declared to be a falsifier of history and a neo-Nazi polemicist. For transcripts, reports submitted to the court, and witness testimony, see www.hdot.org.

A SPELLING

1. Philologos, "Should Anti-Semitism Be Hyphenated?" *Forward*, November 18, 2012.

2. Moshe Zimmerman, *Wilhelm Marr: The Patriarch of Anti-Semitism* (New York: Oxford University Press, 1987).

3. Philologos, "Should Anti-Semitism Be Hyphenated?"

THE EXTREMIST: FROM THE STREETS TO THE INTERNET

1. Jonathan Weisman, *(((Semitism))): Being Jewish in America in the Age of Trump* (New York: St. Martin's Press, 2018), p. 20.

2. Belew, *Bring the War Home*, p. 238.

3. For a deconstruction of the various flags marchers carried at the rally, see "Deconstructing the Symbols and Slogans Spotted in Charlottesville," *Washington Post*, August 18, 2017.

4. Lauren M. Fox, "The Hatemonger Next Door," *Salon*, September 29, 2013.

5. Louis Jacobson, "Donald Trump's 'Star of David' Tweet: A Recap," Politifact.com, July 5, 2016.

6. "A Dark and Constant Rage: 25 Years of Right-Wing Terrorism in the United States," Anti-Defamation League, May 2017; Bill Morlin, "ACT's Anti-Muslim Message Fertile Ground for Oath Keepers," Southern Poverty Law Center, June 12, 2017; Weisman, *(((Semitism)))*, p. 21.

7. Brian Levin, "Special Status Report: Hate Crime in the Cities and Counties in the U.S.," Center for the Study of Hate and Extremism at California State University at San Bernardino, 2016, p. 12.

8. James Comey, "The FBI and the ADL: Working Together to Fight Hate," *FBI: Speeches,* May 8, 2017, www.fbi.gov/news/speeches/the-fbi -and-the-adl-working-together-to-fight-hate.

9. Caitlin MacNeal, "Comey: Twitter Is Like 'Every Dive Bar in America,'" *Talking Points Memo,* May 8, 2017; Weisman, *(((Semitism))),* p. 122.

10. "Aryan Nations," *Southern Poverty Law Center,* www.splcenter.org/ fighting-hate/extremist-files/group/aryan-nations.

11. *Conspiracy Theories in American History: An Encyclopedia,* ed. Peter Knight (Santa Barbara, CA: ABC-CLIO, 2003), p. 758.

12. UPI Archives, "House Holds First Militia Hearings," November 2, 1995, www.upi.com/Archives/1995/11/02/House-holds-first-militia -hearings/9848815288400/; ADL, "Aryan Nations/Church of Jesus Christ Christian," 2013. http://archive.adl.org/learn/ext_us/aryan _nations.html; Kenneth Stern, "Foreword to Paperback Edition," in *Force upon the Plain* (New York: Simon and Schuster, 1996), pp. 7–8; Belew, *Bring the War Home,* p. 236.

13. Arie Perliger, *Challengers from the Sidelines: Understanding America's Violent Far-Right* (West Point, NY: Combatting Terrorism Center, 2013).

14. Kenneth S. Stern, email, July 23, 2017.

15. Bethany Mandel, "My Trump Tweets Earned Me So Many Anti-Semitic Haters That I Bought a Gun," *Forward,* March 21, 2016; Lloyd Grove, "How Breitbart Unleashes Hate Mobs to Threaten, Dox, and Troll Trump Critics," *Daily Beast,* March 1, 2016.

16. Cooper Fleishman and Anthony Smith, "(((Echoes))), Exposed: The Secret Symbol Neo-Nazis Use to Target Jews Online," Mic, June 1, 2016.

17. Jonathan Weisman, "The Nazi Tweets of 'Trump God Emperor,'" *New York Times,* May 29, 2016.

18. Julia Ioffe, "Melania Trump on Her Rise, Her Family Secrets, and Her True Political Views: 'Nobody Will Ever Know,'" *GQ,* April 27, 2016; Josefin Dolsten, "Journalist Flooded with Neo-Nazi Hate after Writing Melania Trump Profile," *Forward,* April 29, 2016; Lauren Gambino, "Journalist Who Profiled Melania Trump Hit with Barrage of Antisemitic Abuse," *Guardian,* April 26, 2016.

19. Laura Silverman, "Trump Backers' Anti-Semitic Taunts and Threats," *Atlanta Jewish Times,* August 1, 2016; Nicholas Kristof, "Donald

Trump Is Making America Meaner," *New York Times,* August 13, 2016.

20. NPR, "Atlantic Editor on Acrimony in U.S.: 'I Have to Imagine That It Actually Gets Worse,'" *Morning Edition,* October 24, 2016, www .npr.org/2016/10/24/498860864/atlantic-editor-on-acrimony-in-u-s -i-have-to-imagine-that-it-actually-gets-worse.

21. Belew, *Bring the War Home,* pp. 237–38.

22. "'Hail Trump!': Richard Spencer Speech Excerpts," *Atlantic,* November 21, 2016, www.youtube.com/watch?v=106-bi3jlxk; "As Trump Disavows 'Alt-Right' Support, Critics Question If He Will Still Normalize White Supremacy," *Democracy Now,* November 23, 2016.

23. Joseph Bernstein, "Alt-White: How the Breitbart Machine Laundered Racist Hate," *BuzzFeed,* October 5, 2017; "Milo Yiannopoulos and White Supremacists at Karaoke," www.youtube.com/watch?v= XLNLPIRS62g.

24. Ben Shapiro, "The Breitbart Alt-Right Just Took Over the GOP," *Washington Post,* August 18, 2016.

25. David French, "The Race Obsessed Left Has Released a Monster It Cannot Control," *National Review,* January 26, 2016.

ANTISEMITIC ENABLERS

1. Nicholas Kristof, "Is Donald Trump a Racist?" *New York Times,* July 23, 2017.

2. David Weigel, "'Racialists' Are Cheered by Trump's Latest Strategy," *Washington Post,* August 20, 2016.

3. Jane Eisner, "Why Trump Likes Jews Like Cohen and Dershowitz— For All the Wrong Reasons," *Forward,* April 13, 2018.

4. "Trump Won't Condemn Anti-Semitic Threats on Journalist Who Profiled His Wife (VIDEO)," http://talkingpointsmemo.com/live wire/trump-julia-ioffe-anti-semitic-threats; Mickey Rapkin, "Lady and the Trump," *DuJour,* May 2016; Weisman, *(((Semitism))),* pp. 15– 16, 143.

5. Weisman, *(((Semitism))),* p. 129; Donald Trump, "I Don't Know David Duke," *Morning Joe,* MSNBC, November 14, 2016 (television), www.youtube.com/watch?v=YBOy8iTBA9g; Glenn Kessler, "Donald Trump and David Duke: For the Record," *Washington Post,* March 1, 2016.

6. Weisman, *(((Semitism))),* p. 147.

7. Ibid., p. 29.

8. Trump did subsequently say that it was a mistake to change it because it was a sheriff's star. Critics pointed out that sheriff's stars, while six-pointed, have little circles at the point of each star. Louis Jacobson, "Donald Trump's 'Star of David' Tweet: A Recap," *Politifact,* July 5, 2016; Bryce Covert, "Trump Tries to Spin Anti-Semitic Symbol as 'Sheriff's Star,'" *Think Progress,* July 4, 2016.

9. Tal Kopan, "Donald Trump Retweets 'White Genocide' Twitter User," CNN.com, January 22, 2016; Ben Kharakh and Dan Primack, "Donald Trump's Social Media Ties to White Supremacists," *Fortune,* March 22, 2016; Weisman, *(((Semitism))),* p. 158.

10. Niraj Chokshi, "Trump Accuses Clinton of Guiding Global Elite against U.S. Working Class," *New York Times,* October 13, 2016.

11. Deborah Lipstadt, "Didn't Slam Anti-Semitism on the Left? Don't Expect Credibility When You Slam It on the Right," *Forward,* November 27, 2016; Yehuda Kurtzer, "Our Friends and Farrakhan: A Plea to Progressives," *Times of Israel,* March 7, 2018.

12. Andrew Anglin, "Happening: Trump Retweets Two More White Genocide Accounts Back-to-Back," *Daily Stormer,* January 25, 2016.

13. "Meet a Supremacist Energized by Trump," BBC.co.uk, September 22, 2016.

14. Aram Roston and Joel Anderson, "The Moneyman Behind the Alt-Right," *Buzzfeed News,* 2017, https://soundcloud.com/audmapp/excerpt-the-moneyman-behind-the-alt-right-buzzfeed-news.

15. Kharakh and Primack, "Donald Trump's Social Media Ties to White Supremacists."

16. Scott Malone and Jeff Mason, "Trump Yields to Pressure, Calls Neo-Nazis and KKK Criminals," Reuters.com, August 14, 2018.

17. Glenn Thrush, "New Outcry as Trump Rebukes Charlottesville Racists 2 Days Later," *New York Times,* August 14, 2017; Tamara Keith, "President Trump Stands by Original Charlottesville Remarks," NPR, September 14, 2017.

18. Samantha Schmidt, "Trump Retweets Right-Wing Provocateur Known for Pushing False Conspiracy Theories," *Washington Post,* August 15, 2017.

19. Thrush, "New Outcry as Trump Rebukes Charlottesville Racists 2 Days Later"; Keith, "President Trump Stands by Original Charlottesville Remarks."

20. Alan Johnson, "Antisemitic Anti-Zionism and the Left," *Jewish Chronicle,* September 10, 2015.

21. James Bloodworth, "Why Is No One Asking about Jeremy Corbyn's Worrying Connections?," *Guardian,* August 13, 2015.

22. Reverend Nick Howard, "The Asymmetry of Racism Awareness," *Standpoint* magazine, January/February 2012.

23. Chip Berlet, ed., *Constructing Campus Conflict: Antisemitism and Islamophobia on U.S. College Campuses, 2007–2011* (Somerville, MA: Policy Research Associates, 2014), p. 14.

24. Jerry Lewis, "UK Vicar Attends Tehran 'Zionist Lobby' Conference," *Jerusalem Post,* October 6, 2014; John Bingham, "Church of England Vicar Denies Backing 'Anti-Semitic Hate-fest' in Iran," *Telegraph,* October 6, 2014.

25. Marcus Dysch, "Sizer: I Am Ready to Meet the Board of Deputies Any Time," *Jewish Chronicle,* April 11, 2012; Jake Wallis Simons, "Jeremy Corbyn Defends a Controversial Vicar Who Was Banned from Social Media for Sharing 'Clearly Anti-Semitic' Material Blaming Israel for 9/11 Attacks," *Daily Mail* online, August 9, 2015; Kiran Stacey, "Jeremy Corbyn Attacked as Newspaper Claims Anti-Semitic Links," FinancialTimes.com, August 14, 2015.

26. "Raed Salah, Head of Northern Branch of Islamic Movement in Israel, Espouses Antisemitic Conspiracy Theories about 9/11, Nazi Propaganda," *MEMRI, 9/11 Documentation Project,* Special Dispatch 3982, www.memri.org/report/en/0/0/0/0/0/0/5450.htm.

27. Yoav Stern, "Islamic Movement Head Charged with Incitement to Racism, Violence," *Haaretz,* January 29, 2008.

28. Video of Corbyn making these comments to be found at www .dailymail.co.uk/news/article-3191679/Jeremy-Corbyn-caught-video -calling-Muslim-hate-preacher-honoured-citizen-inviting-tea -terrace-House-Commons.html.

29. "Banned Hate Preacher Who Strolled through Heathrow Is Arrested . . . and He WILL Be Deported Says Home Secretary," *Daily Mail* online, June 29, 2011.

30. Rajeev Syal, "Jeremy Corbyn Says He Regrets Calling Hamas and Hezbollah 'Friends,'" *Guardian,* July 4, 2016.

31. Dyab Abou Jahjah, "Our Collateral Damage, and Theirs!" Media Monitors Network, November 7, 2011.

32. Johnny Paul, "Dutch Court Fines Muslim Group for Holocaust-Denial Cartoon," *Jerusalem Post,* August 28, 2010.

33. Matt Dathan, "Jeremy Corbyn Denies Links to Lebanese 'Extremist' Dyab Abou Jahjah—as Picture Emerges of the Two Sharing a Stage," *Independent,* August 19, 2015.

34. "Corbyn Agrees BBC Are 'Zionist Liars,'" *Guy News,* April 29, 2016, https://order-order.com/2016/04/29/corbyn-agrees-bbc-are-zionist -liars/; Henry Zeffman, "Jeremy Corbyn Hosted Event Likening Israel to Nazis," *Times* (London), August 1, 2018; Yair Rosenberg, "Jeremy Corbyn's Holocaust Memorial Day Statement Leaves Out the Jews," *Tablet,* January 25, 2018.

35. Heather Stewart, "Corbyn in Antisemitism Row after Backing Artist behind 'Offensive' Mural," *Guardian,* March 23, 2018.

36. Stephen Daisley, "Jeremy Corbyn Is Not an Anti-Semite. It's So Much Worse Than That," *STV News,* August 24, 2015, http://stv.tv/ news/politics/1327077-stephen-daisley-on-jeremy-corbyn-the-left -anti-semitism-and-israel/.

37. Paul Waugh, "Momentum Activist Jackie Walker Facing Labour Expulsion over Anti-Semitism," HuffingtonPost.co.uk, March 8, 2017.

38. Tom Mosley, "Labour MP Shocked by '1930s' Anti-Semitism," BBC .co.uk, September 25, 2017; Jonathan Freedland, "Labour Denial of Antisemitism Leaves Party in a Dark Place," *Guardian,* September 27, 2017; Yair Rosenberg, "This BBC Interview Perfectly Illustrates Brit-ain's Left-Wing Anti-Semitism Problem," *Tablet,* September 26, 2017; "Jeremy Corbyn Supporting Hard Left Campaign Group Refuses to Kick Out Activist Jackie Walker over Holocaust Comments," *Sun,* October 4, 2016.

39. Aftab Ali, "Oxford University Labour Club Co-Chair, Alex Chal-mers, Resigns Amid Antisemitism Row," *Independent,* February 17, 2016.

40. Edward Malnick, "'Anti-Semitic' Activist Selected as Labour Candi-date as Leading Donor Quits Party," *Telegraph,* April 1, 2018.

41. Gabriel Pogrund, Jon Ungoed-Thomas, and Richard Kerbaj, "Vitriol and Threats of Violence: The Ugly Face of Jeremy Corbyn's Cabal," *Times* (London), April 1, 2018; Gabriel Pogrund, Jon Ungoed-Thomas, Richard Kerbaj, and Tim Shipman, "Exposed: Jeremy Corbyn's Hate Factory," *Times* (London), April 1, 2018.

42. Verity Bowman and Pippa Crerar, "Corbyn Ally Says 'Jewish Trump Supporters Making Up' Antisemitic Charges," *Guardian,* July 31, 2018; "Jeremy Corbyn Endorses BDS Movement in 2015 Footage," *Haaretz* and *JTA,* August 19, 2018.

43. Lee Harpin, "Anger as Diane Abbott Repeatedly Dismisses Labour's Antisemitism Crisis as 'a Smear Campaign,'" *Jewish Chronicle,* March 29, 2018.

44. Benjamin Kentish, "Thousands of Jeremy Corbyn Supporters Endorse Letter Saying Jewish-Organised Antisemitism Protest Was the Work of 'Very Powerful Special Interest Group,'" *Independent,* March 29, 2018; Michael Savage, "Major Jewish Private Donor Ditches Labour over Antisemitism," *Observer,* April 1, 2018.

45. Jonathan Freedland, "For Corbyn, Precision and Honesty Are the Way Out of This Wreath Mess," *Guardian,* August 13, 2018.

46. Daniel Sugarman, "Jeremy Corbyn: 'Zionists' have 'no sense of English irony despite having lived here all their lives,'" *Jewish Chronicle,* August 23, 2018.

THE DINNER PARTY ANTISEMITE

1. Julius, *Trials of the Diaspora,* p. xxxii.

2. *Telegraph,* July 13, 1996, as cited in Julius, *Trials of the Diaspora,* p. xxxii.

3. We see evidence of this in other instances. In 2017 a doctor in a hospital went on a shooting rampage and killed another person. The headline in one paper read "Doctor Kills Woman." If the victim had been a man, it would have been "Doctor Kills Doctor" (which was what the woman was); http://pix11.com/2017/06/30/active-shooter -reported-at-bronx-lebanon-hospital-police/.

4. Julius, *Trials of the Diaspora,* p. xxxii.

THE CLUELESS ANTISEMITE

1. If the image of the JAP is less prevalent today and is more commonly recognized as being antisemitic, it is due, in no small measure, to publications such as *Lilith* magazine and a small cadre of academics and activists. "Jewish Women Campaign against 'Princess' Jokes," *New York Times,* May 1, 1987.

2. Riv-Ellen Prell, *Fighting to Become Americans* (Boston: Beacon Press, 1999), p. 178.

3. Some critics see it as a "justification, after the fact, of . . . intermarriage." In other words, who would want to marry such a self-centered, selfish, icy woman? Joseph Telushkin, *Jewish Humor: What the Best Jewish Jokes Say about the Jews* (New York: HarperCollins, 1998), as quoted in Leonore Skenazy, "Were Jap Jokes a Justification for Intermarriage?" *Forward,* February 23, 2011.

4. Abraham Foxman, *Jews and Money: The Story of a Stereotype* (New York: Palgrave Macmillan, 2010), as cited in Skenazy, "Were Jap Jokes a Justification for Intermarriage?"

5. Deborah E. Lipstadt, "Anti-Semitism Plays Coy in 'Jewish Princess' Jokes," *Los Angeles Times*, May 25, 1988.
6. Staetsky, *Antisemitism in Contemporary Great Britain*, p. 4.

A COGNITIVE FAILURE?

1. Eve Garrard, "The Pleasures of Antisemitism," *Fathom*, Summer 2013.
2. Alan Riding, "September 11 as Right-Wing U.S. Plot: Conspiracy Theory Sells in France," *New York Times*, June 22, 2002. Among the most comprehensive efforts to debunk these theories was *Popular Mechanics, Debunking 9/11 Myths: Why Conspiracy Theories Can't Stand Up to the Facts*, ed. David Dunbar and Brad Reagan (New York: Hearst Books, 2011).
3. John-Paul Pagano, "Anti-Racism Erases Anti-Semitism," *Tablet*, June 21, 2016.
4. "The 4,000 Jews Rumor: Rumor Surrounding Sept. 11th Proved Untrue," http://usinfo.state.gov/media/Archive/2005/Jan/14-260933.html.
5. "The 4,000 Jews Rumor," International Information Program, USINFO .state.gov, updated January 14, 2005, https://archive.is/e908N.
6. Steven K. Baum, *Antisemitism Explained* (Lanham, MD: University Press of America, 2011), pp. 134–35; Anne Morse, "The Jews Knew?," *National Review*, September 11, 2007.
7. "Al-Qaeda Accuses Iran of 9/11 Lie," BBC.co.uk, News, April 11, 2008.
8. Jeremy Stahl, "Where Did 9/11 Conspiracies Come From?", *Slate*, September 6, 2011.
9. David Gerstman, "Oberlin Professor Claims Israel Was Behind 9/11, ISIS, Charlie Hebdo Attack," *Tower*, February 25, 2016.
10. Matthew Gindin, "Inside the Twisted Anti-Semitic Mind of Oberlin Professor Joy Karega," *Forward*, March 3, 2016.
11. "Majority of Oberlin Faculty Sign Letter Condemning Colleague's Antisemitic Facebook Posts," *Tower*, April 12, 2016.
12. Colleen Flaherty, "Condemning a Colleague: Oberlin Professors Condemn a Professor's Anti-Semitic Remarks on Social Media; Others Refuse to Do So," *Inside Higher Ed*, April 12, 2016.
13. Yair Rosenberg, "The Real Scandal at Oberlin Is Much Bigger than One Professor's Antisemitism," *Tablet*, March 15, 2016.
14. NIST, WTC Disaster Study, www.nist.gov/el/disaster-resilience/ disaster-and-failure-studies/world-trade-center-disaster-study; Jim Dwyer, "2 U.S. Reports Seek to Counter Conspiracy Theories about 9/11," *New York Times*, September 2, 2006.

DELEGITIMIZING ANTISEMITISM: JEWS CAN'T BE VICTIMS

1. "Prejudice," Etymology Online, https://www.etymonline.com/word/prejudice.

2. Philip Roth, "The Last Days of Herman Roth," *New York Times,* December 30, 1990.

3. Finalized Minutes, UCLA Undergraduate Student Council, February 10, 2015 (approved February 17, 2015), https://usac.ucla.edu/documents/minutes/Minutes%202%2010%2015.pdf; "In U.C.L.A. Debate over Jewish Student, Echoes on Campus of Old Biases," *New York Times,* March 5, 2015; David A. Graham, "UCLA's Troubling Question for Jewish Students Everywhere," *Atlantic,* March 7, 2015.

4. Philip Giraldi, "America's Jews Are Driving America's Wars. Shouldn't They Recuse Themselves When Dealing with the Middle East?" *The Unz Review: An Alternative Media Selection,* September 19, 2017; Bret Stephens, "I Believe Some of Your Best Friends Are Jewish," *New York Times,* September 28, 2017; Sophie Tatum, "Ex-CIA Operative Apologizes for Tweet of Anti-Semitic Article," CNN politics.com, September 21, 2017.

ANTISEMITISM AND RACISM: THE SAME YET DIFFERENT

1. Damien Cave and Rochelle Oliber, "The Raw Videos That Have Sparked Outrage over Police Treatment of Blacks," *New York Times,* July 7, 2016.

2. Ta-Nehisi Coates, *Between the World and Me* (New York: Spiegel & Grau, 2015), p. 17.

3. Richard Fausset and Ashley Southall, "Video Shows Officer Flipping Student in South Carolina, Prompting Inquiry," *New York Times,* October 26, 2015.

4. Timothy Williams, "Study Supports Suspicion That Police Are More Likely to Use Force on Blacks," *New York Times,* July 7, 2016.

5. Carly Pildis, "I Am Woke: Why I Am Finally Raising My Voice against Jewish Erasure in the Anti-Racism Movement," *Tablet,* July 6, 2016.

6. Utah v. Streiff (2016), 12, as cited in *New York Times,* July 5, 2016.

7. Amanda Arnold, "Smith College Employee Called the Cops on a Black Student Eating Her Lunch," *The Cut,* August 2, 2018; Sofie Werthan, "Someone Called 911 on a Black Oregon Legislator Campaigning Door-to-Door," *Slate,* July 5, 2018.

8. Rikki Novetsky, "Conflating Causes: Why No Red Tape's Partisan-

ship Is Stifling," *Columbia Current,* Fall 2014; Mira Taichman and Danielle Rinat, "I Am a Jew, a Zionist, an Obie," *Oberlin Review,* March 15, 2013.

9. Pagano, "Anti-Racism Erases Anti-Semitism."

A TIME TO PANIC?

1. Yair Ettinger, "Four Killed in Shooting at Jewish School in France," *Haaretz,* March 19, 2014.

2. Lizzie Dearden, "Israel-Gaza Conflict: Synagogues Attacked as Pro-Palestinian Protest in Paris Turns Violent," *Independent,* July 14, 2014.

3. Baron Bodissey, "What Really Happened at the Don Yitzchak Abarbanel Synagogue in Paris?" *Gates of Vienna* (blog), July 19, 2014.

4. TLV Faces Staff, "Posters in Rome Read 'Do Not Buy from Jews,'" *TLV Faces,* August 11, 2014; Lourdes Garcia Navarro, "Hate Crimes against Jews on the Rise in Europe," NPR, August 9, 2014.

5. Admittedly the comment was a quote but the paper did not think it necessary to add something akin to "Jewish leader asserts." Jon Henley, "Antisemitism on Rise across Europe 'in Worst Times since the Nazis,'" *Guardian,* August 7, 2014.

6. Micki Weinberg, "In Berlin, Al Quds Day Marchers Steer Clear of Anti-Semitism," *Times of Israel,* July 26, 2014.

7. Micki Weinberg, "Wave of Anti-Semitic Rallies Hits Cities across Germany," *Times of Israel,* July 21, 2014.

8. Monika Schwarz-Friesel, "Destroy Israel: Jews Are the Evil of the World!", (2014, email to the Israeli Embassy in Berlin)—Manifestations of Contemporary Antisemitism (text of speech at ICCA, Berlin), March 14, 2016, www.linguistik.tu-berlin.de/fileadmin/fg72/GIF/Schwarz-Friesel_Speech_ICCA_14.03.2016_Destroy_Israel_-_Jews_are_the_Evil_of_the_World_.pdf; Henley, "Antisemitism on Rise across Europe 'in Worst Times since the Nazis.'"

9. Manfred Gerstenfeld, "'Hamas, Hamas, Jews to the Gas,'" Ynetnews, August 23, 2014.

10. Henley, "Antisemitism on Rise across Europe 'in Worst Times since the Nazis.'"

11. Raphael Ahren, "After Brutal Attack on Rabbi, Berliners Show Solidarity by Donning Skullcaps," *Times of Israel,* September 2, 2012; Rosa Doherty, "'Don't Wear Kippahs in Public,' German Jews Told," *Jewish Chronicle,* April 25, 2018; "Rabbis Push Back against Warn-

ing Not to Wear Kippas in Germany, Urge Action," *Times of Israel*, April 25, 2018.

12. Melissa Eddy, "In Backlash on Antisemitism, a Sea of Skull Caps," *New York Times*, April 26, 2018.

13. Schwarz-Friesel, "Destroy Israel"; Friesel and Reinharz, *Inside the Antisemitic Mind*, pp. xiv–xv.

14. "Jewish Leader Attacks Austrian Far Right as Anti-Semitism Cases Increase," Reuters, February 15, 2018.

15. David Cameron to Chief Rabbi, September 10, 2014, https:// chiefrabbi.org/wp-content/uploads/2014/09/Letter-from-the-PM -PYN.pdf.

16. Hillel Fendel, "European Leaders Speak Out against Increasing Anti-Semitism," *Arutz Sheva*, September 28, 2014.

17. Deborah E. Lipstadt, *History on Trial* (New York: HarperCollins, 2005).

THE OMINOUS CASE OF SALMAN RUSHDIE

1. The themes included the disputed notion that Muhammad had decreed that three goddesses were to be worshipped as divine entities, suggesting the possibility that Islam allowed for some measured acceptance of polytheism. Rushdie also included in his labyrinthine story a brothel in which the prostitutes bore the names of the Prophet Muhammad's wives. For Rushdie's contemporaneous reflections on what happened to him, see Salman Rushdie, "Choice Between Light and Dark," *Observer*, January 22, 1989.

2. Johannes Due Enstad, *Antisemitic Violence in Europe, 2005–2015: Exposure and Perpetrators in France, UK, Germany, Sweden, Norway, Denmark and Russia*, University of Oslo Center for Studies of the Holocaust and Religious Minorities and Center for Research on Extremism (C-REX) (Oslo: University of Oslo, June 2017).

3. "Man Attacked in Berlin for Wearing *Kippa* Is an Israeli Arab," *Times of Israel*, April 18, 2018; Sven Becker and Dominik Peters, "An Author's Quest to Explain Muslim Anti-Semitism," *Spiegel* online, March 28, 2018.

4. Martin Amis, "Rendezvous with Rushdie," *Vanity Fair News*, December 1990, https://www.vanityfair.com/news/1990/12/martin-amis-on -salman-rushdie.

5. *The Rushdie File*, ed. Lisa Appignanesi and Sara Maitland (London: Fourth Estate, 1989), p. 101.

6. "Khomeini Spurns Rushdie Regrets and Reiterates Threat of Death," *New York Times,* February 20, 1989,

7. Chief Rabbi Immanuel Jakobovits, "Paying Due Regard to Our Beliefs," *Times* (London), March 9, 1989; *The Rushdie File,* ed. Appignanesi and Maitland, p. 199.

8. Jimmy Carter, "Rushdie's Book Is an Insult," *New York Times,* May 5, 1989.

9. Michael Ignatieff, "The Value of Toleration," *Observer,* April 2, 1989.

10. Roald Dahl, "A Dangerous Opportunist," *Times* (London), February 28, 1989; Paul Elie, "A Fundamental Fight," *Vanity Fair,* April 29, 2014.

11. Jeremy Treglown, *Roald Dahl: A Biography* (New York: Farrar, Straus, Giroux, 1994), pp. 255–56.

12. Rushdie, "Year Zero," *Joseph Anton* (New York: Random House, 2012), iBooks edition, p. 886.

13. Ursula Owen, "Essay: A Victory for Literary Freedom," *Independent,* September 27, 1998.

14. Edwin McDowell, "Rushdie's Publisher Assails 'Censorship by Terrorism,'" *New York Times,* February 19, 1989.

15. "Iran's Indecent Proposal," *New York Times,* February 16, 1993.

16. Sabah A. Salih, "Islamism, BDS, and the West," in Cary Nelson and Gabriel Noah Brahm, *The Case against Academic Boycotts of Israel* (Chicago: MLA Members for Scholars' Rights, 2015), p. 149.

PIXILATING THE PROBLEM

1. Andrew Sullivan, "BBC Weeps for Yasser Arafat," *New York Sun,* November 12, 2004.

2. Nick Cohen, "Censor and Sensibility," *Guardian,* December 11, 2004; Oliver Kamm, "Offense and Free Speech," *Oliver Kamm Blog,* May 19, 2007.

3. Ursula Owen, "Free to Speak" (letter to the editor), *Observer,* December 19, 2004.

4. Marie Louise Sjølie, "The Danish Cartoonist Who Survived an Axe Attack," *Guardian,* January 4, 2010.

5. Douglas Torin, "How UK Press Shapes Up to Cartoon Row," BBC .co.uk, February 3, 2006.

6. "French Editor Fired over Cartoons," BBC.co.uk, February 2, 2007.

7. "Paper Withdrawn after Cartoon Row," BBC.co.uk, February 7, 2006.

8. Christopher Hitchens, "Cartoon Debate: The Case for Mocking Religion," *Slate,* February 4, 2006.

9. "BBC's Dilemma over the Cartoons," BBC.co.uk, February 3, 2006.
10. Some employees of the press believed that, in addition to fear, the decision was motivated by the university's proposed plans to establish study programs in Muslim-dominated countries. The plans were under way, and the university did not want to jeopardize these efforts. Interview with Jonathan Brent, Kraków, Poland, July 1, 2017. "Publisher's Statement" in Jytte Klausen, *The Cartoons That Shook the World* (New Haven, CT: Yale University Press, 2009).
11. Paul Reynolds, "A Clash of Rights and Responsibilities," BBC.co.uk, February 6, 2006.
12. Chris Tryhorn, "Jack Straw Praises UK Media's 'Sensitivity' over Cartoons," *Guardian,* February 3, 2006.
13. Reynolds, "A Clash of Rights and Responsibilities."
14. Ibid.
15. Hitchens, "Cartoon Debate"; Nick Cohen, "Paris Attacks: Unless We Overcome Fear, Self-Censorship Will Spread," *Guardian,* January 10, 2015.
16. Dan R. Rasmussen, "*Salient* Publishes Danish Cartoons," *Harvard Crimson,* February 14, 2006.
17. Charles Spencer, "Can We Talk about This, National Theatre, Review," *Telegraph,* March 13, 2012.
18. Dominic Cavendish, "DV8's Can We Talk about This? The Riskiest Show of the Year?" *Quilliam,* March 11, 2012.

PARISIAN TRAGEDIES

1. Jennie Schuessler, "After Protests, Charlie Hebdo Members Receive Standing Ovation at PEN Gala," *New York Times,* May 6, 2015; Teju Cole, "Unmournable Bodies," *New Yorker,* January 9, 2015.
2. Adam Gopnik, "Satire Lives," *New Yorker,* January 19, 2015.
3. Jacob Canfield, "In the Wake of Charlie Hebdo, Free Speech Does Not Mean Freedom from Criticism," *Hooded Utilitarian,* January 7, 2015; CM, "Subversion, Satire, and Shut the Fuck Up: Deflection and Lazy Thinking in Comics Criticism," *Hooded Utilitarian,* October 23, 2012.
4. Jennifer Schuessler, "Six PEN Members Decline Gala after Award for Charlie Hebdo," *New York Times,* April 26, 2015; Schuessler, "After Protests, Charlie Hebdo Members Receive Standing Ovation at PEN Gala."
5. Aurelien Breeden and Dan Bilefsky, "Book by Slain Charlie Hebdo

Editor Argues Islam Is Not Exempt from Ridicule," *New York Times*, April 16, 2015.

6. Rachel Donadio, "Provocateur's Death Haunts the Dutch," *New York Times*, October 30, 2014.

7. Ariane Bernard, "Raymond Barre, 83, Former French Premier, Dies," *New York Times*, August 26, 2007.

8. Bodissey, "What Really Happened at the Don Yitzchak Abarbanel Synagogue in Paris?"

9. "Kosher Supermarket Killer 'Told TV Station He Deliberately Targeted Jews,'" *Times of Israel*, January 10, 2015.

10. J. J. Goldberg, "Yes, It's about French Muslims and Anti-Semitism," *Forward*, January 10, 2015; Andrew Higgins, "3 Shot Dead at Brussels Jewish Museum," *New York Times*, May 24, 2014.

11. United Nations Secretary-General, "Secretary-General Press Encounter at the Signing of the Condolence Book at the French Mission," January 9, 2015; Ben Cohen, "'We Haven't Shown Enough Outrage': French PM Issues Blistering Denunciation of Antisemitism," *Algemeiner*, January 14, 2015.

12. There was a tremendous outpouring of criticism and he has since apologized. His apology is certainly welcome, but the fact that he asked the question in the first place is what is striking. Jim Selby, "Tim Willcox Apologises to Daughter of Holocaust Survivor at Paris Rally for Saying 'Palestinians Suffer Hugely at Jewish Hands as Well,'" *Independent*, January 12, 2015.

13. Howard Jacobson, "Pox Britannia," as quoted in Alvin H. Rosenfeld, ed., *Resurgent Antisemitism: Global Perspectives* (Bloomington: Indiana University Press, 2013), p. 37, n. 36.

14. Mass Tea Party—Wake Up America!, "Teaching Kids to 'Shoot Jews' Hamas TV Show Encourages Kids to Shoot Jews on the Record," YouTube, May 8, 2014, www.youtube.com/watch?v=Ck6TCQghpCE; Sharona Schwartz, "Hamas TV's Bumble Bee Character Encourages Children to Do Some Disturbing Things to Jews," TheBlaze, May 11, 2014.

15. Ryan Grenoble, "Brooklyn Coffee Shop Slammed after Owner's Anti-Semitic Rant," *Huffington Post*, October 2, 2014.

16. Serena Dai, "Coffee Shop Owner Who Called Jews 'Greedy' on Instagram Was 'Misunderstood,'" *DNAinfo New York*, October 2, 2014.

17. CNN Politics, "Wright Revisits 'Them Jews' Remark," June 11, 2009.

18. "#Communiqué de Presse—Assassinat de Sarah Halimi: Le Crif stu-

péfait que le caractère antisémite ne soit pas retenu." *Crif—Conseil Représentatif Des Institutions Juives De France,* July 13, 2017; Juliette Mickiewicz, "Affaire Sarah Halimi: Le suspect mis en examen pour meurtre," *Le Figaro,* July 12, 2017; Marc Weitzman, "Sarah Halimi Was Murdered by a Muslim Attacker Reciting Verses from the Quran, But Was He a 'Terrorist'?" *Tablet,* May 25, 2017.

19. AFP, "Paris Women's Brutal Murder Declared Anti-Semitic Act," *Times of Israel,* February 28, 2018.

20. Months after the killing, France's new president, Emmanuel Macron, suggested that the authorities had refused to "see" the evidence that was in front of them. Daniel Sugarman, "Macron Speaks Out on Murder of French Jewish Woman," *Jewish Chronicle,* July 17, 2017; James McAuley, "In France, Murder of a Jewish Woman Ignites Debate over the Word 'Terrorism,'" *Washington Post,* July 23, 2017; "French Intellectuals Accuse Authorities of Covering Up Jewish Woman's Slaying by Muslim Neighbor," Jewish Telegraphic Agency, June 9, 2017.

21. https://en.wikipedia.org/wiki/Killing_of_Ilan_Halimi.

22. "Arab Teenagers Arrested in Beating of Jewish Boy outside Paris-Area Synagogue," Jewish Telegraphic Agency, March 1, 2018.

23. "Slain Holocaust Survivor's Family: She'd Known Her Killer Since He Was a Boy," *Times of Israel,* March 27, 2018; Bari Weiss, "Jews Are Being Murdered in Paris. Again," *New York Times,* March 30, 2018; "Two Charged with Antisemitic Murder of French Holocaust Survivor," AFP, March 27, 2018.

24. "In France, Thousands March in Memory of Murdered Jewish Woman," AFP, March 28, 2018.

25. Henry Samuel, "Macron Hails French Resistance Spirit of Heroic Gendarme Who Swapped Himself for Hostage," *Telegraph,* March 28, 2018.

A MATTER OF ANTISEMITISM, NOT HISTORY

1. For survivor testimonies, see Yale University Library, Fortunoff Video Archive for Holocaust Testimonies, http://web.library.yale .edu/testimonies; University of Southern California, SHOAH Foundation, https://sfi.usc.edu/full-length-testimonies; United States Holocaust Memorial Museum, www.ushmm.org/remember/the -holocaust-survivors-and-victims-resource-center/survivors-and -victims/survivor-testimonies.

2. Many of the witnesses from the areas in which these murders occurred have spoken of what they saw. See, for example, Patrick Desbois, *The Holocaust by Bullets: A Priest's Journey to Uncover the Truth Behind the Murder of 1.5 Million Jews* (New York: St. Martin's Griffin, 2009). See also the interviews conducted by Claude Lanzmann for his documentary *Shoah*, www.ushmm.org/online/film/docs/shoahstatus.pdf.

3. For a collection of interviews, letters, journal entries, and testimony of perpetrators, including from those who put the Zyklon B into the gas chambers and those who participated in the shootings on the eastern front, see Ernst Klee, Willi Dressen, and Volker Riess, eds., *"The Good Old Days": The Holocaust as Seen by Its Perpetrators and Bystanders* (Old Saybrook, CT: Konecky & Konecky, 1991).

4. Many perpetrators who were tried for war crimes after World War II argued that they had no option but to follow orders and kill the victims; otherwise they would have been killed. However, this does not seem to have been the case. As David Kitterman concludes after an investigation of more than one hundred cases of Germans who refused to execute civilians, "the most remarkable conclusion about this investigation is the failure to find even one conclusively documented instance of a life-threatening situation (shot, physically harmed, or sent to a concentration camp) occurring to those who refused to carry out orders to murder civilians or Russian war prisoners. In spite of general assumptions to the contrary, the majority of such cases resulted in no serious consequences whatever." David Kitterman, "Those Who Said 'No!': Germans Who Refused to Execute Civilians during World War II," *German Studies Review* 11, no. 2 (1988): 241–54.

5. Gideon Resnick, "David Duke: Trump Makes Hitler Great Again," *Daily Beast*, March 17, 2016.

6. For background on the Institute for Historical Review and revisionism, see Richard Evans's expert report, *David Irving, Hitler and Holocaust Denial*, which was submitted to the court by the defense in Irving v. Penguin UK and Deborah Lipstadt, *HDOT.org*, www.hdot.org/evans/#evans_3–5.

7. *Jeremy Vine Show*, BBC Radio 2, February 20, 2017. Relevant interview begins at about 1.05, www.bbc.co.uk/programmes/p04tj3gx; conversation with producers of *Jeremy Vine Show*, February 18, 2017.

8. Eliezer Sherman, "Sarkozy: There Are Schools in France Where

You Cannot Teach the Holocaust," *Algemeiner,* June 8, 2015; Alison Smale, "Teaching the Holocaust to Muslim Germans, or Not," *New York Times,* June 17, 2015; Benjamin Weinthal, "German Muslim Students Protest Holocaust Remembrance, Attack Israel," *Jerusalem Post,* January 27, 2017.

9. Yair Rosenberg, "This BBC Interview Perfectly Illustrates Britain's Left-Wing Anti-Semitism Problem," *Tablet,* September 26, 2017, www.tabletmag.com/scroll/245953/this-anti-semitic-bbc-interview -perfectly-illustrates-britains-left-wing-anti-semitism-problem.

INVERTING VICTIMS AND PERPETRATORS

1. Walter Laqueur, *The Struggle for the Middle East: The Soviet Union and the Middle East, 1958–70* (Harmondsworth, UK: Penguin, 1972), p. 54.

2. Seth Frantzman, "The Outrage of Comparing Israel to the Nazis," *Algemeiner,* May 10, 2016.

3. Rowena Mason, "Lib Dem MP Condemned for Linking Israeli Treatment of Palestinians with Holocaust," *Telegraph,* January 25, 2013.

4. Sarah Hull, "Death to Jewish Settlers, Says Anti-Zionist Poet," *Guardian,* April 13, 2002.

5. Peter Foster, "What Are Oxford Dons to Make of Tom Paulin?", *Telegraph,* April 27, 2002.

6. Berlet, *Constructing Campus Conflict,* p. 24.

7. Pagano, "Anti-Racism Erases Anti-Semitism." Extensive quotes from her presentation can be found at William Jacobson, "Vassar Faculty-Sponsored Anti-Israel Event Erupts in Controversy," Campus Watch, *Legal Insurrection,* February 8, 2016.

8. Mark G. Yudof and Ken Waltzer, "Majoring in Anti-Semitism at Vassar," *Wall Street Journal,* February 16, 2016; Ziva Dahl, "Vassar Jewish Studies Sponsors Demonization of Israel . . . Again," *Observer,* February 9, 2016.

9. Yudof and Waltzer, "Majoring in Anti-Semitism at Vassar."

10. U.S. Campaign for the Academic and Cultural Boycott of Israel, "Letter in Support of Professor Jasbir Puar Regarding Right-Wing Attacks on Her Recent Talk at Vassar College," *USACBI,* February 2016; Jason Stanley, "The Free Speech Fallacy," *Chronicle of Higher Education,* February 26, 2016; Ken Waltzer, "BDS Scholars Defend the Indefensible," *Times of Israel,* March 13, 2016.

BRANDING VICTIMS AS COLLABORATORS

1. "Ex-London Mayor Ken Livingstone Reaffirms Remarks about Nazi Support for Zionism," *Haaretz,* September 5, 2016.
2. John Stone, "Labour Antisemitism Row: Read the Ken Livingstone Interview Transcripts in Full," *Independent,* April 28, 2016; "Ken Livingstone Stands by Hitler Comments," BBC.co.uk, April 30, 2016.
3. "Extracts from *Mein Kampf* by Adolf Hitler," *Yad Vashem,* www .yadvashem.org/docs/extracts-from-mein-kampf.
4. "Record of the Conversation of the Grand Mufti with the Foreign Minister, Berlin, November 28, 1941," Document 514, and "Record of the Conversation of the Fuhrer with the Grand Mufti of Jerusalem, November 28, 1941 in the presence of the Foreign Minister of the Reich in Berlin," Document 515, in *Documents on German Foreign Policy 1918–1945,* Series D, Vol. XIII (United States: Government Printing Office, 1954), pp. 876-85.
5. Paul Bogdanor, "An Antisemitic Hoax: Lenni Brenner on Zionist 'Collaboration' with the Nazis," *Fathom,* http://fathomjournal.org/an -antisemitic-hoax-lenni-brenner-on-zionist-collaboration-with-the -nazis/.
6. David Baddiel, "Why Ken Livingstone Has It So Wrong over Hitler and Zionism," *Guardian,* April 6, 2017.
7. Stone, "Labour Antisemitism Row"; Ken Livingstone, "This Is about Israel, Not Antisemitism," *Guardian,* March 4, 2005.
8. Lesley Klaff, "Holocaust Inversion and Contemporary Antisemitism," *Fathom,* December 2014, http://fathomjournal.org/holocaust -inversion-and-contemporary-antisemitism/.
9. David Hirsh, *Contemporary Left Antisemitism* (New York: Routledge, 2017), pp. 11ff., 76–77.

DE-JUDAIZING THE HOLOCAUST

1. Daniel Brook, "Double Genocide," *Slate,* July 26, 2015.
2. Ibid.
3. Florian Peters, "Remaking Polish National History: Reenactment over Reflection," *Cultures of History Forum,* October 3, 2016, www.cultures -of-history.uni-jena.de/debates/poland/remaking-polish-national -history-reenactment-over-reflection/.
4. In July 2017, I visited the new World War II museum and the Solidarity Center in Gdansk, Poland. Conversations with curators,

researchers, and others involved in the building and administration of these two institutions revealed the way history has become completely politicized. Peters, "Remaking Polish National History."

5. Rachel Donadio, "A Museum Becomes a Battlefield over Poland's History," *New York Times,* November 9, 2016; Soraya Sarhaddi Nelson, "Nationalist Polish Government Wants Changes to World War II Museum," NPR, March 25, 2017; Nina Porzucki, "Poland's Right-Wing Government Thinks This WWII Museum Isn't 'Glorious' Enough," Public Radio International, February 23, 2017; "Historians Defend Scholar Who Studies Poland and Holocaust," History News Network, June 20, 2017.

6. Jan T. Gross, *Neighbors: The Destruction of the Jewish Community in Jedwabne, Poland* (Princeton, NJ: Princeton University Press, 2001).

7. United States Department of State, *Intelligence Research Report,* OCL-2312, May 15, 1946, www.wiesenthal.com/atf/cf/%7B54d385e6-f1b9-4e9f-8e94-890c3e6dd277%7D/INTELLIGENCE-RESEARCH-REPORT-DEPT-OF-STATE_022218.PDF, pp. 22–24.

8. Griff Witte, James McAuley, and Luisa Beck, "In Laws, Rhetoric and Acts of Violence, Europe Is Rewriting Dark Chapters of Its Past," *Washington Post,* February 19, 2018.

9. Jan Gross, "Poland Death Camp Law Is Designed to Falsify History," *Financial Times,* February 6, 2018; Jonah Shepp, "Poland's Holocaust Law and the Right-Wing Desire to Rewrite History," *New York* magazine, February 3, 2018.

10. Cnaan Liphshiz, "Poland's Prime Minister Said Some Jews Collaborated with Nazis. Scholars Say He Distorted History," Jewish Telegraphic Agency, February 20, 2018.

11. "Remarks by President Trump to the People of Poland," WhiteHouse.gov, July 6, 2017; Adam Taylor, "Trump Was First U.S. President to Visit Warsaw without Visiting the Warsaw Ghetto since 1989," *Washington Post,* July 6, 2017; Weisman, *(((Semitism))),* pp. 156–57.

12. James Kirchick, "Hungary's Ugly State-Sponsored Holocaust Revisionism," *Tablet,* March 13, 2017.

13. Adam Nossiter, "Marine Le Pen Denies French Guilt for Rounding Up Jews," *New York Times,* April 10, 2017.

14. "Far-Left French Leader Slams Macron for Accepting French Complicity in Holocaust," *Haaretz,* July 19, 2017.

15. Elian Peltier, "France Rethinks Honor for Charles Maurras, Condemned as Anti-Semite," *New York Times,* January 28, 2018.

TOXIFYING ISRAEL

1. Lucy Sherriff, "King's College Investigates 'Hate Attack' against Israel's Ex-Secret Service Chief Ami Ayalon," HuffPost UK, January 21, 2016, https://www.huffingtonpost.co.uk/2016/01/21/kings -college-london-hate-attack-israeli-ex-secret-service-ami-ayalon_n _9037882.html?utm_hp_ref=uk-israeli-palestinian-conflict.

2. Dale Carpenter, "Israeli Academic Shouted Down in Lecture at University of Minnesota," *Washington Post,* November 14, 2015.

3. Julius, *Trials of the Diaspora,* p. 481.

4. "BDS Movement," *BDS Movement,* September 28, 2017, bdsmovement .net/.

5. "The PACBI Call for Academic Boycott Revised: Adjusting the Parameters of the Debate," *PACBI*—Palestinian Campaign for the Academic & Cultural Boycott of Israel, January 28, 2006, pacbi .org/etemplate.php?id=1051; Donna Robinson Divine, "The Boycott Debate at Smith," in Nelson and Brahm, *The Case Against the Academic Boycott of Israel,* p. 136; Gabriel Noah Brahm and Asaf Romirowsky, "Anti-Semitic in Intent if Not in Effect," in Nelson and Brahm, *The Case Against the Academic Boycott of Israel,* p. 80.

6. Mark Yudof, "We Must Defeat BDS Macro-Aggression," *Times of Israel,* December 9, 2015.

7. Cary Nelson, "The Problem with Judith Butler," in Nelson and Brahm, *The Case Against the Academic Boycott of Israel,* p. 195.

8. Michael Bérubé, "Boycott Bubkes: The Murky Logic of the ASA's Resolution," in Nelson and Brahm, *The Case Against the Academic Boycott of Israel,* p. 132.

9. Ashley Dawson and Bill V. Mullen, eds., *Against Apartheid: The Case for Boycotting Israeli Universities* (Chicago: Haymarket Books, 2015), p. 42, as cited in *Academic Freedom, Freedom of Expression, and the BDS Movement: A Guide and Resource Book for Faculty* (Academic Engagement Network, November 2016), p. 14.

10. Judith Butler, "Academic Freedom and the ASA's Boycott of Israel," *Nation,* December 8, 2013.

11. David Hirsh, "The American Studies Association Boycott Resolution, Academic Freedom, and the Myth of the Institutional Boycott," in Nelson and Brahm, *The Case Against the Academic Boycott of Israel,* pp. 122–23.

12. https://rototomsunsplash.com/en/rototom.

13. Herb Keinon, "Matisyahu: Anti-Semitism at Spanish Festival Was

Something I Never Experienced Before," *Jerusalem Post*, August 30, 2015.

14. Emily Shire, "Reggae Fest Demands Anti-Israel Pledge," *Daily Beast*, August 17, 2015; "Jewish Groups Protest Cancellation of U.S. Musician's Spanish Concert," Reuters, August 17, 2015.

15. Asawin Suebaeng, "Taylor Swift, Queen of the Zionists?" *Daily Beast*, February 20, 2015.

16. Bencie Woll and Wendy Sandler, "Another Mona Baker Journal Boycotting Israeli Scholars," Librarians for Fairness.org, August 18, 2007, www.librariansforfairness.org/news_post.asp?NPI=185.

17. Yarden Skop, "Top Scientist Joins BDS Movement," *Haaretz*, May 8, 2013.

18. "Loach Pulls Melbourne Festival Film in Israeli Funding Protest," CBC News, July 20, 2009.

19. Alexander Nazaryan, "Alice Walker Won't Allow New Hebrew Version of 'Color Purple,'" *New York Daily News*, June 20, 2012.

20. David Hirsh, "Open Letter to Claire Potter from David Hirsh," *Engage*, December 17, 2013.

21. Martha Nussbaum, "Against Academic Boycotts," in Nelson and Brahm, *The Case Against the Academic Boycott of Israel*, pp. 43, 45.

22. American Association of University Professors, "On Academic Boycotts," in Nelson and Brahm, *The Case Against the Academic Boycott of Israel*, pp. 31–38.

BDS: ANTISEMITISM OR POLITICS?

1. "The PACBI Call for Academic Boycott Revised: Adjusting the Parameters of the Debate"; "PACBI Guidelines for the International Academic Boycott of Israel," Palestinian Campaign for the Academic and Cultural Boycott of Israel, July 31, 2014, www.pacbi.org/einside.php?id=69+.

2. Ellen Willis, "Is There Still a Jewish Question? Why I'm an Anti-Anti-Zionist," in *Wrestling with Zion: Progressive Jewish-American Responses to the Israel-Palestine Conflict*, ed. Tony Kushner and Alisa Solomon (New York: Grove Press, 2003), pp. 226–32, reprinted in *Tablet*, August 13, 2014.

3. Drew Himmelstein, "Stanford Professors Take Stand Against Divestment," Jweekly.com, March 12, 2015.

4. Nussbaum, "Against Academic Boycotts," p. 47.

5. Steven Pinker, "Against Selective Demonization," *Against Anthro Boy-*

cott, https://www.facebook.com/againstanthroboycott/posts/44800
2548722546.

6. Benny Morris, *One State, Two States: Resolving the Israel/Palestine Conflict* (New Haven, CT: Yale University Press, 2009), pp. 168–69, as quoted in Nelson and Brahm, *The Case Against the Academic Boycott of Israel,* p. 192.

7. Himmelstein, "Stanford Professors Take Stand against Divestment."

8. Richard Pérez-Peña, "Scholars' Group to Disclose Result of Vote on an Academic Boycott of Israel," *New York Times,* December 16, 2013; Mitchell Cohen, "Anti-Semitism and the Left That Doesn't Learn," in Nelson and Brahm, *The Case Against the Academic Boycott of Israel,* p. 159.

9. Mark Yudof, "BDS and Campus Politics: A Bad Romance," *Inside Higher Ed,* December 14, 2015.

10. Kenneth L. Marcus, "Is the Boycott Movement Anti-Semitic?" in Nelson and Brahm, *The Case Against the Academic Boycott of Israel,* p. 257.

11. Jennifer Medina, "Student Coalition at Stanford Confronts Allegations of Anti-Semitism," *New York Times,* April 14, 2015.

12. Julius, *Trials of the Diaspora,* p. 67.

CAMPUS GROUPTHINK: NOT-SO-SAFE ZONES

1. Kimber Williams, "Rushdie Urges Students to Defend Free Speech," *Emory News Center,* February 16, 2015, http://news.emory.edu/stories/2015/02/er_salman_rushdie_lecture/campus.html.

2. Eve Ensler, "I Never Defined a Woman as a Person with a Vagina," *Time* magazine, January 19, 2015.

3. Bari Weiss, "We're All Fascists Now," *The New York Times,* March 7, 2018.

4. Teresa Watanabe, "Q&A: UC Berkeley Chancellor Carol T. Christ: 'Free Speech Has Itself Become Controversial,'" *Los Angeles Times,* September 14, 2017.

5. "Robert Reich: Coulter Should Be Allowed to Speak," *Newsweek,* April 25, 2017.

6. "Wellesley Statement from CERE Faculty Re: Laura Kipnis Freedom Project Visit and Aftermath," *FIRE*—Foundation for Individual Rights in Education, March 20, 2017.

7. Chloe Manchester, "Day of Absence Changes Form," *Cooper Point Journal,* April 10, 2017.

8. Bret Weinstein, "The Campus Mob Came for Me—and You, Professor, Could Be Next," *Wall Street Journal*, May 30, 2017.

9. Anemona Hartocollis, "A Campus Argument Goes Viral. Now the College Is Under Siege," *New York Times*, June 16, 2017.

10. Laurie L. Patton, "The Right Way to Protect Free Speech on Campus," *Wall Street Journal*, June 9, 2017.

11. The Committee on Freedom of Expression at the University of Chicago, *Report of the Committee on Freedom of Expression, University of Chicago*, January 2015, https://freeexpression.uchicago.edu/page/report-committee-freedom-expression.

12. Jay Ellison to Class of 2020, University of Chicago, n.d., www.intellectualtakeout.org/sites/ito/files/acceptance_letter.jpg; Bret Stephens, "America's Best College President," *New York Times*, October 20, 2017.

13. Kenneth Stern, "S.C. Anti-Semitism Bill Isn't Needed," *Post and Courier* (Charleston, SC), April 25, 2017.

14. This is not something new. In the 1970s Yale was roiled by such a debate. Anthony Lewis, "A Report on the Dangers to the Right of Free Speech," *New York Times*, January 26, 1975. I wish to thank Kenneth S. Stern for reminding me of this.

PROGRESSIVISM AND ZIONISM: ANTISEMITISM BY SUBTERFUGE?

1. Matthew Stein, "Students for Justice in Palestine Defends Violence against Pro-Israel Groups, Calls Them 'Fascists,'" *College Fix*, September 17, 2017.

2. Colin Beresford and Alon Samuel, "White Nationalist Group Puts Up Anti-Semitic Stickers on Black Lives Matters Posters," *University of Michigan Daily*, April 26, 2017; Tilly Shames, Director, University of Michigan Hillel, email, April 19, 2018.

3. Diane Lederman, "More than 200 UMass Students Call for Free Education, $15 Minimum Wage, Greater Diversity at Rally," *Mass Live*, November 12, 2015.

4. #SHUTDOWN the #PINKWASHING, change.org, www.change.org/p/goucher-college-shutdown-the-pinkwashing.

5. William Jacobson, "How Student Activists Turned Anti-Rape Group into an Anti-Israel Group," *Legal Insurrection*, December 10, 2015.

6. Rikki Novetsky and Sariel Friedman, "Left and Lefter," *Columbia Spectator*, March 12, 2015.

7. "Tufts University Activists Publish Guide Calling Israel a 'White Supremacist State,'" *Jewish Telegraphic Agency*, September 8, 2017; Alex Joffe, "Labeling of Israel and Its Supporters as White Supremacists and Fascists Emerges on Campuses," Scholars for Peace in the Middle East, September 29, 2017.

8. Yitzhak Santis, "At CUNY, Students Blame Israel for Tuition Hikes," *Tower*, November 11, 2015, www.thetower.org/2556-at-cuny-students -blame-israel-for-tuition-hikes/.

9. Mira Taichman and Danielle Rinat, "I Am a Jew, a Zionist, an Obie," *Oberlin Review*, March 15, 2013.

10. Yair Rosenberg, "New York University's Students for Justice in Palestine Blames Police Shootings of Blacks on Israel," *Tablet*, July 8, 2016.

11. Janet L. Freedman, "For the Women's Studies Association, the BDS Vote Was Over Before It Began," *Forward*, November 30, 2015.

12. "Introduction," in Nelson and Brahm, *The Case Against the Academic Boycott of Israel*, p. 21.

13. Yair Rosenberg, "Four Reasons the Chicago Dyke March's Banning of Jewish Stars Was Anti-Semitic," *Tablet*, June 28, 2017.

14. Facebook page: Andy Thayer, January 22, 2016, www.facebook .com/andy.thayer1/videos/10207721271646993/; Paul Miller, "LGBT Conference in Chicago Turns Violent from Anti-Israel Protesters," *Observer*, January 2016.

15. Yair Rosenberg, "Stanford Student Senator: Saying 'Jews Control the Media, Economy, Government' Is 'Not Anti-Semitism,'" *Tablet*, April 7, 2016.

16. Winston Shi, "On Gabriel Knight and What Anti-Semitism Really Means," *Stanford Daily*, April 7, 2016.

17. Howard Jacobson, "Pox Britannia," as quoted in Rosenfeld, *Resurgent Antisemitism*, p. 37, n. 26.

18. David Clark, "Accusations of Anti-Semitic Chic Are Poisonous Intellectual Thuggery," *Guardian*, March 5, 2006.

19. Tariq Ali, "Notes on Anti-Semitism, Zionism and Palestine," www .counterpunch.org/2004/03/04/notes-on-anti-semitism-zionism -and-palestine/, August 19, 2015.

20. Jonathan Freedland, "My Plea to the Left: Treat Jews the Same Way You'd Treat Any Other Minority," *Guardian*, April 29, 2016.

21. @lsarsour, October 31, 2012, https://twitter.com/lsarsour/status/ 263651398250545152?lang=en; Tally Krupkin, "Linda Sarsour at Racial Justice March: 'It Is Not My Job to Educate Jewish People

That Palestinians Deserve Dignity,'" *Haaretz*, October 2, 2017; Debra Nussbaum Cohen, "Why Jewish Leaders Rally Behind a Palestinian-American Women's March Organizer," *Haaretz*, January 25, 2017; "Young Man Asks Challenging Question to Linda Sarsour—Here Is Her Response," www.youtube.com/watch?time_continue=436&v=uMisnUF14io.

22. "Nation of Islam," Southern Poverty Law Center, n.d., www.splcenter.org/fighting-hate/extremist-files/group/nation-islam.

23. Elad Nehorai, "Memo to the Left: Denounce Anti-Semite Louis Farrakhan," *Forward*, March 2, 2018.

24. https://twitter.com/TamikaDMallory/status/970032405577961473.

25. www.instagram.com/p/BNDLpbGFrlc/?taken-by=msladyjustice1&hl=en.

26. *Forward* and Aiden Pink, "Women's March Co-president Attends Louis Farrakhan Rally—Again," *Haaretz*, March 1, 2018.

27. www.facebook.com/womensmarchonwash/posts/1848805725132698.

28. Daniel J. Roth, "Women's March Leaders Slam ADL, Call Group 'Islamophobic,' Anti-Minority," *Jerusalem Post*, April 18, 2018; Yair Rosenberg, "Women's March Organizer and Farrakhan Fan Tamika Mallory Attacks the Anti-Defamation League," *Tablet*, April 18, 2018.

RESPONDING TO THE PROGRESSIVE "CRITIQUE"

1. Debra Nussbaum Cohen, "At Summit to Counter BDS Movement, J Street Feels the Heat," *Haaretz*, March 30, 2017.

2. "Antisemitism Tracker Organized by State," *AMCHA Initiative*, August 22, 2017; Judy Maltz, "Jewish Group Releases Blacklist of U.S. Professors Who Back Academic Boycott of Israel," *Haaretz*, March 30, 2017.

3. Jane Eisner, "Why Accuse Israeli Singer Noa of Backing BDS, When She Rejects It Outright?" *Forward*, February 22, 2016; "JNF Canada Drops Event over Singer Noa's Alleged BDS Support but Achinoam 'Noa' Nini, No Stranger to Controversy over Her Politics, Says She's 'Completely' Opposed to Israel Boycott," Jewish Telegraphic Agency, February 21, 2016.

4. Amir Tibon, "Portman's Boycott of Netanyahu Borders on Antisemitism, Israeli Minister Says," *Haaretz*, April 22, 2018.

5. Jonathan Lis, "Israel Set to Pass Law Banning Pro-BDS Foreigners from Entering Country," *Haaretz*, January 30, 2017.

6. Mark Yudof, Chair, and Kenneth Waltzer, Executive Director, Academic Exchange Network, to Menachem Ben-Sasson, President, Hebrew University, May 30, 2017.

7. Revital Hovel, "Israel's Attorney General to Examine Shin Bet Detentions of Left-wing Activists," *Haaretz*, August 14, 2018; "Israel's Shin Bet Reportedly Barred 250 People from Entering Israel in 2018," *Haaretz*, August 15, 2018.

8. Pini Dunner, "BDS Is Not Pro-Palestinian, It's Anti-Semitic," *Los Angeles Jewish Journal*, August 15, 2015.

MYOPIA: SEEING ANTISEMITISM ONLY ON THE OTHER SIDE

1. "Jewish Leaders Statement Against Attacks on Linda Sarsour," *Medium*, May 31, 2017; Rabbi Barat Ellman and Rabbi Ellen Lippmann, "Linda Sarsour Is a Friend to Jews," *New York Daily News*, May 7, 2017; Bari Weiss, "When Progressives Embrace Hate," *New York Times*, August 1, 2017.

2. Aiden Pink, "Will Ties to Louis Farrakhan Spur Jews to Shun the Women's March?," *Forward*, March 6, 2018; Rabbi Sharon Brous, *Facebook*, March 5, 2018, www.facebook.com/RabbiSharonBrous/posts/10155756338029678.

3. Glenn Kessler, "DNC Vice Chair Keith Ellison and Louis Farrakhan: 'No Relationship'?," *Washington Post*, March 9, 2018.

4. Shachar Peled, "Bannon Addresses ZOA, Urges Jews to Join 'Insurgency' against Anti-Trump Republicans," *Haaretz*, November 13, 2017.

5. Weisman, *(((Semitism)))*, p. 144.

6. Joseph Bernstein, "Alt-White: How the Breitbart Machine Laundered Racist Hate," *BuzzFeed*, October 15, 2017; Melanie Phillips, "The Alt-Right Smear," MelaniePhillips.com, March 17, 2017; Lloyd Green, "The Zionist Leader Who Can't Quit Steve Bannon," *Daily Beast*, August 30, 2017; Armin Rosen, "ZOA President Meets with Top Trump Aide," *Tablet*, January 26, 2017; "White Nationalist Richard Spencer Gives Israel as Example of Ethno-State He Wants in U.S.," *Haaretz*, October 19, 2017; Weisman, *(((Semitism)))*, p. 90.

7. Jack Moore, "Israel's Netanyahu Hasn't Condemned Hungary's 'Anti-Semitic' George Soros Posters. Here's Why," *Newsweek*, July 11, 2017; "Hungarian Jews Slam Prime Minister's Praises for Hitler Ally," Jewish Telegraphic Agency, June 26, 2017; Peter Murphy, "Meeting of the Minds: Netanyahu Visits Hungary," *Yahoo!*, July 16, 2017; Mai-

rav Zonszein, "Israel's War against George Soros," *New York Times,* July 17, 2017; Eszter Zalan, "Orban and Netanyahu Set Aside Anti-Semitism Concerns," *EU Observer,* July 18, 2017; Max Bearak, "Hungary Accused of 'Hatemongering' in National Survey Targeting George Soros," *Washington Post,* November 8, 2017; Larry Cohler-Esses, "George Soros Denounced by Hungary as 'Satan' Seeking to Destroy 'Christian Europe,'" *Forward,* October 2, 2017.

8. Noa Landau, "Netanyahu Pushes Hosting Visegrad Group in Israel in Talks with Senior Hungarian Official," *Haaretz,* February 13, 2018.

9. "Polish Official: Israel Ashamed of Jewish Passivity in the Holocaust," *Haaretz,* February 10, 2018.

10. Anshel Pfeffer, "Orbán Is Coming to Israel to Meet His Soulmate Netanyahu. Here's How He's Taking Down Hungary's Democracy," *Haaretz,* July 17, 2018.

11. Polish Government, "Joint Declaration of Prime Ministers of the State of Israel and the Republic of Poland," June 27, 2018, www.premier .gov.pl/en/news/news/joint-declaration-of-prime-ministers-of -the-state-of-israel-and-the-republic-of-poland.html; Raphael Ahren, "Does the Israeli-Polish Holocaust Law Agreement Defend Truth or Betray History?" *Times of Israel,* July 4, 2018; Jeffrey Heller, "Yad Vashem Center Criticizes Israeli-Polish Statement on Holocaust Law," *Reuters,* July 6, 2018; "Full Text: Yad Vashem Historians Against Israeli-Polish Statement on 'Holocaust Law,'" *Haaretz,* July 5, 2018.

12. Jonathan Lis, "Right-Wing Israeli Lawmaker Meets Member of Austrian Party with Nazi Roots," *Haaretz,* February 12, 2002.

13. Hillel Ben-Sasson, "Attacking Soros: Israel's Unholy Covenant with Europe's Anti-Semitic Ultra-Right," *Haaretz,* July 12, 2017.

14. Nussbaum Cohen, "At Summit to Counter BDS Movement, J Street Feels the Heat."

15. Ben Sales, "A State Legislator Called J Street Anti-Semitic. Right to Left, Jewish Groups Disagree," *Jewish Telegraphic Agency,* April 5, 2017.

16. Nussbaum Cohen, "At Summit to Counter BDS Movement, J Street Feels the Heat."

MISSING THE FOREST FOR THE TREES:
A DENTAL SCHOOL AND A FRATERNITY

1. For background on this practice, see Jerome Karbel, *The Chosen* (New York: Houghton Mifflin, 2005).

SPEAKING TRUTH TO FRIENDS: BEYOND VICTIMHOOD

1. Simon Rawidowicz, *Israel, the Ever-Dying People, and Other Essays* (London: Associated University Presses, 1986), pp. 50, 53–63.

CELEBRATING THE GOOD IN THE FACE OF THE BAD

1. Deuteronomy 31:6.

INDEX